LIVING THE
CHÂTEAU
DREAM

Dick and Angel Strawbridge

SEVEN DIALS

First published in Great Britain in 2021 by Seven Dials,
an imprint of The Orion Publishing Group Ltd
Carmelite House, 50 Victoria Embankment
London EC4Y 0DZ

An Hachette UK Company

1 3 5 7 9 10 8 6 4 2

Copyright © Dick and Angel Strawbridge 2021
Illustrations by Sam Steer
Images by Sean Lewis, Marry Me Marie, Jon Davo, Martin Weibe
All © Dick and Angel Strawbridge

A CIP catalogue record for this book is
available from the British Library.

ISBN (Hardback) 978 1 8418 8535 3
ISBN (Export Trade Paperback) 978 1 8418 8536 0
ISBN (eBook) 978 1 8418 8538 4
ISBN (Audio) 978 1 8418 8539 1

Typeset by Born Group
Printed and bound in Great Britain by Clays Ltd, Elcograf S.p.A.

MIX
Paper from
responsible sources
FSC® C104740

www.orionbooks.co.uk

LIVING THE
CHÂTEAU
DREAM

Also by Dick and Angel Strawbridge

A Year at the Château

To Arthur and Dorothy,

Every day you both inspire us to 'suck the marrow out of the bones of life'.

We are incredibly proud of you both and your passion for everything you do.

Love Mummy and Daddy.

XXXX

Contents

Preface

Before we get started, you need to know one thing: when you see words in bold, that's me, Angel, telling the story.

And when you see them like this, that's me, Dick. Right, let's get going.

*

On 31 December 2014 we settled one-year-old Arthur and baby Dorothy down to sleep. We poured ourselves a drink, and sat on our balcony wrapped up in a blanket, looking out at Southend Pier. It was windy and wonderful. We chatted about what a year we'd had and how, after four years of looking in France for our forever home, Château-de-la-Motte Husson had found us. We reassured each other that the children were now at the perfect age to move and that

we would tackle every twist and turn that was thrown at us with the same energy that we always had. We got excited about visiting French supermarkets, drinking the wine and eating the baguettes and how we would learn a new French word every day. There was still a lot to do before our move on 30 January 2015 but we could not wait.

As you get older, you really feel that time flies by. A year later, after we'd settled Arthur and Dorothy into their beds and were awaiting New Year's Eve 2015, it seemed we had proved it beyond doubt. The year had truly shot by and it was not until Angela and I sat in our salon with a drink in hand that it really hit us what a year 2015 had been. We struggled to remember all we had done; we had changed the whole direction of our lives. We had become custodians of a forty-five-room French château, a magnificent building that had no electricity, heating or sewerage. Over the past year, we may have only scratched the surface of what needed to be done but we had accomplished all the basics and now had utilities from the twenty-first century; we were comfortable. That very special evening, as we sat on the sofa, we held hands, ate cheese and drank port and reminisced about our first year at the château, and then explored our dreams for our lives ahead.

Introduction

The clocks turned midnight. It was our first New Year's Day together in our forever home. Anything and everything felt possible. Our celebrations were more of a snuggle than a party but we had achieved a big milestone. It was a new year and we both felt the anticipation and excitement of the unknown.

The first morning of the year started frosty but calm. We could hear the birds singing and all four of us sat together in bed chatting. We talked to Arthur and Dorothy about the science of 'a year' – what it meant for a new year to start. At one and two years old (nearly three!), 1 January was most certainly just another day to them but Arthur grasped the concept of a year, and he definitely knew his birthday was soon!

As we sat together in bed, we were filled with happiness knowing the move to France had been the right decision. It did not matter that the electricity to our suite came via the extension lead from the downstairs hallway, nor that the wallpaper was falling off and the paint was hanging down from the ceiling! We were broke but happy, and in our home that was filled with love and laughter.

Our future was in our own hands. We had stopped filming after our wedding and had no idea of when the TV show would air, or even if anyone would watch it, or like it! We were getting used to having time to ourselves again. It felt odd. We are not used to *not* having deadlines but we needed to progress with our vision to turn the château into a magical place, both for our family and for the others we wanted to share it with. So, as the dawn rose on a new year, we set about making that happen.

This was our first winter in a habitable château. I'd tried to convince Angela that a warm jumper was better than lots of central heating but I'm not sure I was successful! Our suite was tatty but snug and we had to come to terms with the fact that the château was made up of 'zones' of different temperatures. If we spent time in an area we kept it warmer but we were very aware that the heating was expensive to run, though we didn't know exactly how much it would cost. Thankfully, the old coach house had a set of stables that had been filled with firewood that I reckoned would last for a couple of winters at the very least – even though some of it was soft wood that was very rotten. When I picked up logs that were light I knew that they wouldn't burn for long and we got through a lot of it very quickly. However, at this stage there was still a reasonable supply of oak logs to keep the home fires burning.

I grew up in a time when it was not unusual to find ice on the inside of your bedroom window on a cold night – that's what curtains were for, to keep the cold out of your room. There was no such thing as double glazing and radiators upstairs were a rarity. I remember the initiative to go smokeless (in the early 1970s) and our family home getting a coal stove, complete with a back boiler, that used anthracite, which would stay lit all night if stacked before my parents went to bed. (Those memories raise a couple of questions – how many people are aware that anthracite is not just a colour on a modern paint palette? Who remembers putting a shovel of 'slack' on the fire to keep the embers burning through the night?) Similarly, loading our modern wood burners at the château with logs and turning them down keeps them lit through the night and they burst easily into life in the morning, so the cycle of the winter months involves bringing in a fair amount of logs and tending the fires. Particularly during the first year when fuel bills were unknown and a lurking fear . . .

When you walk in through the front door of the château, the airiness of the entrance hall and the majestic staircase leading up and giving you the option of going left or right sets the scene and never fails to impress. You could fit a small house easily in that volume, but as it is so open, it is a challenge to keep it warm.

As they were ugly, we did not have thermostatic valves on any of the radiators and so I developed the ritual of walking around turning radiators off as we retired and on again as we surfaced, in advance of the family moving into parts of the château. I particularly enjoyed walking around in the morning and last thing at night. In the morning, as I left the suite, the drop in temperature would be very noticeable on the landing outside. Downstairs, I'd turn on the radiator and stoke or light the fires. It was lovely and peaceful, and it allowed me to absorb the quiet. We started 'breakfasting' in the suite and my efforts meant the château was up to temperature by the time everyone came downstairs for a second breakfast or to start working.

In the evenings, I have always done a quick check outside and then made sure that all the windows and doors were secure. Having a château just made the task a little bigger. But I really enjoyed the couple of minutes' walk around that confirmed all was well. By the time I was upstairs to join in the children's bath time regime, I was relaxed, and even though we often went downstairs again to continue working we could theoretically nod off with the children ... something that happened all too regularly.

During the winter months, it was normal for us to keep some heat on in our suite, which is always the warmest place in the château. However, when the temperatures hit the serious minus figures, we would have some heating on elsewhere in the château through the night – usually the radiators in the hallway and the salon, with one on in the honeymoon suite with the doors open to allow some heat to head upstairs, which, along with the tanks and pipes in the attic, were sufficient to keep us frost free. We had done the necessary work to live in a twenty-first-century way, we just weren't convinced that we were able to pay the bills if we were not frugal and, equally importantly, we didn't want to be wasteful.

But before anyone thinks winter in a big draughty château is all hardship, it is really important to explain the beauty we are surrounded by. Not many people know, but stormy weather makes an old building talk to you. We had plugged as many draughts as we could but there was still lots of creaking and the odd bang to remind us that the château was there protecting us from the elements. We have often been asked whether the château feels spooky but that thought never crossed our mind. From the first day we walked in through the front door it has felt welcoming and, although I know I'm not attuned to spectral or otherworldly forces, no one who has visited us has been anything but positive about the feelings and energy here – it's a lovely place to live.

Hard frosts take the château to another level of amazing. Arthur and Dorothy have never ceased to enjoy standing on the ice formed on a puddle to wait in anticipation of it giving way, or sliding on it if it's too strong, and, after walking around on crispy grass, returning to a blazing fire in a warm salon with rosy cheeks is an experience to savour. When the moat freezes over, it changes our view of life completely. It is like being held in our castle by the ice queen and all you want to do is shut the gates and have a family duvet day and play!

CHAPTER I

The Building Years

The château is large and grey and in the depths of January it complements the skies beautifully. It is big and dark and cold looking but that only tells part of the story. Inside, it was now warm and light and full of laughter, even if only in the 20 per cent we were properly occupying. In the depths of winter, the wood-burners in the salon and *salle à manger* always acted as a focus. Their roaring flames changed the high-status, high-ceilinged rooms into our home, which was snug. But you only had to move outside the main reception rooms to the entrance hall to be reminded that the château was still a 'work in progress'. The wind howled through the house, mainly via the large double entrance hall doors. There was a small piece of glass missing that was taped over and when the wind was fierce the doors played melodies, reminding us of how much work was still ahead of us. Our bedroom was definitely more shabby than 'shabby chic', and, despite my fanatic cleaning, there was always dust lurking to cover every surface.

But it was our dust, our forever door to fix, and if ever there was a moment when the list felt too long, we stopped and Dick reminded me that you eat an elephant a bite at a time. We couldn't have been happier and we knew we couldn't have worked harder. We knew what we had achieved so far was nearly impossible – but that didn't make our to-do list any shorter.

We were living our dream. We had done it. We had bought the most beautiful building in a stunning setting and it was our home. Even after the first, very challenging year, we knew this was where we were going to live the rest of our lives – all our investment was for Arthur and Dorothy, and their families, too. We could picture their grandchildren playing and talking to them about the old days . . . in French?!

We are, however, realists – optimistic definitely, but we are grounded. There was so much more to do and we understood that we had only actually set the foundations for our dream life. When we paused, caught our breath, stopped to smell the roses, we felt the warmth of being in our dream place, so we tried as often as possible to take those moments. They were not rare but not frequent enough. We were still in the 'building the dream' phase, not the chilling out and enjoying it phase!

After our ridiculously busy first year at the château, it took a while to get used to stillness. The Christmas decorations were packed away and put in the attic. (We had our own attic to store things! I mean, that took a bit of getting used to and we often had to pinch ourselves that it was all real.) Mum and Dad went on a well-deserved holiday and, now that we were turning the corner to another new year, we knew it was time to start getting busy again.

Finding our new rhythm and achieving our balance of family, business and no-guilt downtime was not easy, though. There was a heaviness on our shoulders that we needed to be busy to ensure our dream succeeded.

But we had a plan. In fact, we always have a plan. We are not naive and know that plans are only the starting point and that they will change, but to come up with a plan we had to agree what we wanted to do and that involved talking and a fair amount of thinking. We knew I was going to have to take jobs that took me away from the château until our businesses here could sustain us. With not much spare cash and lots to do, it made sense to do things that didn't cost a lot! Working in the château tended to be expensive so it was completely logical for me to get out and spend some time exploring the walled garden.

For any gardener, a walled garden is a dream. But the area was a mess. The main entrance is over the moat and to the left. The garden is the best part of an acre and the walls are orientated so the main path runs from north-west to south-east. Two sides are ten-foot stone walls that are eighteen inches thick and the other two are mainly tall two-storey outbuildings, which give the whole area a feeling of being solid and permanent, although all the roofs needed to be replaced. Set back from the outside of the walls, some forty or fifty metres, are rows of tall oak and lime trees, to act as a windbreak. I knew all about wind turbulence from my experiences siting wind turbines and it dawned on me that the combination of these trees and the buildings was the reason the garden was still most of the time . . . Strong winds get deflected up and over these barriers and cannot dip down to blow around the garden. Bird song is positively loud in the walled garden, it seems to be focused, and the expanse of the walls of the buildings means you can hear someone at the château shouting for you even if you cannot see them – very useful when meals are served!

9

There were a very few old fruit trees that had survived the garden being neglected. We had three pear trees that had obviously been trained against the walls, another two that were apparently randomly placed, not at the edge or in the middle, and a single cherry tree that was at least forty feet high; it was a monster. In addition to all the brambles and nettles that formed a low entanglement that it was impossible to walk through, we had a bunch of rogue sycamore trees. I know of no one who would plant sycamores on purpose but some had trunks eighteen inches in diameter, which means they had been there for years. I thought of them as our biggest weeds and couldn't wait to get rid of them.

I started gardening with my father when I was about five years old. To start with, it was much more about spending time with him than actually gardening. I think I was there to potter and collect stones rather than for the horticulture but somehow over the years I absorbed a fair bit. I love time in the garden and somehow you feel like you are relaxing even if you are doing something seriously strenuous.

There are other benefits and the summer before I headed off to the Royal Military Academy Sandhurst, I was all for getting a gym membership to bring myself to the level of fitness I knew I would need, but my dad put it very simply: 'Don't be an idiot, Richard, just get out and dig the garden, it'll sort you out.' I dug for Northern Ireland and also went running, and ended up in good shape!

You learn when you spend time with knowledgeable people. As well as growing vegetables with my father, I also visited my grandparents every weekend – it was the sort of thing you did back then – and they both invested lots of time in their garden. Indeed, when they lived in Newtownards, my granny used to grow and sell flowers to the flower shops up in Belfast and it was from her I got my appreciation of roses and scabias, both of which are stunning cut flowers. So through osmosis, and then years of converting barren military quarters' gardens into veggie patches, I achieved a good working knowledge of gardening, but my knowledge of walled gardens was limited. I knew the principles and had visited some but I had little practical experience.

The concept of a kitchen garden, the 'potager', originated in medieval France, but I'd always thought of potager as a thick, substantial vegetable stew eaten by peasants in the past, and my lack of French meant I'd never put the two words together. But despite this ignorance, we were the owners of a walled potager and I couldn't wait to do it justice.

The big breakthrough came when we had a visit from our neighbour Jacques De Baglion, whose family had been the previous custodians of Château-de-la-Motte Husson. He walked around the moat with Inox, his Labrador, and we ended up in the walled garden surveying the wreckage of a once beautiful place. In our now comfortable Franglais, we discussed my theory that there had to be a set of paths that 'crossed' the garden and more that went around near the outside to define the beds by the walls. Jacques got very excited and took me through the layout, explaining how the old fruit trees had actually lined the paths and how the paths met the three gates in the walls. He admitted his memory of it was a bit hazy as it was the best part of forty years since the garden had last been in its glory. His visit left me inspired and when he'd gone , I went off to get a 'grape' to go in search of our lost paths. (Okay, who doesn't know what a 'grape' is? My Irish grandfather and my father always called a garden fork a 'grape' and I have called it that all my life, though I find I now have to be trilingual and translate into English and French!)

Where to start? Obviously the paths had to lead to the gates but in the middle of the far wall was an overgrown tower that must have been a focal point. There were also a couple of old fruit tree stumps slightly off to one side that must have lined a path in the past, so I confidently marched into the middle of the garden and stuck my grape into the ground and jumped on it to sink it in . . . nothing. I moved to a spot in line with the side gate into the garden and what would have been a greenhouse . . . but again, nothing. I started spiralling out and finally I felt the tell-tale crunch of gravel down about six inches over towards the moat in line with our tower. I grabbed a spade and dug a trench across what I felt was a path. I discovered one made from the same slightly orangey-coloured grit we had in front of the château and, interestingly, it was curved so it was high in the middle and lower at the outside edges. The weeds and decades of leaf matter that had become soil had truly covered the paths; the edges were down a good nine to twelve inches, so my path-finding probing only worked if I hit the centre of a path. But I had a working technique and a garden to plot out. Very quickly I knew I had a cross and a rectangular outside path about six feet in from the walls but, in truth, at that moment I still only had an overgrown garden with paths that had yet to be reclaimed.

There followed a lot of sweating despite the cold, crisp weather and, over the course of a very special week, I cleared the first part of our pathway. It went from the main entrance to the garden to the outside path, then dog-legged to the left to join the main trans-garden part of the cross path. I had a lot of help from Arthur and Dorothy and I think even Angela enjoyed these hours out in the fresh air, though she did like making the point that she wasn't a 'land girl' (yet!).

Seeing Dick in his garden melted our hearts. He had been incredibly patient during our first year but I often heard him talk about how he could not wait to get in there and start to reclaim the garden. Even to this day, he says he would have bought the château just for the *potagerie* and I fully believe that. Neither of us is good at doing nothing and in this time of uncertainty (our wedding

and events business was yet to prove successful and we did not even know when our television series would be aired, or if anyone would watch it!), Dick was using the garden to keep himself busy and, well, because he loved it! It was a reminder of why we moved here. The truth be known, I was there for the family fun and to see Dick in his element, and Arthur and Dorothy were there to play with mud. We were no help. But huge support. Probably.

Our first potager tree planting came about by chance. We were at the local supermarket and there was a huge area taken up at the entrance by lots of fruit trees. It was obviously 'fruit tree planting time' and so we grabbed a bargain, or eight.

I had never seen fruit trees being sold in a supermarket before! And that is one of the reasons we love French supermarkets. If it's in season, you know about it as you have to walk a full ten metres to pass the seasonal displays. I honestly believe that even if you don't have a garden, you get a sense of what is being planted at that time of year just by visiting supermarkets!

The trees were lovely to look at, each was sold in a hessian bag, and we picked up four initially because that's all we could fit in the trolley. Dorothy was in the front seat and Arthur was in the main body. But at €6 each (that was about £4), they were such a bargain we couldn't miss the opportunity. So Arthur and Dorothy walked for the rest of the shopping trip and we got more trees.

As a family, we went out into the garden and, using the roughly scraped pathway as our guide, we planted what was to be the part of our avenue of fruit trees. We all dug the holes and, with great ceremony, put in a mixture of French apple and pear varieties – we'd decided that the cherries and plums had to wait as they were over twice the price, so we left gaps for them.

I love having everyone in the garden working. Somehow Angela always dresses the children to be functional but makes them look too cute to work. Dorothy had the most gorgeous red double-breasted tartan coat on with a faux-fur collar, which I would have said was for wearing to Sunday school, with matching wellies and hat. But this was not a spectator sport and Dorothy took a spade that was obviously too big for her and started scooping out a hole. It all looked a bit dangerous to Mummy but as the spade was unwieldy, Dorothy started to use her hands. To further the team effort, I loosened the soil and gave her and Arthur trowels. Surprising to say, they were both actually helpful! They obviously needed a hand making the hole a bit deeper but their playing progressed the planting of our fruit trees and they proved themselves.

Everyone had been hard at work digging holes, even Dorothy. And, as I was digging, I was watching everyone simply being happy and content. All with rosy cheeks ... It really was one of those days that we had dreamt of when we'd decided to move to France. Late morning, Dick had put on a casserole with seasonal vegetables and every time I went back to the château it was full of mouth-watering aromas that made you hungry even if you had just eaten!

Yes, the garden had a long way to go, but we had started. Together. When the trees were in, it was a very special moment and I felt quite tearful. We were making our history, inspired by the original paths, and it was our garden.

That evening, we embraced the French love of seasonality. Winter is very definitely the time for warming casseroles. Root vegetables were in abundance and some of the most enticing cuts of meat are a must for the slow cooker. We love them all. In addition to the *jarret de boeuf* – shin – we like using *la pointe de poitrine* – brisket. It is a very reasonably priced cut and is often sold for *pot au feu*, which is a very common dish here. It was just what the doctor ordered after a long day in the garden!

....

POT AU FEU

*The clue is in the name – **pot au feu** literally means 'pot on the fire', which is actually cooking in a saucepan. The principles are simple: the elements needing more cooking go in first...*

Ingredients

1kg brisket or *plat-de-côtes* (short rib)
1 onion, quartered
2 leeks, roughly chopped
4 carrots, roughly chopped
1 turnip, cut into eight
3 cloves of garlic
1 bay leaf
a sprig of thyme
a few sprigs of parsley
2 cloves
6 peppercorns
1 tbs salt

Method

Place the beef in a large pot. Cover with water to a level about 2.5cm (1in) above the meat. Bring to the boil, turn down the heat and simmer for one hour, skimming off the foam from time to time.

Transfer to a slow cooker and add the remaining ingredients. Slow cook for a further six to eight hours.

If you wish, you can serve the broth separately but just before service we fish out the aromatics, cut the beef up and then put it back into the pot, which we put on the table. I love it with buttery mash potatoes that 'dissolve' into the broth. Or, dipping in a buttery baguette also hits the mark – though, from what we've seen, it appears the French aren't great dippers?

Interestingly, I was brought up with a degree of confusion about what was a swede and what was a turnip. In Northern Ireland what we call a turnip is called a swede in England, and English turnips are not really talked about at all . . . Thankfully, as we have learned more French, the confusion has gone: a turnip is a navet *and a swede is a bloke from Sweden!*

....

January had flown by and, before we knew it, Arthur's birthday was here. His first official birthday in France! After Arthur's second birthday party in the UK (the day before we left for France), which was packed with family and friends, and our recent wedding celebrations that seemed to last for weeks, I think we were all after something gentle for our little man's third birthday.

Arthur is a water baby, as is Dorothy, so we managed to book ourselves into a Center Parcs, two hours west from here, called

Les Bois Francs. Because it was January, it was empty and cheap and the pool was hot! However, the negatives were that most of the facilities were closed . . . That did not stop us having fun and I managed to get away with going on the kiddies' slide for hours on end without being told off by the lifeguards.

It also felt nice having a change of scenery. We had been very château-centric in our first year and, as magical as it is, there was a constant anxiety always to get things done.

Arthur received his first Nerf gun, a selection of superhero goodies and his most treasured item to this day: a plastic trophy he won for going on the red water slide the most times in an hour. We wrote on it with a Sharpie: 'Winner 2016 – Arthur Donald Strawbridge', and Arthur was the proudest little three-year-old you could imagine.

I'd never been to a Center Parcs and I wasn't quite sure what to expect as I had a vision of Butlin's in a wood – though, to be fair, I'd never been to Butlin's either! We arrived in exactly the right mind set and had a ball. Indeed, we spent so long in the pools, under the fountains and going up and down every conceivable shape of slide that we invariably finished our pool sessions white and wrinkly. But it was great fun and the children laughed and smiled and were thoroughly pooped each evening.

One aspect of the park was a bit of a surprise; I suppose it was part of the 'eco' ethos but there was very limited lighting on the many roads and tracks that connected all the cabins, which looked the same. The children weren't old enough for bicycles yet and so our trip back to the cabin by foot in the dark early evening usually involved us taking a 'direct' route rather than following the roads. I laughed until I nearly peed myself on many occasions but I particularly remember pushing Angela up the bank of one ditch as she was pushing Dorothy's pushchair ahead of her and getting a tad grumpy with me, while Arthur stood on the top (already having been helped up there) making a sage comment along the lines of, 'I'm not sure this is the best way, Daddy . . .'

*

With our mini-break over and the garden underway, we knew we needed to knuckle down and think 'business' . . . It had taken a while to get into the right frame of mind as this was a task where you needed to be fully functioning and focused!

Angela is an entrepreneur and has no shortage of the characteristics needed to be successful in business. She has vision, motivation, passion and confidence but, very importantly, she is also a good decision maker. We have had many discussions about what we should do and when faced with numerous options, we look at the objective, then decide the best way forward for us as a family, according to our resources. With the myriad of tasks the château presents on a daily basis, we truly understand that 'you eat an elephant a bite at a time'.

My first business mentor told me, 'Plan, plan, plan. If you don't, you plan to fail.' I have found writing up your thoughts in one place really allows you to set out your objective and map the journey to get there. Planning in pre-Dick days honestly kept me focused and on track. Then I met Dick . . . the most organised and thought-out human you will ever meet. He not only plans but annoyingly he recognises all the pitfalls in a plan. I can't lie, I like to plan with pure optimism, while Dick is an optimistic realist. But together, we plan quite well.

Before we even bought the château, we had a plan. You can't just buy a château and expect the money you have left (£20,000

in our case) to go far. Dick had a National Geographic show commissioned, which meant that we knew funds were going to come in in the first year. That was all part of the planning. We also planned for Dick to continue being a TV presenter until we established the business here at the château, which we never for one moment thought would happen overnight. But our end goal, our objective, was to create a live/work life where we could be here for Arthur and Dorothy. So, how does one achieve that?!

Firstly, we needed to work out exactly what we wanted to offer our guests. This meant that every detail needed to be pored over. When it comes to weddings, there's an infinite number of ways of coming up with a pricing structure. We were of course limited to the rooms we had available, well finished, which was a grand total of one: the very lovely honeymoon suite. But that was all we needed to get started!

After many evenings of discussions, we decided on three initial offerings: weddings and special celebrations; luxury weekend getaways and corporate strategy days (Dick's forte).

Apart from attending weddings, I was unsighted as to how much work they would involve but I knew Angela would have the details all covered well in advance of our first one, so I was not worried. When it came to our luxury weekend getaways, the principles were easy: we wanted to provide the sort of weekend we'd love to go on. It was all about luxury, decadence, more luxury and then, to finish it off, more decadence. However, that was quite an open-ended idea, so we thought we'd start off by holding 'food lovers' weekends' – or FLW – to confirm how the weekends would go.

When it comes to the service, Angela is all over it. I had been a finalist in *Celebrity Masterchef*, I've worked in restaurants, run restaurants, presented over seventy cookery shows and written half a dozen cookery books, so it's fair to say I know my way around the kitchen. And to cap it all – I love my grub! We were both confident that anyone who attended our FLW would be wined and dined, but we sat down and discussed in some detail our USPs –'unique selling points'. We set down the agenda for a weekend getaway that celebrated France and our region. We made the decision even before we moved to France that we were to be about quality rather than quantity. Fewer, more memorable weekends were our aim and we enthusiastically discussed at length what we would offer.

Our weekends were initially to be for one couple and would commence on a Friday evening. They were to be received in the salon with nibbles and a lovely, very easy to drink red sparkling wine. They would then be shown to their room where they were to relax and prepare for dinner. The honeymoon suite was to set the standard for each suite. There would be a bar and a fridge stocked with soft drinks and local sparkling Loire wines in their private salon. Their tower room was a quiet place to sit and chat and the bathroom had a large shower and a bath big enough for two to relax in, as well as an armchair if only one person wished to bathe. (How many conversations have taken place with one of you perched on the closed loo seat chatting to the other wallowing in the bath? For us it had been lots, hence the obligatory armchairs.) Obviously, a huge, very comfortable bed was the centrepiece of the bedroom.

Dinner was to take hours and the many courses would showcase regional and local foods. Digestifs and petit fours would round off the evening. Saturday was a leisurely start followed by a trip to the market to buy whatever ingredients looked good and then home for a much-needed lunch, some relaxation around the château grounds, then a casual evening of cooking and dining down in the family kitchen in the *sous sol*. The menu would be determined by what we had bought and what our guests wanted to try.

A late and leisurely breakfast would take place on Sunday morning followed by onward travel. We felt it was a good mixture of being pampered and having a chance to experience château life. And we were excited to welcome guests into our home to do it.

When we first moved to the château, we were all in – we sold everything we had, including my old and much-loved Fairway taxi called Ethel Red and our shared VW family car. We knew we needed every bit of extra cash. It did mean, however, that we were car-less, apart from the time when we were making the television series, when we were loaned a car by Citroën. Since filming had finished in November 2015, we had been sharing my parents' car but it was obvious that we needed wheels of our own.

Cars are very expensive in France, though interestingly we found the insurance costs seemed to be less. Over the years, I've driven most things from tanks to articulated lorries, cranes to forklifts and motorbikes to buses, so my needs were not that important when it came to choosing our vehicle, but there were some important factors, after the obvious one: that it had to be safe for the family. Firstly, the cost; secondly, the fact that it had to be big enough and, finally, Angel was adamant it had to be an automatic. With that in mind, we scoured the classified ads.

Being broke at the start of 2016 is part of our journey. Most people would be after moving to a new home and having their wedding. We had the additional costs of starting the restorations of a forty-five-room, nineteenth-century château ... enough said. With everything going on, we had not really paid much attention to the fact that our neighbour Bertrand had not yet submitted his bill for the work he did on our sewerage system, so when the €12,000 bill came in, we had to borrow some money from our family. The fact

that we were car-less and waiting for work was all part of the early stress. So our families added a few thousand extra to allow us to buy a little run-around car . . .

It's nearly impossible to get anything in France roadworthy for €3,000, especially from a dealership, so we looked on a reputable second-hand site. That I had become used to driving the lovely automatic Citroën for the past year, combined with obviously driving on the opposite side of the road and the very fact that many French drivers just do not use roundabouts like we do (I'm sure you're meant to stop at roundabouts . . .?) meant I'd lost a little bit of confidence. Arthur and Dorothy's safety was my number one priority and, in light of the above, I thought it might be in everyone's interest if we looked for an automatic. Dick and I did not see eye to eye on what was acceptable. Though this only caused an issue whilst we both had to agree . . . As I was clearly the tricky customer (or, in my defence, the less confident customer), Dick left it to me to find something I could drive, for under €3,000. In France.

In *my* defence, I only passed the responsibility onto Angela after she said the fully serviced, very reasonable, low-mileage Audi A2 I had found was ugly and the wrong colour . . .

And I went on to find the ugliest little grey car you could imagine, but I loved it because it felt comfortable and safe. The seats were high and there was next to no bonnet sticking out, meaning parking was easy. I could fit a potty in the footwell and the boot was the perfect height for changing nappies. It was Dick's worst nightmare. It went 0–60 in about five minutes and Dick chuntered from the moment we got it until the moment we had enough cash to buy another car.

*

When I look back, I realise that I have always been ambitious and motivated. But falling pregnant was a game changer for me. I instantly felt I wanted to spend more time being a mum. I wanted to spend those first precious moments with my babies guilt free (or as guilt free as possible).

When Arthur was seven months old and I was two months pregnant with Dorothy, I was hosting a tea party for a regular client of mine. She said to me, 'I don't have many regrets but if I had one, it would be that I worked too much when the kids were young. You just cannot get those years back.' I knew she was telling me to slow down. It was all the sign I needed and exactly what my gut had been telling me. Dick most certainly had his thoughts on the matter but, having spent a decade building up my business, the Vintage Patisserie, I needed to be ready. It was the end of an era.

But the new era had dawned upon us! I knew it was right to restart the next chapter with a new business. We would take a bit of the Vintage Patisserie and a bit of Dick's rustic and delicious cuisine and make something new, something that was both of ours.

I knew that, first things first, we needed a website. I am of an age that I remember the Yellow Pages. I did not know of the 'internet' until my late teenage years and it changed the way we did everything. I have no idea how a French château would have showcased its business overseas, or in fact to anyone, back then. Our platform needed to be wonderful; it needed to represent the magic of the château. Now, that's easier said than done!

I had a little bit of experience here, having done two sites from scratch. One was a highly illustrated interactive site where you could design chocolates and cakes, the other, which followed this, was my Vintage Patisserie website. I find a gentle mix of illustration and stunning photography to be the best combination and I think it is important for your homepage to wow visually but also be informative. There are obviously people out there who do this for a living, but with barely any funds in the bank this was a DIY job and we called in a favour from our artist friend Sam, who luckily happens to be quite a fantastic web developer too. There were a lot more details to think about but we had started and it felt good.

The Vintage Patisserie website remained live and during the transition period, whilst the new site was being built, I would send replies to anyone who enquired telling them about our new wedding business and food lovers' weekends. As most tea party enquiries were for hen parties, weddings were not necessarily what they wanted and with the FLWs at £1,000 per couple all-inclusive for the weekend, they were far more expensive than my previous tea parties, but we believed they delivered in value.

And then I got an email from Jane Lockhart. Jane had emailed about a hen party but after I had replied explaining the situation and our new ventures, she booked her and her partner Alun in for our first food lovers' weekend.

Selling the first of anything is always a complete buzz. I've sold all sorts of things, including vintage clothing, clothes I have made, T-shirts I have printed, cupcakes, chocolates, china, cake stands. But whether it's a £2.50 cupcake or a £1,000 weekend at the château, there is nothing quite like the thrill of that very first sale.

I ran down the stairs in excitement to share the news with Dick. We had done it. We had secured our first paid weekend and we celebrated with a cup of tea and a trip to the bakers to buy some éclairs for Arthur and Dorothy.

Whilst Angela had been working hard on getting our business ready to launch, I had been working on a TV series in Northern Ireland to build a replica of the first plane to fly in Ireland, which had been built and flown by Harry Ferguson, the Ulsterman of tractor design fame. As I was heading back to Northern Ireland to complete the project, and for our creation to hopefully fly, we decided to make it into a family trip and spend a couple of days with my mother and sisters.

There are lots of ways to get to Ireland from France; we opted to take a ferry overnight to Dublin, followed by a couple of hours driving north. It's a long crossing but we thought amusing the children on the ferry should be easy as there were play areas. And we hoped they would sleep for the majority of the crossing anyway – how naive were we . . . The Irish ferry boat was very friendly and we all enjoyed a meal before heading off to get our beauty sleep in the four-berth cabin. Our plan was for Angela and Dorothy to share one bottom bunk, Arthur to have the other and for me to be on a top bunk. It couldn't have been simpler but for the fact that Arthur kept rolling out of bed! It was purely by chance that Angela and I were chatting after the children had fallen asleep and I managed to reach across and catch Arthur as he simply rolled off the bed . . . I checked all the stuff we had in the cabin to find a safe way of barricading him into the bunk. There was no wall-making capability but I did manage to build the equivalent of a high-trapeze safety net between the bunks using luggage, sheets and our spare clothing. However, there was no way I was simply going to sleep above Arthur and wait to see if the 'net' caught him. Instead, I had the pleasure of sleeping with our boy, who was impressively capable of pushing unwanteds out of the bed and also appeared to like doing starfish impressions. It didn't take long to establish that the best way for me to protect Arthur and get a night's sleep was for me to occupy a couple of inches of the bunk and to have most of my body 'floating' between the beds on the net construction.

But despite the deprivations of the night, we awoke smiling and laughing the way families do, had a big breakfast and headed off to a wonderful couple of days with the family and some filming as well!

The excitement of turning up at Granny's house was fantastic. Dorothy was a baby when we had last visited, so for her it was like her first visit! From the moment we entered the house, Granny and the aunties did not stop pampering us. I remember Jenny saying, 'I want you to be rested and to have a break.' I had a complete twitch being looked after but I knew they meant what they said, and as they never got much of a chance to spoil the children, I tried my best to sit still.

During Dick's time at work we explored County Antrim together. We drove for hours along the coast and ate picnics in the car whilst listening to the constant pitter-patter of rain.

Once Dick had finished his job, we got some quality time all together. One of the highlights was when we ate potatoes grown by Dick's sister, which went straight from a growing bag for a quick wash and then into the pan. This was a first for me and it was really true what Dick had said, they are so sweet! We had planned a day out at the Belfast Zoo. The zoo was opened in 1934 and sits on a secluded location on the north-eastern slope of Cavehill. It's a very special place and, as Granny said, there are lots of hills, so you will need your pancakes!

This was the day when Arthur and Dorothy learnt what it is to have Granny's pancakes with Granny in Northern Ireland! It involves sitting on a stool at the breakfast bar in the kitchen and taking warm buttermilk pancakes fresh from the griddle with too much butter and whatever topping your heart desires – though maple syrup and possibly some crispy bacon is hard to beat. My mum revelled in her role as pancake maker, as she has done for every one of her grandchildren, and Arthur and Dorothy knew they were in for a treat as they could see how excited I was. As the pancakes come off the griddle you can't eat them straight away – they are too hot and need to rest a couple of minutes to be perfect, and for that they are put into a folded tea towel. We nearly had a mutiny from Arthur when he thought he wasn't allowed one, but watching Granny pouring out the next four onto the griddle amused him for long enough to cool the first batch, then it was onto the plate, butter and a drizzle of maple syrup, brought back from Canada by my brother Bobby, who lives there (not 'maple-flavoured' syrup!).

As I cut the first pancake into strips to share, it started to disappear. Arthur and Dorothy didn't say a thing. I think my mum was a bit worried that they wouldn't like them, but though the second piece being put into their mouths before they had finished chewing the first may have been bad manners, it was also a wordless compliment! Granny was turning the pancakes out four at a time with practised skill on her trusty griddle that has been about as long as I can remember, so it wasn't long before she had so many that our little ones were properly stuffed and she had a pile for everyone else to tackle without getting a look from Arthur and Dorothy, who were very sticky with a light covering of buttery maple syrup! I had to stop them eating as we were all getting a bit worried that people that small were eating that much – the results could be unpleasant and my sister Deanna, who was going to be playing with them, is a bit squeamish. Arthur and Dorothy made their appreciation of Granny's pancakes clear by asking for them every time they felt a bit peckish!

....

GRANNY'S PANCAKES

Best served hot with butter or with maple syrup and bacon and a full fry-up. If you ever have any left over, they fry up really well as part of an Ulster Fry, which is a breakfast guaranteed to keep you going all day.

Ingredients

Butter, to cook
225g soda flour (make your own with 450g flour to 1 tbsp
bicarbonate of soda and ½ tsp salt)
2 eggs
300ml buttermilk (or sour 300ml of milk with ½ tsp lemon
juice)
1 tbsp sugar

Method

*Heat the griddle and season with butter on a piece of kitchen
towel. Beat the ingredients in a jug and when the griddle is hot
pour out four pancakes. When you can see the bubbles coming
through they are ready to turn over.*

*Once cooked, stack in a folded tea towel to keep warm. The big
challenge is to make them faster than they can be eaten.*

....

It must have been the rest Jenny and the girls had given us, or possibly the change of scenery, because when we arrived back home, we were bouncing. I threw myself into cleaning and cleared out the original drinks cabinet that is behind a door in the *salle à manger*. I organised our drinks cabinet, our drawers, and I was looking at the château through our guests' eyes. Although our suite was shabby, rationalising clothes and toiletries felt like we were being busy and it just made me feel better!

The website had a final push and, after months of poring over every detail, our platform to communicate the magic of the château to the world was finished. Our château site was cream, dark green and gold. It felt elegant, not too fussy, clear to use and packed a punch with stunning photography from Dick's daughter Charlotte. It captured the imagination. The fonts were hand drawn and dark green, which gave it a really personal feel. We wrote all the copy ourselves in the first person so it was chatty yet informative, and when we looked at it, we smiled. This was a new beginning! We paid Sam later that year and to this day it's a favour that we will never forget . . . On 4 March, our website went live and we shared our offerings with the world. Within ten minutes, we had received our first wedding enquiry! It was from an old client of mine, also called Charlotte. To be clear, Charlotte was not old, but she used to work for a very well-known beauty brand and the Vintage Patisserie used to make personalised gifts for many of the glossies and newspapers as a press relations exercise for their brand. Charlotte would basically use me whenever she could and I loved her for that. She gave me my first ever grown-up, personalised chocolate order: 1,000 boxes! I had a tiny tempering machine in my kitchen and I pretty much stayed up for five days straight to get the order complete. Those were the days, pre-Dick, when I was a one-man – well, lady – band!

Charlotte talked about how she and Richard, her fiancé, had been waiting for the right wedding opportunity to come along but she now realised she had been waiting for us to start our business! It felt very reassuring. We continued to chat about the timeline and how next year would be good because they were planning on having a baby! I immediately put my tuppence in . . .

'Please, please listen to me, Charlotte. Have your wedding *before* your baby. It's the one day in your life that is completely about you. As wonderful as it would be to have a little one in tow, it will not be the same . . . You have the choice!'

And that was that. Charlotte booked her wedding with us for that August! Our first wedding. In just five months. After the complete excitement and buzz, the terror kicked in. There was a *lot*

to get sorted. Apart from finishing the honeymoon suite to guest standard, which would need to be complete in time for our first food lovers' weekend, we needed toilets for eighty, a team front and back of house, suppliers, extra cutlery, more organisation, a sound system, comfy chairs – and that was just the few things that sprang to mind!

Getting the website up to start attracting customers had been our highest priority. We were confident we could make the château work for us but the relief that we felt when we had our first wedding booked in was a 'sinking to your knees and closing your eyes' level of relief. However, typical of our lives in France, we were on a rollercoaster. Having a wedding here meant being ready for a wedding here.

It's very different having friends and family come to your own wedding compared to a paying customer and their guests. We needed more facilities and we needed to be completely professional. Which meant we needed a team that knew what to do.

Angela had warned me there was *some* snagging to do in the honeymoon suite but I wasn't too worried about that (duh!). We also needed guest toilets, including at the orangery (the two sheds and bath to pee in with the old long drops we had for our wedding wouldn't do at all), and the rest of the orangery needed to be perfect and needed to have power. Any area guests would go needed to be perfect, the service needed to be perfect, the bar needed to be perfect, the food needed to be perfect . . . The list went on but every task had one thing in common: they needed to be perfect, and fast.

CHAPTER 2

Our First Easter Together

Although we were only a few months into 2016, it had most certainly been an eventful time. Having a reason and drive to push our home onto the next stage really put a spring in our step. Our bookings felt like a huge achievement and milestone, and the atmosphere at the château mirrored our emotions. Easter fell on 27 March in 2016. Dick's mum Jenny had sent us back home with a big box of Easter treasures. There were some Cadbury's eggs but, more importantly, family heirlooms – hanging eggs that had been painted and découpaged by the family decades ago and the cutest wooden bunnies with 'This way' signs. There were also plastic decorate-yourself eggs of all colours and sizes, and stickers galore that to this day we have not used as they look so great. There were also packets of specialist food-dye powders . . .

Easter is a very important celebration in France. It says a lot that our local convenience shop in the village opens every day except Easter Sunday. For me, growing up in Northern Ireland, Easter was a simple celebration that involved eating too much chocolate and having a breakfast of magical boiled eggs. Thinking back, most of the eggs we had were white, whereas nowadays they tend to be brown ... Decorating eggs was something done every year and my mother was a dab hand at producing wonderfully dyed eggs for all nine of us (Mum and Dad plus seven kids!) for Easter morning breakfast. At school, every youngster would bring blown eggs in to be elaborately converted with glitter and odds and ends to rival any Fabergé egg. We used to all blow our eggs, though I wonder how many youngsters know the knack today? I'll test Arthur and Dorothy next year!

The previous Easter, Dick had been in America working to bring funds in so we were excited this year to finally be spending our first Easter together at the château as a family. That week, Dick and I had gone on a date to the supermarket and stocked up on French packets of foiled Easter eggs, small enough to be hidden on our Easter hunt and also small enough to go into the plastic eggs Jenny had sent us back with.

Supermarkets have their own tradition – they celebrate what is happening in their entrance way with displays that woo you. The last time we were wooed and shared this excitement was in January when it was tree planting season, but now, in March, the Easter displays were majestic. Stacked higher than either of us could reach were bags upon bags of foiled eggs in every colour you could imagine. There were chocolate chickens and bunnies and lambs and ducklings all looking rather artisan, wrapped in cellophane with curled, hand-tied bows and handwritten script in icing, wishing us '*Joyeuses Pâques*'. I simply could not get over how reasonably everything was priced. In addition, there were towers of Ferrero Rocher, Lindt and, my personal favourite, Mon Chéri. I ignored Dick adding them to the basket so I could act surprised and delighted when I received them.

I was so very much looking forward to sharing my joy of winter lifting together. This year we would walk together as a family and look at the trees blossoming and nature starting to bud. The transformation of our home in spring is incredible and like no other. One day there is frost on the ground and the next day there are dozens of primroses and daffodils on the banks! Seeing our first primrose together was a moment of intense joy. I had not realised how much I missed Dick last year when he was working in America. I had completely played it down as I was being brave, but sharing this moment together brought it all home.

It was raining on Easter Sunday, so we created an indoor egg hunt. That has now become a tradition for us, as it only takes something to happen two years in a row for it to become a tradition in our house. And as this was Dick's first Easter in the château, he got to hide all the eggs, and that gave it a whole new level of celebration!

Arthur was just three and Dorothy was soon to be two and she was walking very well for her age. We used Jenny's plastic eggs filled with chocolate eggs, as well as some extra little eggs hidden around the ground floor (the main floor). They both had little wicker baskets and on the day they wore little fluffy gilets. I have the video on my phone and it's so wonderful to watch them both still with the toddler walk. It's unsteady, a little bit wobbly and enough to make any gushy parent's heart melt.

That afternoon, Dick made an Easter roast dinner fit for a king, my parents joined and it was great family fun. We painted eggs and ate far too much chocolate. Then we put on our wellies and went for a walk, jumping in muddy puddles.

Easter brought us a few days' rest, which was enough to feel like we had celebrated together but also gave us just enough time before Dorothy's (and my) birthday to get a little bit of work done.

Dick often tells me that he subscribes to the aphorism that you achieve 80 per cent of the outcome with 20 per cent of the input. Of course, the inverse is that you have to do the remaining 80 per cent of the work to make things perfect, so though I knew Dick thought the honeymoon suite was finished, I also knew the final 20 per cent would take another round of 80 per cent effort, as it included:

- Re-painting the salon area (I'd made a bad call with the green and re-covered most with a lustre sand paint).
- Moving the furniture around for a more elegant set-up – we quickly discovered that the stunning rococo chairs in the salon were not child friendly, and with Arthur and Dorothy rather energetic, it seemed best we swapped.
- Buying a mini-fridge and installing it into the stunning side cabinet (which meant Dick cutting the back out of one of the cupboards).
- Finding a new, larger and rustic kitchen table from Emmaus, our local charity shop, and adding the matching table back into the honeymoon suite (this table matches the side table already in there).
- Sanding and varnishing the floors – a job that never got done in time for our wedding.
- Painting and filling all the skirting boards, including replacing some – a huge job, which we simply ran out of time for before our wedding.
- Buying a coffee machine and ensuring the room had everything functional for actual guests. Coffee is very important in Dick's world and it has to be right!

- **Buying towels, dressing gowns, soap dispensers and welcome toiletries . . .**

The honeymoon suite was urgent and important to get done, so despite the fact I chuntered a bit, I understood our need to complete it and, once finished, it was lovely to know that this suite and the reception rooms were in good order. The list of jobs to be done was long, as the honeymoon suite was to set the standard for what we wanted to achieve for our guests. There was a significant amount of dressing to be done but it was clear there were also areas to fill, sand and paint, where skirting did not sit flush on a less than smooth wall or chased-in cables were not quite invisible. Thankfully, the list did not involve a lot of capital expenditure but it did all add up to a significant amount of work. And my beautiful wife has never been known to accept the engineering concept of 'near as damn it'.

It's necessary for me to publicly admit to some of my shortcomings. I don't like, or do, painting, decorating or hanging wallpaper, and I can think of nothing worse than hanging a row of pictures that have to be equally spaced, on exactly the same level, and somewhere that has not yet been quite decided. I will move a sofa around to find the perfect spot, but having seen it from every angle (more than once), and when the movements start to be millimetric, I usually say 'two more moves then I'm done'.

Angela had sourced half a dozen pictures – I think they came from magazines found in the attic – and had put them in simple frames. All we had to do was put them on the wall(s). I can do the sums that determine the number of different ways six pictures can be arranged; however, in the salon of the honeymoon suite there were other variables . . . The doors and windows are such that the wall spaces are not regular sizes and the light hits them all differently. I started to get that pain behind my left eye that chaps get when they know they have to do something and smile. We'd been together for more than five years and had been through the most demanding first year in France but I think the hanging of those pictures is one of my darkest memories . . . I just didn't get it. I kept thinking of the old saying my dad used to quote: 'Patience is a virtue, possess it if you can. It's seldom in a woman and never in a man.'

I'm not sure how long it took us, and the amount of the time has probably increased in my mind since, but we did get there in the end! After two or three days, I think, we had three pictures equally spaced and aligned horizontally on one wall, at the perfect viewing height, with a forth in the middle of the adjacent portion of wall, beside the window, again aligned horizontally, with the remaining two on the wall opposite the three, but vertically aligned and horizontally complementary . . . obvious really!

*

Angela and Dorothy have birthdays on consecutive days at the beginning of April. They are both Aries, which apparently means they are allowed to be bossy? As Angela's day comes first, I am forceful in reminding her that we have to be allowed to celebrate her birthday too. She so wants Dorothy to have the best day possible that there is little time for organising Angela's day. It's slowly sinking in, but for me it's not a discussion point.

My treat this year was going to Emmaus, followed by lunch in what we now call the 'Mushroom Restaurant'. It was just Dick and I, holding hands and being able to spend an abundant amount of time looking in the clothes and linen section! On 7 April 2016, as we walked into Emmaus, the staff ran over to us. We had spent a large amount of time and bought a copious amount of stuff there over the past year. My first thought was they knew it was

my birthday! But alas, no – they had a stunning gigantic oak and gold-plated armoire that was ten feet high and would not fit in any normal house! They knew us well enough by now to know that we would be the perfect customers for this set. It came with a matching bed, two chairs and a side cabinet. At €600 for the entire set it was a complete bargain. In London, you would have paid thousands for the bed alone and if you broke the costs down to individual items, it was cheaper than something you would buy flat-packed! That's how we justified the expense, which we hadn't been planning on, and we were not cash rich. For an extra €50 they would deliver the following week. Happy birthday to me!

We then carried on our journey . . .

Outside the town of Bagnoles-de-l'Orne, in the woods, there is a Michelin-starred restaurant and hotel that we had booked into for a long lunch and night away. It was about forty-five minutes away and had been Michelin-starred since the late 1990s. We knew all the chef's priorities lay in seasonality, local produce and regional specialities. We were a bit surprised, however, by just how much emphasis was put on using mushrooms and fungi . . .

Eating out in a Michelin-starred restaurant is never cheap but lunch can be more reasonably priced so we planned a long and leisurely lunch and a chilled evening. Lunch started not long after midday and we chose the house aperitif that was a fruity sparkling drink that was way too easy to drink. The arrival of a plate of appetisers set the scene and we smiled, knowing this was going to be great. The appetisers were six different bite-size morsels, each arranged on a platter. We often take notes when eating out, partly to remind us of what had been served but also as inspiration for new dishes for us to try at home, but there were a lot of new French words describing some of the dishes and it was only afterwards, by plugging into a translation app, that we found out exactly what we had eaten.

As usual, we took it in turns to decide what to try next and the richness of the foie gras choux, followed by lightly pickled *trompettes de la mort* that were not at all sharp and then the peppery smoked duck were savoured, and somehow the first aperitif had evaporated. The second was exactly what was required to enjoy the wild mushroom macaroons, a barely smoked eel mousse and, finally, a very delicate cold artichoke and garlic soup.

By the time we were moved through to the restaurant for our tasting menu, we were very mellow and smiling. It was with great ceremony that each course and its paired wine were served. We had decided that we would have one menu that was paired with wine and one that was not. Obviously, we were aware of the cost but we also wanted to enjoy our brief holiday rather than spending most of the afternoon and evening asleep! The wines did not disappoint. We had not heard of many of the vineyards, but each glass was delicious.

We started with *foie gras de canard* served with rhubarb and pink peppercorns on a bed of leaves that we just could not identify (they were peppery and I'm sure were weeds) and a fragrant mushroom oil. Then a small plate of girolles and asparagus cooked with squid ink.

Two fish dishes followed. One of roasted cod served with a spinach purée, pea shoots and purée, turnips and black garlic, and a flat fish that I think could have been a flounder that came with nettles, peas, wasabi and baby onions.

We then had our meat dishes and we didn't realise at the time but our 'pigeon' was actually thin strips of squab, served with morels, powdered herbs and an egg yolk. Then veal smoked on hay with new potatoes and a veal sweetbread confit.

Pudding came as a shock – it was the most beautiful collection of desserts, the centrepiece of which was a blown-sugar balloon with a macaroon and mousse inside – both of which were made from mushrooms. The balloon came surrounded by *trompette* sorbet, a selection of glace fungi – mushrooms in syrup and honey cream – and I could have sworn there were truffles in the pudding somewhere (though not the chocolatey ones!). We both giggled like school children when Angela had problems swallowing one of the syrupy mushrooms and could not bring herself to chew it. As we had our coffee and petit fours, we decided that mushrooms for pudding was something we would probably avoid in the future . . .

By eight o'clock that evening, we were peckish and contemplating whether or not to go down to the restaurant but instead we decided to go for a walk around the beautiful art deco town of Bagnoles-de-l'Orne. We wandered hand in hand and stopped for an amazing pizza and beer and laughed and chatted to the other clientele. It was definitely a day of culinary extremes but we thoroughly enjoyed both and we headed back to the château the next day recharged.

The next day was Dorothy's second birthday. It feels quite a treat to have Dorothy's and my birthday so close; it's like a double celebration and this year the circus was in town – an expression I'd happily use every day if I could! And we knew this because on every lamppost there was a flyer saying so.

The French circus is very different to anything found in the UK. There appeared to still be animals involved. I fully understand the need to ensure good animal husbandry and that circuses have had a bad reputation, however, I have memories going back to the early sixties of family outings to the big top where we were in awe of every act, and being so close to wild animals that could eat us, or the trainer, as they 'performed' in the hastily erected cages was unforgettable.

The circus was positioned on some wasteland on the outskirts of Laval. It had the biggest big top tent you can imagine. As we parked up and walked to get our tickets there were animals tethered all around. Lots of them were more domesticated than wild and they were munching on the long grass. There were llamas and alpacas, a couple of camels, a cow, some variant of a buffalo and goats with large horns, and a collection of horses and ponies. They all looked very chilled, if a bit out of place on the fields on the edge of town.

The fabulous and colourful hand-painted artworks were everywhere. But I was a little uneasy, I had never been so close to so many tethered animals. They appeared to be tied by ropes to trees or stakes on the other side of the path. Arthur and Dorothy thought this was simply incredible. Interactive, one could say! I, on the other hand, was working out where we could run to in order to be safe should one escape . . .

My level of concern grew during the performance when there was a cage erected and lions came to within a few feet of us. I didn't realise circuses did that anymore and I had the children hugged close and slightly behind me to protect them.

The last time I was personally at a circus was when I was in my early twenties with my dad in Essex. It was the early 2000s and let's say it was what you would expect from a circus of those times. Clowns, tightrope, trapeze artists, fire. Basically, a theatrical show of incredible circus performers.

I've since had a couple of lovely encounters with circuses. I went on a trip to Zippos Circus to have a tour of the archive and saw an endearing side to circus life. It would make you want to run away with the circus! We have also visited Giffords Circus on a number of occasions, which, to me, epitomises everything stylish about circuses.

We bought our tickets and some popcorn and proceeded in. It was amazing to see just how busy all the performers were – the tickets were sold to us by the lady who then did the trapeze, and the jugglers showed us to our seats and then became part of the clown troupe. The children and Angela and I loved it; it was a day out from a different era. We were uncomfortable about the fact there were big cats involved in the circus but we have not seen the same sort of circus travelling and performing in our area since that day. It appears we were some of the last people to experience such an old-fashioned circus with 'wild' animals as France changed its laws on what is acceptable with respect to circus animals.

A couple of years ago, we had a family circus set up in the village. The tent wasn't very big at all but they were scheduled to perform three times a day for a couple of days. It was amazing – every act was performed by the same four or five people (there was juggling, the trapeze, clowns . . . indeed, every act you would expect!). Even though the audience, which ranged from classmates of the children to the little old ladies of the village, was limited to about forty, the troupe performed their hearts out. The animals were cats (yes, domestic moggies!), dogs and donkeys, but the show was wonderful and we cheered as hard as we could to show our appreciation for their hard work.

*

Spring was certainly with us and the world was heating up. The walled garden had to be dug over, weeded and planted if we were to start enjoying the fruits of our labour. It was over thirty-five years since I'd used gardening as a workout before going off to join the army and, though the heart was willing, my body was complaining after a day's digging and there was simply so much to do. So Angela and I had a talk and decided it made sense to invest in a rotovator, a useful machine with rotating blades that really helps in soil preparation.

It is surprising just how many places sell them, and they vary in size, power and obviously price. We invested in a simple, rugged machine. It did not have all the gears and add-ons of some others but it was powered by a reasonable-sized Briggs & Stratton engine and as all parts can be replaced/fixed, it should last for years, if not forever ... There is an old saying, I think it may be Irish: 'I've got my grandfather's hammer. It has had three new handles and a new head, but it's my grandfather's hammer.'

Just to put this into perspective, I'd never even heard of a rotavator!

I love our rotavator, and the love affair started that spring. We got our money's worth in the first couple of days as I followed it up and down, after having cut the vegetation with the lawnmower at maximum height – first pass scraping the weeds, the second dislodging them and the third releasing the soil from the roots. After the fourth or fifth pass, the blades were digging in and the soil was there to be adored. I stopped and picked it up and smelled it. It crumbled nicely in my hands and the earthy, clean smell confirmed just how lucky we were.

I had bought a box of 'Charlotte' seed potatoes and they had been chitting in the remains of the old tower. When I planted my first two rows I think I did a happy dance. I was only a little late. I'd always marked the planting of our potatoes at home by putting them in on St Patrick's day on 17 March and harvesting the first ones on 12 July, the day of the Orange Order parades. These were easy dates for someone from Northern Ireland to remember and, what's more, they worked. I was going to find out if they worked hundreds of miles south in France.

There was a lot of change and activity taking place in our new home. Dick was completely in his happy place in the walled garden and loved taking the kids in there. They were going from strength to strength and seeing that I think gave me the strength to put a stop

to Arthur's dummy habit. Our little man is a creature of habit. He loved a dummy from a very early age and became dependent on them for sleeping. The thought of trying to break habits, especially when they are linked to children's sleep, can be very scary and daunting! I think I was the one that had built up the situation in my head. But I knew with school looming we needed to have time for the new normal! It could take months for him to sleep again, right?

Wrong. I don't love being wrong, but on this occasion I did! We gathered up all of Arthur's dummies, all eleven of them, and asked him what he would like to buy with them and he said a trampoline! So we all jumped in the car and headed down to our local sports shop . . .

Arthur was not constrained on what his dummies could buy for him and it's interesting that he came up with the idea of a trampoline. I can only assume that he'd seen children playing on one on TV as, up to that point, trampolining was not something that had been on our radar.

The obvious starting point was the large sports shop but it only had trampolines for personal training and making your bits jiggle up and down, which was not what Arthur wanted. That left us a bit stumped but we were sure that we had seen them in one of our local supermarkets, obviously, so we headed off there, and they had a selection! A three-year-old trading in his treasure is not a good person to ask, 'Which one do you want?' Arthur looked at all the pictures and chose one that looked pretty huge. I was steering him towards a three-year-old-sized one, only to discover it was out of stock, so I gave in and we filled the back of the car, with the boot tied down rather than closed, with the best part of 100kg of bouncing fun.

There was no question that the trampoline had to be put up immediately. It was/is a good ten feet across and surrounded by its own cage, so the children couldn't fall off and hurt themselves. The quality was good and, although it took a bit of time to put it together, it was soon functioning, and even today the children love spending time on it. Though it has had its own adventures . . .

On one particularly stormy night it was lifted up and unceremoniously plonked into the moat by the wind. In the short time it was there, the moat froze over and it was encased in four inches of ice. When it was eventually extracted using a pulley system and a large A-frame, the caging was buckled and unusable. So, after a delay, the bouncy bit was brought back to life over a hole dug into the ground, so the trampoline was at ground level. I made all that sound easy, but it was not without issues. Having dug out a crater for the trampoline (I had gone down to the moat water table, which defined how deep it would be!), I was smoothing it down but there was a rock sticking up about two inches to one side. There was no way it could be left like that as it could really hurt a bouncing bottom, so I proceeded to dig it out. I admitted defeat and moved the crater two feet when it became clear that this was a four-foot-long rock forming part of an old wall that we subsequently discovered had been the old chapel. Sometimes the château just fights back.

*

We had been building up to our first paying event at the château and suddenly it was here – it was time for our first food lovers' weekend and the château was ready. We knew we could host and cater, and I believed Angela would be wonderful at it, but we were still nervous because the success of this weekend would shape our future business. We had to make a profit – that was pretty fundamental – but also we had to enjoy it to ensure we had the enthusiasm to continue to grow. Like most things, the planning is so important if you are to succeed, and we had done our best to cover all eventualities. The château was going to be judged, and so were we . . .

Much to Dick's pain, all snagging in the honeymoon suite was completed, a fridge and coffee machine had been bought and I'd happily stay there. Everything that could be polished had been polished. We had even visited Emmaus and made a special hamper of gifts for the guests, including cheese boards, linen and general French kitchenalia! Jane and Alun were due to arrive in Laval on the 12.47 train from Paris and we would be there to collect them.

It had originally been a surprise for Alun but Jane hadn't been able to keep it in any longer. I most definitely could relate to that. I'm a terrible keeper of secrets, especially if it's something really exciting like a trip away or presents. I can see clearly that this comes from my mum and grandma; it's in our DNA. My grandma would use the bottom of her wardrobe to 'hide' birthday and Christmas gifts but she was always so excited that when we visited, she would whisper, 'Go have a look in my wardrobe.' And, of course, being young and impatient, we would dash to her room to have a look. She was so naughty! My mum inherited the wardrobe hiding spot and also the inability to keep exciting secrets. We are very blessed to have an attic to keep gifts in, but I have to admit I still struggle too, although I am desperately trying to break the mould!

We had planned the experience to be completely bespoke for Jane and Alun. Two weeks before their arrival, we had sent them an email. Here it is, with Jane's responses:

Dear Jane,
We have a few questions for you both, when you get a
moment, which will help us plan your weekend:

What are your food loves? E.g., 'shellfish YES, rabbit NO'.
How do you feel about raw ingredients?
We both eat everything (and I really do mean everything!).
We are both big fans of seafood and also rarely eat red meat
so tend to eat that out in restaurants (mainly because I can't
cook a steak to save my life). We mostly eat chicken/fish at
home as it's easy. Alun loves cheese and all things pickled.
In fact, his idea of heaven would be a cured meat and cheese
platter, a bottle of red wine and all things pickled (especially
spicy onions). Sad, I know . . . I just love all food!

Are there any dishes that you have always wanted to try?
Mmm. That's a tough one. I would say any local specialities
would be amazing.

Is there anything else that stands out that we should know
about? i.e., allergies, things you don't eat?
No allergies. Nothing we don't eat.

Is there anything that you would like a lesson in? Bread
making, butchery? Anything at all that you have always
wanted to learn?
Oh yes, bread making would be amazing! Anything cooking
related really, to be honest. Both of us really like to cook
but never get time for it so would be great to do something
along these lines. Perhaps food pickling or conserve
techniques or cured meats / smoking food, etc., that we
could do at home.

With this information and with what we know already, we
can pretty much nail your visit to celebrate everything you
love, including tons of relaxation!

There is no rush for this – whenever you are ready!
Speak soon,
Dick & Angel

We already knew Alun really wanted to learn how to smoke food, so that was on our list of activities and, armed with the above information, we were ready . . .

Our food lovers' weekends all require the same amount of preparation. Angela sorts out the château and I'm kitchen based. But first of all, there is the shopping to get done. This is not our average supermarket trip – it's more fun. I always start with the menu for Friday night; the weekend is a marathon.

Laval is a lovely, clean, not too modern station. I arrived in good time and managed to get a parking slot in the drop and collect zone. When the Paris train disgorges, there are about five frantic minutes when the hundreds of passengers all come out, find their contacts or start their onward journey. I saw the train arrive and got out of the car and made myself look like the person waiting to collect Jane and Alun, who I'd never actually met. I wasn't at all nervous, though I did smile to myself that I had no idea who was coming and that two strangers may end up being kidnapped and given a lovely weekend! My solution was to be very obvious: to make eye contact, smile at everyone, look British somehow and exude 'your chauffeur'. Somehow, we did connect and, right from the very off, it was relaxed and the fifteen-minute drive back to the château flew by.

It was interesting looking at our home through a completely new set of eyes. We were so aware of all the imperfections that it was easy to forget the initial impact the château has. As I turned into the drive, Jane and Alun saw the building for the first time and were taken by the sheer size. We feel the château is a family home, but at first sight it's definitely a château.

When Jane and Alun arrived at the steps up to the front door of the château, Angela came down to say hello. She'd obviously been watching out of a window for our arrival. We took in the view for a couple of moments, then we ushered them into the salon where we served a local sparkly red with some spicy seeds I had prepared, which are so tasty and a bit different to olives or other expected nibbles.

I knew roughly when they were to arrive so I lit a candle and checked and re-checked that everything was tidy. We are not a hotel, where there is a reception and then your guests entertain themselves for the duration. We were part of the package and we'd be showing them our home and this part of France. I was nervous; this was very different to anything we had done so far. Receiving our first paying guests was a big moment.

We intended to make sure that there were lots of different elements to the weekend so that it lived up to the expectations of food lovers. We had never been served sparkly red or spicy seeds, and neither had our guests, so we started as we intended to continue. Conversation was easy and lively, and even though we were working we had a glass too – after all, we were celebrating the launch of our new business!

....

SPICY SEEDS

Ingredients

A mixture of seeds, the ratios can depend on what you have in – pumpkin seeds, sunflower seeds, pine nuts and sesame seeds are all great
Light soy sauce
Finely chopped fresh chilli (optional)

Method

Put the pumpkin seeds, sunflower seeds and pine nuts in a cold pan and turn on the heat. Don't put more than a couple of layers of seeds into the pan. (So it all depends how big your pan is!)

This is a great time to practise your 'cheffy' tossing in a frying pan, or you can stir them, but they will start off slowly, then the seeds will take on colour very quickly.

When the seeds are colouring but not yet dark brown, take the pan off the heat and shake on a good amount of soy sauce. It'll steam as the pan is hot so keep shaking to coat the warm seeds. Add in your chilli and ensure it's well mixed.

Allow to cool. If you are worried about the seeds being overcooked, take them out of the still-hot pan and pour the lot into a large bowl to cool.

When cool, store in an airtight container. Serve in a bowl with a small spoon to allow people to put some into their hands. They are also great on bread and butter as it's like a salty, spicy peanut butter without the peanuts or the gooey texture!

....

We discussed what we were going to do over the weekend and the menu for the evening in detail and showed Jane and Alun up to their suite. We find that when being shown upstairs, people naturally stop at the bottom of the double stairs and look up. The landing is up above and behind you, so your neck creaks as you look up and over. Maybe the pause is to brace yourself for the climb, but most likely it's to determine which way to go.

We all went up; I carried the bags. The honeymoon suite was immaculate – every snag Angela could think of had been sorted and I know she was as proud as I was when we showed them into their suite for the weekend. It was what we had dreamed of doing. We'd created a suite we'd love to stay in, and it was spacious with wonderful views. To be honest, if we stayed somewhere like it, complete with a stocked free bar, we would probably have ordered room service and not surfaced . . .

They were the first people, other than friends and family, to see the rooms or to stay at the château, so we were analysing every facial expression or comment to see what they thought. From what I saw, they loved the rooms and were a bit surprised at the extent of the suite.

My shoulders must have dropped a couple of inches when we saw a genuine 'wow' on their faces. It was actually a lovely moment as we were seeing the château through the eyes of another, something that had not happened since our wedding. But even since then, so much improvement had taken place.

They did surface for dinner, which was scheduled to take hours, and our menu for the evening was full of dishes we thought they would enjoy, because we did! A long gin and tonic served in our Tyrone crystal glasses is a great aperitif, especially on a lovely May evening when the light is just changing to become golden.

I know that Angela likes people to settle at the table and get a drink before we serve so I didn't even start cooking until they were comfortable and had a glass of wine. Our dining table extends to hold sixteen but we don't fold it all away for smaller numbers; we just sit side by side to be more intimate. With the floral decorations and the candlelight shining on crystal, the table looked decadent and twinkly, and so we started our service.

We started with an amuse-bouche of duck gizzards with rose jelly. The slightly salty confit duck and the sweet aromatic jelly go so well together that it's almost a shame to just serve one, but it is an amuse-bouche, and I'm sure some great performer said always leave them wanting more?

The soup course was white aromatic onion and garlic, served with an egg yolk and crunchy *herbes de Provence* croutons. The raw, just-warmed egg yolk is the surprise in this dish that adds richness and goes so well with the salty, crunchy croutons. Of course, we always have lots of fresh baguette to go with the soup so there is no excuse not to have a clean plate.

Then it was on to the fish course . . .

. . . .

SCALLOPS AND *BOUDIN NOIR*

This dish is all about the way the flavours come together.
Boudin noir *is the French equivalent of black pudding but it is positively creamy in texture and does not have the coarse grains or bits of back fat. It comes in a variety of flavours: some with chilli, some with added apple or onions; however, our favourite is the 'traditional'.*

Ingredients

3 scallops and 3 slices of *boudin noir* per person
Olive oil
Balsamic vinegar to deglaze the pan
Mixed green salad to serve it on
Bamboo skewers

Method

Trim the scallops and put in a bowl. Season and drizzle over some olive oil. Toss to ensure they're covered well in the oil. Take the individual skewers and poke them through the sides of the scallops and the boudin noir.

Just before service, heat a frying pan until hot. Place the skewers in the pan. You will see them cooking from the bottom up. When they are 'cooked' to about a third of the way up carefully turn the skewers over – the scallops and boudin noir *will be seared and a little crispy.*

Cook for the same amount of time on the second side and then put the skewers onto a warm plate. Deglaze the pan with some balsamic vinegar and serve the skewers on the mixed green salad with a dribble from the pan to dress it.

....

I was keeping them well watered whilst Dick was keeping the food flowing. As I was topping them up, we were hearing lots of 'enjoyment of cuisine' sounds – anyone who enjoys cooking for people knows that appreciation is fantastic. I kept going back to tell the chef. We were on a roll. So, after the fish course, we settled down for a delicious main of . . .

SLOW-COOKED DUCK BREAST WITH A PLUM AND PORT REDUCTION, PURÉED CELERIAC AND SEASONAL VEGETABLE BROTH

Ingredients

Duck breast – two is enough for three or four people,
depending on the size
500ml port
3 tbsp plum jam
Celeriac
Butter or cream
White pepper
Carrots
Parsnips
Sliced bulb of fennel
Stock
Runner beans
Peas

Method

Score the duck-breast skins and place in a sous vide for four hours at 56°C, or they can be pan fried rather than slow cooked. Take the breast out of the sous vide, dry and place skin side down in the pan, then turn the heat on. Allow the fat to render and when crispy turn over and turn off – it's ready.

Reduce the port to about two tablespoons, then pass the jam through a sieve and combine the two.

Peel, chop and boil the celeriac until cooked. Drain it and add butter or cream and white pepper. Allow to sit in the pan with the lid on for five minutes and then purée.

If your carrots and parsnips are big, cut and shape them into smaller torpedo shapes. Cook in butter for five minutes and add in the fennel and cook for a further two minutes. Add the stock to cover, bring to the boil, add the remaining ingredients, then simmer for two minutes.

To plate up, pipe the celeriac purée into the middle of a shallow bowl. Slice the duck breast and fan the slices on top. Put the vegetables and broth on the other side of the bowl and nappe *the duck breast with the plum reduction.*

....

We love having cleared plates come back into the kitchen, as it's obvious we're doing something right. The meal flowed well and Jane and Alun seemed to be smiling and enjoying the evening, which continued with more courses. First we served them a sorbet – apple tends to be our sorbet of choice as we are in the cider region – as it's a great palate cleanser. Then came dessert, which was pears poached in a rosé wine syrup with star anise, and milk chocolate ganache, served on a poppyseed shortbread. Then we served some local cheeses. In France, the cheese course is served before the dessert and usually involves cheese or a choice of cheeses eaten with a knife and fork. We love the British way of ending on cheese and crackers and grazing while the *digestifs* are taken or until we have had our fill.

We served red and white wines throughout the meal but instead of staying with the local reds that have very little body, we bought a selection. It was great fun but the only way to ensure they were good was to go for a Premier Cru or Cru Bourgeois, depending on the region. We assume that the producer must have jumped through some hoops to achieve the classification and we haven't been disappointed yet.

As we were highly organised, dinner went very smoothly. Angela did service and I would pop in before each dish to explain the provenance of the ingredients, talk 'cookery' and field any questions. I cooked an extra portion of every dish that we shared in the service kitchen.

We both believe you have to be attentive to your guests but give them enough time and space to enjoy themselves as a couple. Even from our first evening, it was simple for us to work together on the service. On FLW, it was lovely for Angela to sit down in the kitchen with me and I'd serve her a meal similar to our guests, but maybe with a few more morsels I know she loves . . .

My job was very enjoyable and at the start of every course I ensured our guests' glasses were topped up with wine and water and brought new cutlery and finally the food. Then we liked to give them some space. There is a balance between being attentive and being in the way, so I washed the dishes from the previous course whilst Dick plated me up some of what they were having. There is a small table on hinges in the service kitchen so Dick and I used that moment to sit and breathe. I also learnt very quickly to have a mirror and my lippy next to me, so I could refresh!

Angela knows that I don't eat much when I'm cooking so she allows me to serve her when our guests are happy. I'm genuinely not hungry when I cook but I come from the Keith Floyd school of cookery and always have a tumbler of wine on the go. And I taste things to see that the seasoning is good or that the textures are working, so I do eat something.

At the end, we joined our guests for the cheese course and a glass of wine/port. We chatted through what the weekend had in store and marvelled at the cheeses, which were local and delicious. We served them with baguette, butter and some of our homemade quince 'cheese' (it's so thick it is difficult to spread but we love lumps with our cheese). Despite the ample amount already eaten, they proved there is always a little gap for some cheese.

Finally, sometime after midnight, we adjourned to the salon for them to enjoy coffee and petits fours, which were small, very rich truffles, and digestifs. This allowed us to set up the dining room for breakfast.

Funnily enough, no one was particularly hungry at breakfast the following day, but it was a food lovers' weekend, so I'd been out to buy fresh baguettes and a selection of pastries. In the vestibule connected to their salon, we left fresh croissants, butter, apricot jam and freshly squeezed orange juice, to give them enough energy to come downstairs for a breakfast of coddled eggs.

As we didn't know what flavours Jane and Alun would like we did a selection: smoked salmon, Parmesan cheese and spinach, and salted.

. . . .

CODDLED EGGS

Egg coddlers are a British creation from Royal Worcester. There is a ceremony in them, which takes eating the humble dippy egg to a whole new place. But the process is easy!

Ingredients

An egg per coddler
Butter
Flavourings, such as smoked salmon, air-dried ham, spinach,
grated Parmesan
Salt and black pepper

Method

Put on a saucepan of water to boil. Generously butter the inside of the coddlers and place your flavouring in the bottom. Crack in an egg, season and screw on the lid.

Place the coddlers in the simmering water, which should reach the level of the bottom of the lid, and cook for six minutes.

Take out of the pan, dry and loosen the lid before serving with buttery soldiers.

....

After breakfast, we had decided that a trip to our local market was essential, so we all headed into Laval. This trip was pretty important as we hadn't planned or provisioned for lunch or dinner! The market spreads around the irregularly shaped 'square' and is a mixture of professional and local producers' food stalls. There are lots of fish and shellfish, fruit and vegetables, cheese, charcuterie, meats, farm produce and delicatessen stalls, as well as some tables that are obviously individuals selling their excess produce. Some weeks there are lots of seedlings for sale and even poultry. To add to the market atmosphere, you can also buy a hat, an outfit or even a bed if you venture down to the stalls on the periphery of the square. Around the square there are cafés and bars that are open early, with people standing around having a glass of wine and freshly shucked oysters at ten in the morning. Obviously with nothing too important to do. It's all very relaxed but the shoppers can be seen looking and checking all the stalls before buying.

The trip was a success. A lovely walk around looking at the ingredients and talking about what we would like to try and what they'd like to learn to cook resulted in several shopping bags of fresh veggies, lots of cheese (the stallholder was a proper showman and so we ended up with a wedge of very tasty waxy cheese with a line of ash through it that lasted for weeks), dried meats and pâté, a couple of lovely live crabs and, surprisingly, some chicken breasts, bought with the challenge of doing something tasty and impressive. We popped into Chez Martine for our obligatory coffee with the locals before heading back to the château.

Subsequent FLW have set all sorts of challenges as a result of our trips to the market. Guests to France always love the selection of produce on display. So many people are worried about cooking fish and seafood so our Saturday evening fish courses have involved the preparation and cooking of just about every fish we have seen – crabs, lobsters, cockles, clams, monkfish, plaice, razor clams . . . It's fair to say that there is also a fascination with the offal on display. One particularly adventurous FLW involved tongue served with a piquant, slightly spicy sauce; it was delicious!

We returned to the château for a lunch of fresh baguettes, cold meats, pâtés, salads and cheese, all served with a light local cider. The afternoon was all about relaxing and we reconvened at about five o'clock in the family kitchen in the *sous sol* to start preparing dinner. The descent down the servants' stairs sets the scene and you enter the darker area where the work gets done . . . A slight twist to our decadent weekend getaway was that we intended for our guests to cook for us using the ingredients they had bought – and, of course, the husband or wife who did not normally do the cooking would be put in charge of a particularly challenging dish! When we had finished our *mise en place* we headed up to get ready for our evening.

When eating with friends, I always work on the principle of getting them involved with the food early, so by the time Angela had drinks served and nibbles on the go, our massive pan was bubbling and we popped in two very impressive spider crabs. In the time it took them to cook, we had made our hollandaise. The family kitchen is big enough for eight to dine around the table but is intimate enough so those cooking can still be part of the conversation. The island has the hob on it, which allows anyone tending the pans to face the people sitting down, and when they take a seat to eat it's in the chairs that have their backs to the island. Being surrounded by our mixed copper and vintage *batterie de cuisine*, it is a lovely place to cook and to socialise. I have a rule that no crystal or special glasses or crockery are allowed, so it's tumblers and our vintage plates and bowls – though I have allowed linen napkins rather than just kitchen roll to try to alleviate Angela's twitch!

The crabs filled a massive platter and you could see a slight hesitation – however, credit where it's due, as moments later our guests were cracking open legs and claws and, after I had pulled apart the bodies, Angela convinced them of the merits of the brown meat and soon bread was being dipped into shells and hollandaise and crab was being savoured by all. Eating a crab is not something to be rushed and we each marvelled at the amount of meat hidden in the body where the legs joined. Every tiny morsel was savoured. The first course took over an hour of chatting and enjoying before I even thought of putting on the chicken we had prepared.

After the crab was cleared away, which was no mean feat, the chicken was ready and looked and tasted lovely. We had met our remit to do something interesting with chicken breast with a chicken and spinach roulade.

....

CHICKEN AND SPINACH ROULADE

Ingredients

½ onion diced
2 cloves of garlic, crushed
50g butter
¼ freshly grated nutmeg
Big bag of spinach – dry and with thick stalks removed
2 large chicken breasts
Salt and black pepper

Method

In a large frying pan, gently soften the onion in half of the butter. After the onions have softened add the garlic. When cooked, add in the nutmeg and season. Add the spinach and allow it to gently wilt, then put it into the food processor and blitz. Check the seasoning.

Trim the sinew end of your breasts and butterfly them – if that sounds difficult, it's not. Just lay the breast flat on your board, pointy bit towards you and with the thickest side pointing to your knife hand. With a sharp knife, cut the breast horizontally through the middle of the thickest part, stopping at just over halfway so you don't ever see the knife blade through the flesh. If you peel back the part you have sliced, you can see why it's called butterflying – the two sides are identical, like a butterfly. Place on a large piece of clingfilm, cut sides down, and put another bit on top. Gently tap with a rolling pin to flatten. You'll be surprised how big you can make it. Thin is good but not too thin as it needs some structural integrity.

Peel off the top layer of clingfilm. You need to spread the spinach mix on the breast but it does not want to be too wet, so I spoon the spinach into a sieve to drain it first, keeping the liquor, then spread the drained mix on the breast.

You now have a large, flat chicken breast covered with a layer of the spinach mix, so it's time to make the roulade . . .

Use your fingers to start rolling along the long side – there's always a long side. Once you have made the first part of a roll, if you lift up the clingfilm the chicken should roll onto itself and, if you keep lifting, eventually you will have a 'Swiss roll' – a chicken roulade!

Place your roulade in the middle of a fresh piece of clingfilm about three times the length of your chicken roll.

Roll the chicken up in the clingfilm. Hold the clingfilm both sides about two inches from the roll and then keep rolling the clingfilm in the direction you rolled the chicken up, lifting when you reach the far side of your surface, then come back and roll again – keep doing this and, as long as you hold the clingfilm, the roll will tighten and shape your roulade – it does work! Tie off the ends of your clingfilm and your roulade is ready for cooking . . .

Pop the roll into a pan of simmering salted water for fifteen minutes and it will be cooked through. Take out of the pan and carefully cut open your wrapping – save the juice to add to your leftover spinach to make a tasty sauce to nappe *over the sliced roll.*

....

This had to be served with new potatoes and we introduced them to *Noirmoutier* potatoes, which the French claim are better than

Jersey Royals. They are grown on a small island a couple of hours south-west of us and I have to say they are special!

For pudding we kept it simple and had fresh French strawberries mixed into a mess, with meringues, cream and strawberry coulis. Yummy and quick to make. We chilled with our digestifs and ended feeling very mellow.

Late that evening, Jane and Alun looked relaxed, content and well fed. There was a tiny table and chairs outside the château that I bought in a panic when I realised there was nowhere for them to sit should they wish to sit outside. It was for two people but looked ridiculously small – though I can still see them sitting there in my mind's eye and the memory makes me smile when I look back. They were lit by moonlight with blankets around their shoulders, smiling.

The following morning, after more French patisseries, freshly squeezed orange juice and Dick's creamy scrambled eggs (he claims he got the recipe from a James Bond novel?!) served with crispy *boudin noir*, the weekend was near to an end. We felt it had gone well and I think we lived up to the promise that this weekend was for food lovers. It was nice to reflect that we had opened up our home to our first paying guests. This was a taste of the future and we loved it. The château was built to entertain and we planned to carry on that legacy.

We all hugged and said our goodbyes. They both thanked us and said it had exceeded their expectations. Jane mentioned that she knew words could not describe how special the weekend had been and when they left it was like saying goodbye to friends.

At times like this, we could not thank my mum and dad enough. They are the unsung heroes of our enterprise as they provided the loving childcare for Arthur and Dorothy that allowed us to work and entertain without the stress of worrying about the children. Multigenerational living makes such sense and allows a special bond between grandparents and grandchildren.

Although Dick and I had had a couple of late nights and early mornings, we were revitalised when the children came running up for their hugs. So we headed out for some fresh air. Our walk around the moat reminded Dick that the alders needed to be trimmed but that was soon forgotten as we started picking the wild daisies that were growing over two inches tall. Dick said they were ox-eye daisies, and with some clues even the children worked out why . . .

To get all the way around the moat we needed to make a traumatic crossing of the rickety bridge that spanned where the stream entered the moat (another job for the 'to-do' list!) but, carrying a child each, we crossed safely and headed around behind the walled garden and through the woods. It's amazing what a little fresh air will do. We were completely mellow and we spent the rest of the afternoon as a family, walking, talking, playing with LEGO, telling stories and finally sleeping!

*

Although we could count on a couple of fingers our bookings, shortly after our first one we received another, then we started to have an actual order book. It was lovely to receive an enquiry on behalf of four managing directors of four different CIS-based companies who wanted to get to know one another and explore if there was scope for them to work together in a way that would benefit them all. I was very excited as a large part of my second career working for a large multinational company involved solving problems and facilitating strategy meetings, and to top it off this would involve hosting the event here at the château.

We had to come clean and say that apart from the honeymoon suite, the accommodation would be rudimentary, but the food would be great and the wine would flow and we would have a ball . . . Funnily enough, this didn't bother Archie, who was organising the event and who had already claimed the HMS! So we were going to have our first management team-building weekend that was planned to be a mixture of *Scrapheap Challenge*, a food lovers' weekend and *The Apprentice* . . .

This was to be a working weekend but it was also all about getting to know one another, so the activities had to reflect that. When they all turned up early Friday evening, they already knew each other after the journey together. We gave them a guided tour and then we had a lovely meal and firmed up plans for the weekend. A trip to the market, a 'scrapheap challenge', fishing and cooking were all on the cards for Saturday with a strategy session planned for Sunday morning.

Our meal ended with the obligatory cheese course and a serious quantity of my rather lovely malt whiskeys; however, we were all up bright and breezy on Saturday. After breakfast, a trip to the market and a beer with the locals, we returned for a quick lunch and then the chaps wanted to help with something around the château. A quick chat confirmed that, even though they were keen to get out the chainsaw and be creative in the woods, they had not got a lot of experience with some of the tools I had, so I set them the task of re-building a two-metre bridge across a part of the moat. There was a path around the moat but where it borders the marshes there was a gap that meant going all the way around involved leaping or using precarious stepping stones – not easy with Arthur and Dorothy in tow! Our new bridge would allow sedate perambulations around our estate.

The task was tackled with gusto and when I went to inspect the work and check they were all in one piece, I saw we had a piece of art that was definitely interesting to look at. The gap had been spanned, so that was a result. The mix of logs and branches was not actually safe to walk on but it was possible to cross the gap, just! To be fair, when I put a scaffolding plank across it, we used it for a long time with very few casualties.

We had initially planned the cooking that evening to be very simple but the choice of fungi at the market had seduced us so, as well as barbecuing a marinated shoulder of lamb with salad and the trimmings, we had mushroom risotto on the menu. Our lead chef for the evening had never cooked anything but wanted to become the mushroom risotto expert.

I took them through basic knife skills and we prepared our vegetables. For all our food lovers' experiences, when there is a hands-on element, we always go through the safety points first and when we start drinking, I tend to take the knives off everyone and pass them the produce after I've prepared it. We were having a party so by the time we had prepared the fungi the knives were back on the rack.

Our risotto was probably the most photographed bit of cooking I think we have ever done with updates being sent to unbelieving family back home.

....

MUSHROOM RISOTTO

Ingredients

1.5l stock
1 jar of dried fungi, roughly chopped (*forestière* mix is much
cheaper than porcini)
100g butter
1 large onion, chopped
2 cloves of garlic, chopped
400g mixed mushrooms/fungi, roughly cut, leaving some
shape in the pieces
400g risotto rice – we use baldo or arborio
50g goat's cheese
100g crème fraîche

Method

Put the stock in a pan and bring it to a gentle simmer. Add the dried fungi and allow to simmer for several minutes to rehydrate them.

In a deep-sided frying pan, melt half of the butter and gently cook the onion and garlic until soft. Add the mixed mushrooms and cook gently for another four minutes. Add the remaining butter, then pour in the risotto rice and stir everything together. Cook for a couple of minutes until the edges of the rice grains start to become translucent.

Add in a ladle of the hot stock and mushrooms, stirring until the rice has nearly absorbed all the liquid, and repeat. Keep stirring and adding the stock until all the liquid has almost been absorbed and the rice is cooked through.

When you add the last ladle, stir through the crumbled goat's cheese and crème fraîche. Increase the heat, then turn off and cover for a couple of moments. Stir well before serving.

....

Having eaten our risotto starter and kept our hunger at bay, we had our fishing competition. Experience does not tend to help with the fish in the moat and the biggest fish we have seen pulled out have been caught by children and people trying for the first time, much to the chagrin of our experienced fishermen! We use sweetcorn as bait as it is not messy to use and it works. It was lovely to watch our guests competing on the western side of the château as the sun was going down. It was peaceful and idyllic and the smell of the barbecuing lamb shoulder ensured we were soon ready for our next course. The conversation was punctuated with laughter and friends taking the mickey out of each other. And there were even lots of fish caught! Initially I acted as the ghillie, baiting hooks and taking fish off the hooks, but very soon everyone was self-sufficient and the competition was fierce.

On Sunday morning I facilitated a strategy session where we explored the opportunities the companies had to work together and issues each had within the sector. It was surprisingly lively after a couple of days' eating and drinking and we did have some 'Eureka!' moments, when suddenly the future seemed more certain and rosy. By the afternoon, we parted having achieved our aims and also having had lots of fun – a very definite win-win.

Our business was growing but all revenue streams had to be used if we were to have the funds to continue our work on the château, so I headed off back to the UK to film a documentary for BBC Four on Arthur Ransome's 'Land of *Swallows and Amazons*'. I think the choice of presenters who were able to sail gaff-rigged dinghies in the Lake District, cabin cruisers on the Norfolk Broads and Thames barges on the Orwell was somewhat limited. Luckily for me, I fitted the bill and it involved heading off for filming, adventures and a bit of sailing.

When I was up in the Lake District, I had to present a piece on the medicinal leeches that were harvested up in some of the ponds in Victorian times and it felt like the scene from the *African Queen* (remember Humphrey Bogart coming out of the water after towing the boat? Angela had no idea what I was talking about!). As I lifted my leg out there was a huge leech pulsating as it sucked blood from my calf. After repositioning a couple of times to get the best shots, I declared enough was enough and I had to scrape it off with a credit card! You don't use a cigarette and burn it off apparently or it regurgitates yuck into your blood – who knew? I also learned that leeches use an anti-coagulate when they feed: my calf bled for about an hour and I ended up with a squelchy boot but we did have enough footage to continue working!

Cash flow is key to any business and we knew the extent of work to be done in order to get the château ready for our first wedding. We had always planned for Dick to carry on working whilst we grew the business. It was the only way. When Dick left, he always put Arthur in charge of protecting everyone. It was very sweet and Arthur took his role very seriously. Dorothy jumped at the chance of sleeping and laying like a starfish in our bed and I often ended up on the edge of our huge bed!

But the pace also changed when Dick was away, it slowed down. My focus was fully on the children and it forced me to stop some of the other work (well, until they went to bed). We played lots outside and on our new trampoline. Those eleven dummies had really paid for themselves! The children could bounce for hours. It was great exercise and really tired them out.

The grounds were constantly changing, with the grasses, flowers, lavender. And the château was heating up. I put a table outside for the children to paint on and we would sometimes spend the entire day surrounded by fresh air. I loved the trees and their shade, and meals were often served picnic style.

Bath time was always at 6pm and they loved to share and splash. Then we would call Daddy to wish him sweet dreams and afterwards I would sing Dorothy to sleep and then Arthur. Normally they were both fast asleep by 7.30pm and I would call Dick back for a real catch-up on our day.

It did not matter if Dick was away for two days or two weeks, the excitement levels of him arriving home were the same. I always liked to clean the house (I hated the idea of Dick coming home to mess) and Arthur and Dorothy would wait by the window. Then we always had a cup of tea. Even at three years old, Arthur loved a cuppa too and if we were very lucky Dick would have brought back some custard creams!

That evening, after we had put the children to bed, we sat on our warm stairs outside of the château and shared a port. It was good to be back together as a family. We talked about his job, that we missed each other and that we were doing okay.

After months of uncertainty and talks of the show being moved to More4, we finally had a date for the series to be aired on Channel 4. Our commissioner, Lizi Wootton, had spent lots of time on the edit; she loved the project and was adamant it should go out on the main terrestrial channel. Initially, there were only going to be three programmes in the first series, summing up our first year. Though subsequently, what was filmed was catalogued and more detail used so the series then became four programmes.

To say we were nervous was an understatement. Thankfully, people seemed to really enjoy our adventures and emails started to flood in. Thousands of requests came in one week. It was overwhelming and very humbling. Angela set about reading and answering every one and even today she still reads every email we receive and tries to answer as many as possible. I am in awe of her work ethic. The first episode of *ETTC* got just under a million viewers and everyone was 'delighted'. However, we didn't actually get offered a new commission until after the third episode had aired and we had proven – by our growing audience – that people really did want to watch what we'd been up to.

It may be hard to believe but it was not a given at the time that we would accept the request for more programmes. Our move to France was all about our new lives and we were actually still wondering how to achieve our two-hour lunch break dream. After lots of talking, we decided a second series was the right thing to do. We had so much more we wanted to achieve and the first year had been organised chaos, so going forward it needed to be . . . different.

Once we had said yes, we were excited to start filming again and carry on capturing our journey – mainly so one day Arthur and Dorothy would have a record of what we all did together to show their children!

With all that we had going on, I knew that I needed help getting the walled garden in good order. But rather than paying for someone to help, we made the decision we'd use nature's rotovators, which had the by-product of beautiful, very tasty pork! Enter Stumpy Bum, Tufty and Chunky, our Piétrain weaners.

Our friends Johnny and Nadine were over from Los Angeles staying with us and Johnny and I put a wooden crate in the back of our car and headed an hour and a half south to pick them up. I chose gilts (young female pigs) as they can be kept longer than young boars that produce more hormones as they mature. I had it on good authority that boars can produce 'pissy' pork if left too long and that was not going to happen. The drive back was aromatic and when we transferred the girls to the walled garden, they were a tad smelly and dirty – pigs aren't normally 'dirty'; muddy, yes, but they are surprisingly clean animals. We had the electric fence up and ready to contain them. Without it they would wreak havoc and dig up everywhere they could get to. They had to understand that the white strip was an electric fence but, as always happens, the first belt they get can send them in any direction – usually away from the pen. This happened but a couple of squeals later, they treated the fence with respect and stayed within its bounds. We'd given them a massive amount of the garden and I'd turned the tower that was a folly into their pigsty with a couple of pallets to keep them from damaging the walls and enough straw to make them comfy.

Right from the very beginning, we all loved the pigs. I already knew I'd enjoy keeping them because I'd raised my first pigs more than ten years earlier. We had to be very strict with the children about the electric fence but we all enjoyed feeding and watering them and we socialised the pigs by stroking them as they were fed, so it wasn't long before they'd come over to get their tummies scratched. When we fed the chickens or pigs, we'd call them so they learnt to come, which is useful when you need to control your animals. For the chickens, we use a clucking noise a bit like the cockerel makes to tell the ladies he's found food. Sort of a clucking version of 'chuck chuck chuckieees'. It works really well. For pigs, it's a very different sound; here at the Strawbridges', it's more of a hog call; that is, a long 'shoooiee ... Shoooiee.' Angela thought I was joking but it wasn't long before she was a regular Dr Doolittle and she loved popping over the electric fence and tickling our pigs' tummies.

*

I was definitely on a learning roller coaster. We had pigs and they were really cute. But at first I was terrified of them. I had a *Babe* vision in my mind but soon realised that they could knock me off my feet. I never thought I would say it, but after feeding them a few times I completely loved them. They were so thankful for food. My mum loved giving them leftovers, it was so satisfying! The fence did, however, take a bit of getting used to. I was petrified that the kids would forget and walk into it. But like animals, they learn fast, thankfully, because of my constant 'stay away from the fence' tune.

The girls grew quickly and they did an amazing job rotovating a huge expanse of the garden. As the summer progressed, we chose a hollow they had created and filled it with buckets of water to provide them with a wallow, which they loved. It was important, as light-coloured pigs can get sunburnt, so the mud was their factor 50 protection. I once worked with a lass who was a very strict vegan but she was employed to manage animals, amongst other things. I asked her how she reconciled her veganism with the fact the animals were destined to be eaten and she said her aim was to give them the best life possible. I thoroughly agreed.

I knew the pigs were destined for our bellies and that was fine. Well, I hoped I was going to be fine with that (it was a first!). These were our first pigs, they were my first pigs ever, and it really surprised me how much personality they had. They became part of our rhythm, checking and feeding them, after the chickens. We loved it and I found myself in wellies more than ever. We also enjoyed telling pig stories to our friend Sophie. At our wedding, Sophie – who had match-made us – and her husband Will, gave us some money specifically to buy pigs, so every now and again we would FaceTime Sophie with them to say hello.

We knew that there was so much still to get organised for Charlotte and Richard's wedding and although we were deep in wedding planning, for this beautiful moment we were enjoying the great outside.

Having time in the first half of 2016 had allowed us to plant the garden and put down some of the foundations for our future potager. As a family, we spent many happy hours pottering around outside. The trip to the walled garden is always full of anticipation about seeing what's happening. I love it in the sun, the rain, frost, snow, wind, fog – it doesn't matter, it's just facets of an amazing place. I have on my phone a picture of Angela, Arthur and Dorothy all riding on a garden trolly as we headed over to the entrance of the walled garden. It's my favourite picture and I still love walking over there with the family.

At the weekend, we walk over and let out the chickens and geese. Sometimes we all do it together and other times it's any two or three of us. For the children, it's part of the rhythm of living here. We do not take our harvests for granted but in the early days every bit of fruit or vegetable was a minor miracle. Arthur and Dorothy understood the benefits of entering the garden first when the strawberries were ripe as they could have their first pick, literally.

We had herbs in abundance and we planted a significant amount of salad bowl lettuce, mixed salad leaves, spinach, peas, beetroot and other quick-to-harvest plants near the gate for ease of gathering. Any weeds or vegetables that were not good were thrown to the pigs, who devoured them greedily. I think the pigs knew Arthur and Dorothy were a source of food as they always threw things over the fence to them. Watching a small child open a pea pod they have picked is so lovely. When they understand how to get inside, each pea is taken out one at a time and eaten in an almost ceremonious way, as they concentrate on their fine motor skills. Arthur and Dorothy had the added excitement of taking the empty pea pods and giving them to the pigs, who loved them. We could easily spend twenty minutes nibbling the peas and feeding the girls.

CHAPTER 3

The Château's First Wedding

Every season in our little part of France is special but there is something relaxing about summer. The days are long and the weather is warm; you grow accustomed to the trees being green and the flowers blooming. With the drier months, gradually the water level in the moat starts to drop. The changes are first obvious when large rocks start to appear and our herons perch on them to fish, and around the back of the château to the north-east gradually a stony beach of sorts is revealed. Then quite suddenly you notice the moat is shrinking...

Early summer is when you would expect all the activity of spring to be bearing fruit and nature is abundant; week by week, more produce matures and becomes available for the table. France is more geared towards enjoying hot summers than the UK, which always seems to be as surprised by sun in the summer as it is by snow in the winter. Everyone is expected to take a holiday and, apart from the holiday destinations, August, when it arrives, is quieter than you believe possible. When the temperatures rise, people find it hard to work as productively. Looking out the window at this time of year is like a siren's call enticing you away from the mundane in search of pleasure. But we didn't yet have the luxury of a proper work-life balance. Our dreams were coming true, our wedding business was really happening and now we just had to do the work to ensure that Charlotte and Richard's dream wedding was all they had wished for!

Towards the end of June, Charlotte and Richard came to say hello. They had a family home in France a couple of hours away so it made perfect sense to come and see us. Seeing anything in real life is always different; a building's surroundings, atmosphere, light, feeling and smells all make a difference.

When anyone new is meeting the château in person for the first time I'm always terrified and excited in equal measure. The sun was shining and the skies were blue and, after a big welcome, we stood with Charlotte and Richard and looked up. 'It's even better in real life,' Charlotte said. We were delighted to hear that! We then showed them around the château and the grounds, had some lunch and chatted about everything involved in their big day. Richard explained to Dick how important Scotch eggs were to them and Charlotte explained her colour scheme. With all the important information covered, it felt realer than ever.

As we said our goodbyes, Richard said, 'This place has a magic about it.' It was not because of its look, he added, but because the château is calm and happy and feels like home. We agreed. It was lovely to hear.

When they left, Dick and I sat down and wrote our priority list together with a plan to start working through them. It's probably not a surprise that we had different priorities, however . . .

Charlotte and Richard's wedding was only a couple of months away and there was a raft of work to be done, especially at the orangery. The nearest mains power was in the château and laying a trench all the way over was a non-starter, as it would have been hundreds of metres long and would have to go across the front of the château, over the bridge and then cross country to the orangery. Apart from the mess and disruption, the cost would have been too much for us to bear and, quite importantly, we didn't have enough power for the château, never mind sharing it with other buildings. Even if you are not a techie you will understand that the total power available on the island would have tripped if we'd connected five 3kW heaters. For the techies, we had a single-phase supply that regularly suffered reduced voltage – I measured down as low as 180V when making the case to have a new three-phase connection, so with a 63-amp trip we had to be very aware of how we loaded the system ... End of techie bit!

So we made the decision that we'd harvest the sunshine. I'd done it lots in the past and it would involve generating electricity on solar panels, storing the energy in batteries, then converting it to useful 'mains' power when required. We'd always had aspirations to make the château more sustainable but we were pragmatists about how we could invest our funds in the early days. Though we tried to futureproof all the work we had done, this was to be our first pure eco project. I sourced the necessary components as cheaply as possible, which involved getting them on the internet – the panel, the charge controller, the monitoring system and the pure sine inverter. Even though deep-cycle batteries were significantly cheaper in the UK, I couldn't get anyone to ship them to me. After some difficult conversations with a battery supplier, I managed to order three. I'd done the sums and the system should have been able to charge in a week and provide sufficient power for a 'reasonable' sound system and lights for a wedding function.

Obviously, downstream my calculations were tested, especially at the wedding that wanted a five-piece electric band with sound that would have taken the glass out of the windows . . . Then we had to compromise. I said 'no'.

Installation was interesting. Carrying a solar panel five metres up a ladder was great fun! Positioning it was simple: it sat on the gutter of the south-facing roof and everything else was in the loft. The loft was great – the hatch had a pulley system for hauling things up there. We'd never ventured up before and I discovered it was full of lovely old terracotta pots and a lot of old straw. The wooden floor was not strong and there were a couple of holes but it was dry, so I set about connecting up our new system.

The batteries were charged by the French sunshine and when we needed electricity, it was taken from the batteries and turned into alternating current – just like you get in a domestic plug. There was a spaghetti field of cables in the roof that connected to sockets, lights and switches. There was a very small, discreet monitoring panel mounted on the wall that said how long the batteries would last at the current rate of usage ('current' – there's a techy joke, there!). It was comforting to discover that the lights could be left on for days when the batteries were fully charged and our PA/music system was good for at least twelve hours, which boded well for our parties but had yet to be tested . . .

After we had received an initial deposit from Richard and Charlotte, we discussed how the money needed to be used wisely . . . Lights and power are of course very, very important but I am sure you can guess that most of the other things Dick and I considered essential were slightly (massively) different.

The bargain chairs we had purchased from Emmaus for our wedding were just grand. On the whole, we had great-quality, hardy pews to enjoy our wedding breakfast on. What let them down was their seat pads . . . many were filled with straw and were tatty and caught on any delicate dress. I had therefore elevated this to a 'priority job' and had been looking for a good, sturdy material to upholster the seats with. I could probably get four seat covers out of one square metre, plus I needed foam, a type of filling called Dacron and lots of staples.

I found a collection called 'New York' – an art deco velvet chenille with a simple but elegant fan design. It came in twelve colourways and was exactly what I was after but the problem was the choice! There was Broadway (a deep burgundy), Harlem (purple), Central (mustard), Liberty (mint green), plus Rockefeller, Brooklyn, Staten, Empire, Hudson, Queens, Albany and Hampton. I could not decide, so I got some of each. If our chairs were to be eclectic, I thought it was better to celebrate it.

. . . .

HOW TO REUPHOLSTER A DINING ROOM CHAIR

You will need
(quantities will depend on what you are upholstering /
how many)

Sandpaper
Chalk paint and brushes
Furniture wax
Steel wool (optional)
Dacron
Seat foam
Fabric – upholstery quality
A staple gun (with 8mm staples)

Method

Step 1: Take a seat

Pick up the chair you wish to upcycle and lay it on its side. If the seat comes out, you'll want to remove it now – a few knocks underneath it should do the trick. If your seat isn't removable, cover it with some masking tape and plastic sheeting before we start painting.

Step 2: Paint away

Preparation is key. Usually this will involve sanding and priming your surfaces; however, if you buy chalk paint, it may be a simple clean and one coat! Chalk furniture paint is super versatile and will give your upcycled chair a lovely smooth finish, even on untreated wood. And the best thing is, you can't really go wrong – if you don't like the colour, you can easily paint over it.

(Top tip: Sometimes I like to sand back the second colour a bit and reveal some of the old paint underneath.)

Step 3: Wax on, wax off

Once the paint is on and dry, your chair transformation is well underway. You'll want to ensure the paint is sealed by adding a layer of wax to it. I like to use clear wax to give it that fresh look but darker ones may be better if you're looking for a shabby chic effect. Don't hold back as you brush the wax on – a nice even coat will work wonders for the next step. And remember to wipe away any excess.

Step 4: Grab some steel wool

For a subtle aged effect, rub the freshly waxed chair with some steel wool. You can also use sandpaper but I prefer the softer effect of the steel wool and wax. Using the wool, rub off as much or as little of the paint as you like. Take your time until you've got your desired effect.

(Top tip: Once you've got it looking how you want, add another layer of wax to seal the paint and achieve a perfect finish.)

Step 5: Reupholster your chair

If you want to refresh your seat covers, start by removing the pins from the back of the seat. Then, with a bit of force, the old material should come away. At this stage, check to see if the existing foam needs replacing or repairing.

(Top tip: I usually add a little bit of Dacron to the middle of the seat for extra body to plump it up.)

Step 6: Material and staple gun at the ready

Next, lay your new material over the seat. If you have a pattern or design, make sure it's positioned properly and the right way up. Then, carefully flip your seat over. Using a staple gun, add one staple to each side of the seat. Flipping the seat back over, you can then check your placement and that the fabric is not creased, before adding the rest of the staples. Then, starting with the corners, staple the edge of the material all the way around.

Step 7: Finishing touches

Now for the final steps. Trim away any excess from the underside of your seat and check it's all looking neat and smooth. Carefully fit the seat back into the chair.

If your seat pad is not removable it's the same process as above, but on the corners, you cut a line (so four in total, one for each leg) to the leg and neatly fold the material underneath and staple into place. Most seats will have the staples attached underneath but if you have one that requires staples on the side, and therefore showing, that's where you glue or tack in beading and braiding over the top to hide them.

Once you get going, it's so satisfying and much easier than it sounds.

....

There is a lot of investment needed when setting up a business and we were spending what was necessary. Angela has always been in charge of how things are to look. Of course I have opinions but Angela always has a vision that is made up of lots of details so I am content to do the necessary infrastructure work and wait to see the beautiful outcome. When I saw the material arrive, I thought, 'That's a lot of work,' and 'I quite like the eclectic look,' – but I think 'eclectic' was an excuse to have a mish-mash of different materials. Suffice to say, Angela did not compromise and so our chairs were to be unified and made gorgeous.

Each chair took around fifteen minutes and we needed eighty. Looking back, it was a big investment of time but a crucial one. Many of the chairs are still in use to this day and it goes on the list of the things that Dick chunters about!

On Charlotte and Richard's visit, we talked pig roast and Scotch eggs. I knew exactly what they were after. Our vision was to provide a weekend wedding celebration that allowed the family and guests to congregate and renew, or make, acquaintances before the main event. For that, we had decided that we would have a pig roast as a nod towards the old French custom of having a roast wild boar at a wedding celebration.

The idea was easy to think of but the clock was ticking and this was our first pig roast, which always takes more effort and time. Once it was set up, it would be easy for future events. But we had to execute the plan. I was happy I could cook a pig on a spit over an open fire – indeed, I'd done it several times, the first being back in the mid 1980s. However, it is a long task and requires constant attention, so I was looking for a more failsafe way of doing it. I had noticed a large heating oil tank in one of the outbuildings that I was sure could be upcycled, so I set myself the task of building our château pig roaster. Needless to say, things didn't run as smoothly as I had hoped.

Moving aside the detritus that half hid the tank, I put the sack trolley under it to move it to somewhere more convenient for working on. I'm a dab hand with a sack trolley; one of my first summer jobs was emptying forty-feet containers using one to transfer goods around a warehouse. So I lined the trolley up and prepared to move the centre of gravity over the wheels and . . . absolutely nothing happened. I thought the bloody thing was bolted to the floor but it wasn't. Then it dawned on me. I started tapping the side with my knuckles. It was three-quarters full of very old heating oil. That was a bit of a problem. What do you do with hundreds of litres of old oil?

I went to the *déchetterie* (the tip); they said 'no' without any more advice. I then asked the Mairie's office, who suggested the *déchetterie* . . . I was then given the contact for an expert. He did that amazing sucking-in noise and said it was 'terrible' and gave me a quote for hundreds of euros. If I had not been so environmentally aware it would have been poured into a hole in the ground to soak away, but . . . Time was ticking so I thought I'd store it and sort it out later, but that in itself was a big old problem. What containers to use and how to get it out? There was no tap at the bottom, just a plug. The only powered pump I could find was battery powered and after a couple of minutes it was 'tired'. I syphoned off the top but it wasn't long before every 25l and 50l container I had was full so I had to hand-pump the oil out, then take it to where the old hot water tanks were in another outbuilding. This was my solution to a lack of containers, and it worked. We still have some but I've used oil to start a bonfire on more than a few occasions.

Eventually we had an empty drum that I could move but I knew the residue would be a problem. In my mind, I had designed the roaster but I needed to cut the heavy gauge steel and there was going to be heat, sparks and volatile fumes (it's when heating oil is warmed that it becomes volatile) and I didn't fancy an explosion while I was working on the tank! So I took the tank around behind the outbuildings for a controlled burn. We were being filmed for the second series of *Escape to the Château* at the time and I thought this would make for some good footage! Our cameraman Sean wanted to get the best possible coverage and after I had lit the straw in the mouth of the plug hole (all the other pipe connections had been taken off to allow air in and out), he started to move in to get a better shot. I restrained him and about fifteen seconds later, we had a very impressive whoosh as the warmed gases ignited and a jet of flame shot out the plug hole . . . I fed in some more straw and twigs and the fire burned the inside of the tank to render it safe – job done.

After that it was easy. I cut out a door big enough for the biggest pig that would fit and I even remembered to place the hinges and drill the bolt holes before cutting the door completely free – so much easier. The spit was a 30mm pipe with holes drilled through it for skewers to be put through the pig and the spit – that way, when the spit is turned the pig turns. That sounds simple but if it's not secured properly then you have the issue of a hot, partially cooked pig that cannot be rotated! I welded an old child's bicycle tyre to the spit to make the turning easier and the lone reflector on the wheel is how we determine if the spit has been turned . . . If you rotate the spit on the hour then you put the reflector to the twelve o'clock position. We rotated by quarter-turns every fifteen minutes, so if I passed at quarter past the hour and the reflector was still at twelve then I knew it had to be turned so would do it. Likewise, anyone looking at the wheel would know when it was last turned – simple but effective!

I made the decision to cook with hardwood logs and, as we had cut down some pear and cherry trees, we kept these logs aside for our roaster. We baste with cider and the smoky logs make the skin nearly black. The taste is amazing but you don't get the crackling. For me, however, the skin is there to protect the meat and lovely smoked spit-roasted pork is the objective.

Rearing and eating whole pigs is an area that is completely Dick's responsibility. I was out of my comfort zone and did not even pretend I wanted to be involved. So when Dick asked me to measure our pigs for the roaster, I was surprised. I did say, 'Stop pulling my leg,' but he insisted that he needed to know as he was worried they were too big. So I grabbed my tape measure and off I went. In the background, I heard Dick shout, 'Be careful they don't try to eat your shoes!' As I looked down, I realised that I had very gold mermaid shoes on that possibly looked delicious, and most probably they were different enough that our very inquisitive girls would be keen to see what they tasted like!

Once I was in the pig area and was struggling to get the tape measure in a position to determine their length from nose to tail, I should have realised that Dick was completely pulling my leg. Of course Stumpy Bum, Tufty and Chunky would not stay still for one moment and every time I carefully approached them, they moved! Not to be beaten, I changed my tactic. I would stay still and let them come to me. And they did . . . and I managed to measure Stumpy. She was 1.1 metres, if I remember, although I secretly hoped they would be too big for the roaster as I had begun to enjoy keeping pigs!

Summer was in full swing, and the château was glowing. The grounds were bursting with flowers – poppies, roses, lavender – as was the meadow, which was full of stunning grasses and daisies. We were having fresh eggs from our chickens most mornings and had started enjoying our first home-grown produce. We were weaving in work and things really were getting done around the château. Our dream was happening. We were in it, right this second. Arthur and Dorothy were going from strength to strength, with their personalities developing daily and clear to see. My mum and dad had really got into the rhythm of French living too. Mum had discovered lots of new foods that she loved and simple things like finding the best place to buy prawns made her day. My dad found a new all-time favourite bread and fell in love with getting the lawn-mower out! Although busy, life was happy and balanced.

The children often spent all day outside, playing on the trampoline, finding bugs and playing with mud in the walled garden. Come the evening, they were exhausted and would fall asleep rather easily, which allowed Dick and I to sit on our front stairs and have a glass of port together. The stairs outside the château embraced the heat and sitting on them felt like a hug. We would sit side by side and, as the crystal port glasses are so small, we'd bring

Winter 2016.

First day
of school.

ARTHUR

The
oneymoon
uite round
wo.

The cloakroom
before.

The cloakroom after.

Our first wedding.

out the decanter to have it at hand for our top-ups. All around, the solid stone walls and steps were giving off the heat they had collected throughout the day, in preparation for another glorious day tomorrow. We had the whole château and all the grounds but we were sublimely happy to just sit on a step, holding hands and chatting through progress, sharing all the little things that may have been missed as we had beavered away. Sometimes we would only have five minutes, but however long it was, it grounded us. Maybe it was the port, maybe it was because we had stopped, but whatever the day had thrown at us, when we stood up, we felt invigorated.

It is obvious that my dad loves being a grandad. He is so patient and just loves spending time playing with Arthur and Dorothy and they love making things together. So one day he had an idea that the children needed a sandpit, and once the seed was planted my dad set about making the best sand pit they could dream of.

If you imagine any child's sandpit, the dimensions that spring to mind are probably not in metres . . . Steve decided that this sand pit had to be big enough for both children to play in and possibly with a couple of friends when they got older. From need, to concept, to prototype, to painted pit, to new fitted roof to stop cats visiting was several weeks, and when the final, wonderful sandpit was filled with the first ten 25kg bags of play sand it was in a position, in the coach house garage, that we knew would not be changed without a lot of thought. The children loved it and its construction is such that it was built to be around for many years. Steve even managed to finish it before the kids went back to school!

I was still on a high after Charlotte and Richard's visit, but even though I wanted only to think about flowers, balloons and cakes, my big worry was that eighty guests would need somewhere to go and powder their noses. I'm a firm believer that many venues are let down by this facility and if I'm going to be brutally honest with you, I can actually remember many events by their terrible bathrooms! Let's face it, we all have the best chats in the cloakrooms putting on our lipstick!

We had allocated the old bureau at the back corner of the ground floor to be our cloakroom when we first moved in but with the clock ticking there was a bit of pressure as this was not a small or a quick job and involved the entire room being plumbed, cubicles sectioned, toilets installed and, of course, it needed to be made pretty.

Toilet cloakroom size became our first topic of conversation. Dick had done his research on how big toilets need to be and I also had an idea of the size I would like them to be.

Simple facts: toilet cubicles have to be big enough not to be claustrophobic and soundproof enough not to be embarrassing. The area available for cubicles without impinging on the windows and their reveals theoretically gave us plenty of space for three toilets – so we decided to make two and make them nicer. After a lot of discussion, we decided that the cubicles would go all the way to the ceiling but would have a false roof. The ceilings on the ground floor are high and without a false roof it would be like sitting in a lift shaft ... I worked out what was required and my builder mate Steve and I laid it all out and started erecting the stud walls. When a couple of plaster boards were up, and it was obvious what went where, we called Angela in ...

It was so obvious as soon as I walked in that the walls going all the way up to the ceiling just didn't work. The room was like a corridor. I just didn't like it at all. Dick said he knew from the moment I walked in that I hated it ... that's probably why I didn't even have to argue much to get a flat roof over the cubicles that left the shape of the room and all the coving in view.

*

Regular trips to Emmaus was a part of our family routine and with the house a little upside down with renovation and organising, it was a nice break for everyone. Arthur and Dorothy loved it and it was not like going shopping. We saw and bought things that you just don't find in the regular shops and if you don't get something when you see it, it probably won't be there next time or ever again.

Although the excitement is finding the unexpected, I was actually after more taxidermy for the top of the cubicles in the cloakroom. There is around 1.5 metres between the top of the cubicles and the ceiling and I thought it would be nice to showcase a wildlife scene. But it was actually a rather big space, so anything would help. We would often find taxidermy in Emmaus at a very good price.

On one Wednesday morning, we turned up and did our usual look around the kitchenalia section together (which, bizarrely, is where you would find the taxidermy). Then, as we were about to split up, me going to the 'Bizarre' and Angela going to the clothes and fabrics section, Angela spotted a collection of children's bicycles, scooters, trailers and tricycles. We'd never seen things like this before and there were lots of them. There were no pedals and the children obviously propelled themselves using their feet. We didn't know until Arthur started school but all the primary schools have a collection of these little bikes and scooters that the reception children sit on and gradually build up their balance until they are ready for pedals. These had all seen some serious service but were still working and, what's more, Arthur and Dorothy loved them.

We bought a selection for next to nothing – they varied from trikes with trailers that looked a bit like Roman chariots, to mini two-wheeled bikes to scooters. I hadn't actually put two and two together and was wondering where Arthur and Dorothy could ride them, then Angela declared the racetrack around our entrance hall open. There was nowhere outside smooth enough for them to ride but the hall was perfect, though I did put the salon and *salle à manger* off limits!

For €15, I truly believed we had the bargain of a lifetime. These sturdy 'wheelers' were built to last and I guessed that Arthur and Dorothy had grown out of their Rupert Bear walker and the trundle buggy and block trolley they used to push each other in. Although I knew it was no good for the floors, I missed the kids charging around the house. The fun and laughter fills the house and is addictive – so I knew a bit of charging about would make it feel truly alive again! The floor would need re-doing anyway before the wedding; well, at least, that was my justification to myself, so I thought, let's have a bit of fun!

The parquet flooring has at its centre a flower design set in an octagonal shape. Around that are more octagons of wood getting ever bigger ... It was a ready-made racing circuit for children! Arthur and Dorothy both found a favourite vehicle very quickly. Arthur chose a three-wheeled scooter and Dorothy a trike and they loved racing in circles again and again and again. We would often stand in the middle and pretend they were spinning us around and making us dizzy. And, in fairness, although it started as a joke, by around twenty turns we genuinely were pretty dizzy! Or we would chase them, which never ceased to create laughter and terror. Both Dick and I were always on hand to ensure that the château's version of *Wacky Races* was safe. They never tired of it. And then, before the kids went to bed every night, they would park their vehicle along the side of the back staircase, which became called 'the garage'!

Finding the round, white ceramic 'school sink' in a *brocante* – a French flea market – for €50 was a delight. It was the kind that would have been used by four or five kids at the same time in school. Slight problem was that it didn't work, but luckily I knew a very clever man who could sort that.

I also picked up an art deco mirror for next to nothing, which inspired a very crisp-looking art deco wallpaper that I used on the cubicle. I tried to keep the colours fresh and clean because this was a bathroom first and foremost. For the personal touch, I découpaged the inside of our doors with vintage magazines I had found in the attic. I used PVA and water, a 50/50 mix; it works every time and really brought our simple door to life. I stacked old suitcases next to the sink so you could place your bag there whilst washing your hands and added a couple of Lloyd Loom chairs we had lying around. It's habit that people go to the toilets in pairs, so having a 'waiting chair' felt sensible. Around the sink we used metro tiles, because I knew that area would be used heavily and I did not want the walls to look grubby – tiles allowed me to wipe clean after every event. There was an original safe still in the wall, which we kept and tiled around. It's actually very beautiful and useful for keeping spare toiletries in!

Practicalities aside, I added a little bit of fantasy with taxidermy and used bamboo from our grounds to create a geometric foliage display. It came together nicely, though at this moment, I was simply delighted that we had toilets for the wedding.

Having magazines in a loo is not a new idea but I thought sticking them on the doors was pretty novel, and there was no doubt about it, the large circular sink was also really interesting. That didn't mean it would be easy to install or that it would be in perfect working condition. It was just different. Installation raised a couple of issues. Firstly, the plumbing was all up inside the column that the sink was precariously perched on, and secondly, well, the huge sink was precariously perched on the column. As usual with a 'fix', I took everything apart and cleaned it to see what state it was in. Seals were replaced, washers turned upside down to give them new life, waste pipes were fitted and it was ready to turn on. Minor leakage, which was dealt with by PTFE and tightening, and we had a sink that squirted water out of half a dozen spray nozzles at once. Securing it was a minor engineering challenge that involved cables going down through the middle to a beam in the ceiling below and being tightened until a big, unsteady man could lean on the edge without movement. I was happy it worked; Angela was happy it looked good. Result.

I rest my case. My husband can fix anything! By the middle of the summer, our meadow, which stretches between the driveway and the orangery, was looking magical. Amongst actual grass, there were lots of wild ornamental grasses, yellow flowers, cornflowers, poppies, sage, clovers, dandelions, wild carrots (which do not smell nice!) and other flowers that I was always on a mission to identify. With the summer heat, the colours had started to become muted – the greens, browns, reds, lilacs, pinks and taupes were all soft shades that matched Charlotte's colour palette beautifully. It was stunning and the perfect backdrop for wedding photos.

One day, Dick took the children for an adventure into the grass. I was working outside the orangery and could hear endless excitement and laughing but I couldn't see any of them. The adventure was everyone sneaking up on me through the grasses, commando style, but the laughter gave it away. At first I pretended to carry on working so that they could scare me but they took forever to reach me so I decided to stop what I was doing to join the fun. I got down on all fours and crawled my way over to them to try to surprise everyone. It ended up in one of those very funny moments where we all knew what the others' game was . . . no one scared

anyone but everyone thought everyone else's efforts were hilarious. Then the children decided to jump on Dick whilst he laid on the ground. Arthur first, then Dorothy. Instead of piling on top and crushing my poor husband, I stood back and took pictures . . . 'Could you just do that again, kids?'

There are times in life when you are completely in a moment and are overcome with happiness. That was one of those very special times. We were creating a magical place for our family and for a business and that was always our masterplan. Everything was looking stunning and we were ready to welcome our guests.

Planning events is in my DNA. I love it. Hosting and making people smile. I've done many things in my life and yet had never actually thought of doing the thing that I love the most. It was about fifteen years ago, when I hosted a press party for one of my new business ventures, that it finally dawned on me. The business was focused on making customised T-shirts, each wrapped up like cakes. For the launch, I put cocktails in teacups and made cute little cakes. My team wore black vintage dresses with aprons I had made. One of the journalists stopped me and said, 'I think the way you have hosted this event is brilliant, so quirky. I would pay for you to come and do it at my house. Why don't you set yourself up a website and I'll be the first person to cover your new business?' And with that she wandered into the crowd . . .

One month later, true to her word, the journalist covered the story and doors opened that I never thought existed. In over a decade in hospitality, I have learnt that, aside from wonderful customers, it's essential to have a good team, organisation, logistics and suppliers. They are your backbone. Each one must be nurtured. By the time I had stepped down from the Vintage Patisserie I had all of the above nailed. And although I knew I could step into the new role at the château seamlessly, I had to rebuild the team, processes and suppliers. With my pidgin French I knew suppliers were going to be tricky, but finding the right ones was essential.

Flowers were top of the list. Charlotte had a chalky blush palette, full of soft colours, and she wanted all the blooms to be very pretty and billowing. My first job was to put a wishlist together from Charlotte's inspiration board. I had to think about season, balance and form, as well as how it would combine together and the availability.

When I had my list, I then translated every flower on it into French and printed a picture of them all. I was taking no chances. I transferred this onto a clipboard (they always make me feel quite official) and drove to our local florist in Mayenne. It was the last week in July, which was a lucky accident because I got my order in just before they closed for August. I was starting to see a rather painful pattern here . . .

The florist was very classical and I would say 'French' in its fashion. Like patisseries, florists here have their style, which is more 'put together' and less rustic. There were lots of lovely displays with carefully twisted grasses and lots of symmetry. It was very nice and I couldn't help but be wowed by the fragrances and colours that hit me from every direction. I had come prepared and was ready to place my first flower order.

Except, the first issue was that the florist was not used to taking any orders that were not ready-made bouquets. I had to explain that I was making them up for the wedding myself – something the florist was not happy with for some reason. Then there was an issue with availability; there were several items on my list that the florist did not know whether she could obtain. I was relaxed about this. I had given myself plenty of options. But then – and this was completely my issue – there was the price of eucalyptus foliage. At €1 a stem, I nearly had to sit down, and I probably would have if there had been a chair. Note to self: we need to start growing this beautiful plant that many consider a weed.

Nonetheless, my first florist order was done. Not as smoothly as I had hoped, but it was done. The florist would be back from her August holiday just before the big day so I was very lucky to have got my order in before she left. I was due to collect them on Thursday, 1 September, the same day Arthur was due to start school. It was all happening!

When it comes to the food for any event at the château, we believe it's all about the ingredients: they have to be seasonal and the sourcing is all about the food miles. Local food is very important to us. We are not extremist in our views and we will buy bananas and other fruit and vegetables that are outside our locality, but the principle is simple and important to us. Though to be clear, I have never aspired to grow enough to support our business. If you sit down, do the sums and think about it, you realise that we'd be too occupied with growing to do anything else, and that wouldn't fund the château . . . That said, we use our own produce if we have sufficient, particularly for small events.

I truly believe you can't compete with homegrown fruit and vegetables and we love tasting our produce together. It was a serious ceremony when the four of us dug our first ever potatoes and produced a meal that transported me back to my childhood with all seven children and Mum and Dad around the table, and Dad looking very pleased with himself as we tucked into our boiled potatoes with butter and scallions.

The shallots that had been pushed into the soil had transformed into bunches of scallions and all we had to do was wash our freshly dug potatoes and boil them in salted water. If you take a freshly dug potato straight to the sink and wash it – not peel it, just rub the mud off with your fingers – the skin will partly come away and you will end up with potatoes with natural sugars that have not turned to starches yet (I'm not sure of the science in this but I was told it nearly half a century ago and truly believe it!). Pop them into boiling, well-salted water until cooked. When they are strained put them back in the warm pan with a knob of butter that looks big enough to be very bad for you. Put the lid on, leave for about five minutes, then, holding the lid, give them a good shake to mix the butter through. Serve and make sure no butter is left behind in the pan! Sprinkle on chopped scallions and be prepared to add more salt or butter. Enjoy! That means don't do any veg or proteins – just savour the potatoes, butter and scallions. If these are your own potatoes, you will know heaven.

We also had to plan how we would handle the proceedings for the big day. We decided very quickly that what we would offer was a 'celebration' and that the formal part of the proceedings would be vows taken under the direction of a celebrant. We had been through the process required to get married in France for our own wedding the year before and, apart from the requirement to be resident for forty days prior to the wedding, we knew there was an awful lot of paperwork and certification, the majority of which had to be translated into French by a court-accredited translator. But, as with all things, we started with a lot of research.

There were online courses to become a celebrant that helped you to understand your responsibilities and taught you how to speak in front of guests and conduct the ceremony. It was obvious that this was going to be my role and I decided to produce a set of words and order for a celebration that were bespoke to us and that we would customise for every couple, making changes depending on what they wanted. Angela and I looked at many different ways of doing things and, over a period of several months, I wrote up the outline for what we consider to be a relaxed but important ceremony. We made sure there was a lot of time for anecdotes and for different family members to join in, as wanted. Angela is our number one point of liaison with the couple but I also talk to them about every aspect of the ceremony ahead of the day and it has always been my job to make it all run smoothly – I love it!

Our first big day was rapidly approaching but items on my list that still needed sourcing or sorting included:

- The arrangement of china
- The bar and ice for drinks
- Buying soup spoons (we had used teaspoons for the soup course at our wedding, which was quite fun!)
- Napkins, which also needed to be embroidered with the guests' names
- Logistics for travel on the day
- And last, but certainly not least: staff for the day

It's a wonderful idea serving everything on vintage china and it makes for an eclectic meal, but storing vintage china safely is that little bit more tricky. Aside from all items having to be hand washed, each item must also be carefully wrapped. There are certain catering racks that you can buy for exactly this, but at around £6,000 for the items we required, we just did not have the money at this stage. We were hand to mouth and every penny had to be for complete essentials or for front-of-house items.

We had a tiny team at the château consisting of Tina, who would turn her hand to anything, for two days a week and Steve, our plasterer/tiler, as and when we needed and could afford him. Certainly not enough for eighty guests. I have always thought that for good service, you need one member of staff for every ten guests. So I was looking for around an extra five members of front-of-house staff. In the kitchen, we also needed a team and used our English-based contact Jai, who assisted Alan, our friend who catered for our wedding. Jai offered to bring over a good friend of his and they both brought their girlfriends along to work in front of house. We also hired two locals and called over a couple of friends from the UK to assist (one who happened to be living in Paris). We knew bringing people over from the UK would never work financially in the long term, with travel and accommodation. We simply could not absorb this into our costs. However, on this occasion, with this being the only event of the year and our first paid wedding, it was needs must and we were happy to only break even to get it right.

They always say it's who you know. Via a good friend of Patrice's (our hairdresser), Sacha was introduced to us. She was looking for work in hospitality and lived locally. I always say if you are a good waitress, you will be good at most things! A good waiter/waitress cannot be underestimated. The hours are long, you are on your feet all day, often running from A to B; you have to be happy at all times (except for breaks) whilst also remembering maybe a dozen or more things at any given moment; you have to make every guest feel looked after but not so much that it feels like you're in their space either. It's the epitome of multitasking. You have to constantly read people, observe body language and genuinely be a people person. Good servers are one in a million. And when Sacha turned up, I knew she was our one in a million.

We knew for this wedding that we did not have a bar area as such, nor enough fridge space, but we had the capability to waitress-serve lots of bubbly, wine, beers and cocktails in teacups. I'd been making ice for weeks to ensure we had enough to keep the drinks nice and cold and we knew we could order crushed ice from our local fishmonger. From the planning of our wedding, we knew the good stuff to serve, so we were happy with this part of the process.

Dick allowed me to go and make the drinks order, which was to arrive on the Wednesday before the wedding.

I should not have been surprised by the drinks order that arrived for Charlotte and Rich's wedding. Angela simply will never put us in the position of running out of anything. Our weddings are not the 'drink at the reception, two glasses of wine during the meal and a glass of bubbly for the toast' kind. Angela's calculations revolve around having enough just in case everyone chooses the same drink and decides to drink it all evening! Some people do drink more than others but half a bottle of wine each is a rule of thumb to compensate for that; in most cases, Granny does not drink as much as the rugby-playing groomsmen. However, to be sure, Angela has always had available half a bottle of bubbly for arrival drinks, half a bottle of bubbly for the post-ceremony drinks, half a bottle of red wine, half a bottle of white wine, half a bottle of rosé and half a bottle of bubbly for toasts, each. Yes – each! Of course, we've never run out but when the wine order arrives it's a feat of endurance to transfer it to the *cave*!

I knew Dick was going to have something to say about the drinks order but you just never know and it's not like there is a twenty-four-hour supermarket at the end of the road. I'd rather be safe than be the wedding that ran out of . . . well, anything.

After the drinks arrived, final prep was happening: the windows were being cleaned, the floors were being scrubbed, clothing rails were going up – including one in the wallpaper museum turret especially for Charlotte's wedding dress – napkins were sewn and ready to be laid out. The château was looking truly stunning. It was finally coming together – just two days before all the guests were due to arrive for our first ever, not-our-own-wedding, big event.

*

At the same time, we had a big day of our own to prepare for. It was also just two days before Arthur started school. In all the madness that was surrounding us, it was a welcome break going to the hairdresser. Arthur and I chatted all the way there about how exciting school was going to be. I'm not sure if I was convincing him or myself, as inside my guts were twisted with worry about his lack of French.

Patrice the hairdresser is very nice. It was certainly the most stylish hairdressers in the area. Patrice speaks some English and did not laugh at my terrible French – in fact, he tried to help! He was gentle and Arthur loved going to see him, although that may have been to do with the sweetie he was given at the end for being good. Patrice was also doing Charlotte's hair for the wedding. I would have carried on using Patrice for future weddings, as he is really great, but sadly he likes to have Augusts off.

On Thursday, 1 September 2016 Arthur started school. I had mixed emotions. Textbook, for sure. He was three years and seven months old and he was a bright cookie. I felt he was ready to mix and make friends and definitely ready to learn. But I was also terrified that he did not speak much French and that I would not be there if he needed to go to the toilet. We spent days saying the words 'Pee Pee' and 'Ka Ka' (which we later discovered were actually *pipi* and *caca*) and in the car that's all we talked about. Arthur had not been left with anyone except our parents before and that was the backbone of my anxiety.

The school was a very caring school but also one that loved rules – a great balance! We had met his teacher that summer when we registered Arthur and she was lovely. Arthur had the chance to play in the classroom with us there. That could have been for him but also us . . . He had his own coat hook, with his name above it, and as soon as Arthur got into the classroom on his first day he ran off to play very happily. We waved goodbye and Dick took my hand and led me out. There was no time to waste, we had wedding guests to welcome.

My first job that day was to collect the flowers I had ordered. On arrival, I had my clipboard in hand and the flowers were there ready and waiting in the back. I was delighted, but on further inspection, I spotted that some of the flowers had completely died. Half the eucalyptus was mouldy and dead and the gypsophila (baby breath) was brown. So I took everything I considered usable and went to pay. The owner was clearly agitated. I explained that I could not use the dead flowers but she argued back, saying that I had ordered them. I then had to explain that I ordered live flowers, not dead ones. I managed to pick up some more flowers from a different local florist and decided that this may not be a great supplier match after all! But I had what I needed for Charlotte's wedding and thank goodness for my over-ordering. In this instance it completely paid off.

I arrived back and walked round, checking everything. I concluded that the house was spotless, the sun was shining and, to be honest, at this point, what was not done was not going to get done! Thirty minutes later, Charlotte and Richard, Richard's brother James and his wife Jane, and their children Ruth and Samuel arrived. It was happening and déjà vu flooded over me from our wedding. The moment when everyone arrives and you realise what is done is done and what's not is not actually allows you to change gear and go into a different mode.

Big hugs and introductions to the extended family were made. And then everyone stepped back and looked up at the château. You can't help but share those moments with your guests. Coming down the driveway, the first thing people see is always the symmetry of the château and it is lovely, but when you are in front of the château and looking up (and my neck always creaks at this point, as you must look all the way up to take it in) it dominates and really makes a statement, just as it was supposed to. We love first-time visitors having a few moments to absorb the château and, as the morning sun moved around to light up the front of the building, it was looking particularly fabulous, offset by blue skies and a scattering of fluffy clouds. The sky looked like a painting artist's favour.

Moments of 'wow' over, and Charlotte changed into work mode. She instructed the boys to get the bags to the rooms and we carried up the wedding dress and hung it up in the wallpaper museum. Wow! When it was unwrapped and revealed, it looked out of this world . . . I always, till this day, I feel it's such an honour to see the dress before the groom. We then ran through all the little bits and pieces that I was to be handed the baton on: menus, service cards, bunting, light-up letters, guest books, cameras, gifts . . . lots of them! Charlotte works in events – that is how we met, after all – and I knew at this moment, it was just her nature to take control. But I also knew she trusted me, so I sent her away to see Patrice for her hair trial whilst we all carried on with the preparation.

Richard, Ruth and Samuel were in the kitchen with me. Their job was to help with the sloe sorbet . . . I did have an electric gelatiere but that would have been too easy to use. So, instead, I'd picked up a wooden hand-cranked ice cream maker that was simple and easy but needed some elbow grease! The principles are easy to understand:

- Ice in the freezer is typically -19°C
- By adding the ice to very salty water, the temperature of the

water drops well below zero but because it's salty it does not freeze

- Putting the 'to be frozen' mix in a metal container in contact with the cold, salty water drops the mixture down below zero so it starts to freeze
- Stirring the actively freezing sorbet mix makes it smooth and scoopable rather than producing a block of flavoured ice

There was more than just work in the kitchen to do and James, who asked for a job, got put in charge of painting the cinema screen, which after a year outside since our wedding looked a bit tired. It might sound silly but we always think playing a part and having a job to do in preparing for the wedding of someone you are close to is rather special.

I'm not sure where the day had gone but, before we knew it, it was time to collect Arthur. My stomach was in pieces with all the emotion. Nerves, flowers, guests arriving, excitement . . . I really hadn't had much time to worry about him and for that I felt guilty. When he ran into our arms, my heart melted. He was smiling, happy and had survived. Or was it more that we had survived?

Dorothy and Arthur had not seen Charlotte and Richard yet, and they had brought them both gifts. That's Charlotte all over, wanting to create happiness. The children were so excited. We still have the 2.5 metre stuffed material toy snake; it lives in the playroom and every time the children play with it, I remember their faces when Charlotte gave it to them. She thanked them 'for allowing her to use their home'. They did not understand at that age and they were too busy playing . . . but I got it. And it meant the world.

Three-day weddings are no mean feat. This one was going to be amazing and tough in equal measures, as everything was new: we

had new processes, new staff, new toilets and, although everything had been planned to a T, we had no idea if the new plans
would survive ... I'm just pleased we were so busy that we had no
time to worry!

Friday, 2 September was going to be a busy day. At 4pm, coaches
full of eighty guests would arrive for a hog roast. In the meantime, we had to take Arthur to school for his second day, prepare
and set the orangery ready for the wedding breakfast, steam all
the dresses, iron all the shirts and do a wedding rehearsal whilst
ensuring everyone was relaxed and happy.

The kitchen was busy. Everything that could be prepared was
being prepared. When the pig arrived, it had a spit unceremoniously inserted and was skewered into place. The fire was set and
there was a pile of logs nearby too, as I was not sure of the burn
rate. There were outlets that I could open and close to adjust the
amount of air getting in but I took no chances and lit the fire in
good time. The lid was open and it burned beautifully. After half
an hour I closed the lid and kept it warm until the pig went in.
We had done a rehearsal and it was all about approaching it so the
point of the spit lined up with the hole. I was glad of the practice
because when we put the pig in the heat was fierce and thankfully
it was in place in moments. Then all we had to do was rotate it
every fifteen minutes and keep the fire topped up, getting it in
the roaster and preparing everything for the following day in the
kitchen.

Richard had to have his Scotch eggs, so we went into production.
This is a great recipe that you can play with to create a really unique
snack. Perfect to take on picnics, serve at a lunchtime buffet or just
to eat secretly from the fridge when no one is looking ... they are
our go-to picnic snacks whenever possible.

SCOTCH EGGS

Ingredients (for six)

500g sausage meat, or a chorizo/sausage meat mix, or a
mixture of 400g sausage meat and 100g *boudin noir* (or soft
black pudding)
Zest of 1 lemon and a pinch of thyme (optional)
8 free-range eggs, of which 2 are beaten and 6 are
medium-boiled and peeled
Flour
250g breadcrumbs
Vegetable oil, for frying
Salt and black pepper

Method

*Mix the sausage meat in a bowl with the lemon zest and
thyme, if using. Divide into six balls. Flatten each with a
rolling pin into oval shapes 12cm long by 8cm at their widest
points. Coat the peeled boiled eggs in seasoned flour and place
them on top of the oval sausage meat discs. Wrap the eggs in
sausage meat until completely covered and then form into
smooth shapes. Dip each ball in flour, then the beaten egg and
then roll in a bowl of the breadcrumbs and a pinch of sea salt.
Deep fry in vegetable oil for eight to ten minutes or until golden
brown.*

*We must have got it right that day because Richard was beaming
from ear to ear!*

Setting up the orangery was simple and relaxing. First, I laid the centrepiece for each table. Old magazines, domino sets, over-sized chess pieces, quirky Avon perfume bottles and anything else that fitted and looked right. Anything went! After lots of moving things around, lots of times, I stood back. Tomorrow it would be finished with the cold and chambréd wines and fresh-from-the-bakers baguettes.

I had received the table plan a couple of weeks beforehand, so I knew where everyone was sitting, and I had a very detailed spread-sheet of what vessels were to be used for what course – much of this stuff would be kept out the back for Dick for service. Like at our wedding, the bride and groom would sit at the centre table with two tables either side and would be at the end of the table looking out over everyone. It was perfect, felt natural and worked well for us. We never had a top table as such but, by default, it was, because the bride and groom sat there. I laid out a vintage china plate as a charger plate, a carefully placed vintage napkin over the top, embroidered with the name of the guest, then a vintage tea cup and saucer and finally all the cutlery needed for the feast, starting with the small spoon for the first course on the outside. Their wedding menu was at the top of the placement, finished with a cutting of lavender from the garden. It looked eclectic and charming. Once I had decided the layout of the place setting, it was a matter of repeating it, eighty times.

In the collection of items Charlotte handed over to me were a lot of very large balloons – soft pinks, blushes, champagne colours. But when I say big, I mean over a metre in diameter . . . and lots of them. Some were to be used for the house decoration and some would hang in the orangery. I had done a quick calculation and worked out that the helium by itself would cost £45 a balloon, so instead we got an electric air blower and hung them from the ceiling! The next day, the bridal party would also be holding these balloons like large lollies but sadly helium was the only way to create that magic! It was all go and coming together very nicely.

But time was ticking on and with only an hour and a half until guests arrived, there was a very important job still to do: the rehearsal.

The pig was cooking well and the sides were all ready so I gave Adam and Jai, my sous chefs, a list of jobs and left the kitchen to conduct the rehearsal. Right from our very first wedding I knew my job was to ensure there was no stress around the bride and groom. When I asked what time the service would start the next day I was told 'midday', to which I answered, 'No, it won't, it will start when Charlotte is ready.' Grooms are safe in the knowledge that their brides cannot escape the island without being seen! And so only when everyone is ready do we take our seats, get into position and await the bride's arrival.

The rehearsal is important to ensure everyone knows where to be when, but it is most important for everyone to realise nothing can go wrong. If there is a problem we'll fix it, and the bride and groom have to be reminded that they're not playing to a tricky audience – everyone there loves them and has travelled all the way to France to share this time with them. I was not worried about officiating and I think my calmness was obvious and hopefully infectious. I was not to know what sort of fast balls can be delivered, but since then we have calmly dealt with a groom spilling red sparkling wine over a light blue jacket – no one ever knew until the speeches – there have been minor dress-related problems and I even conducted one ceremony holding the couple's toddler!

Key friends and family had arrived, the sun was blazing and everyone had a drink in hand. I watched my husband gather everyone together and take charge. Dick is exactly the man to make you feel secure and that everything is going to be perfect. He talked to everyone, explaining that nothing can go wrong as he would be leading and all the party needed to do was follow and enjoy. As soon as Dick started talking, you could see everyone start to relax.

The first part of the choreography to sort was how to get all the bridesmaids and the groom's party into position. We wanted them to look balanced and so there needed to be parallel bridesmaids and groomsmen. Why? Because it will look the best in a picture! Once we had shuffled everyone around a few times, I stood back to check. Perfect! I put a little solar candle on each place to mark where everyone would be standing.

Then Dick started to run through a few things from the cere-mony. There is something so special about the rehearsals. They are filled with excitement and anticipation but also carry the biggest punch of love and happily ever after. It may have something to do with everyone feeling completely relaxed. But I was glad I had glasses on as I had tears of happiness. I was watching the love on everyone's faces. It was happening and it was perfect.

As soon as everyone felt confident with the ceremony, Charlotte and Richard dashed off to get ready for the evening celebration. We had thirty minutes to ensure everything was good to go . . . just enough time to make the coleslaw!

A young man called Nicolas, who Charlotte's mother had seen busking in their local village, was hired to play the guitar and the accordion and the music brought this wonderful moment together perfectly.

As the coach of guests turned the corner, I had butterflies. Everyone was beaming as they made their way to the island, hugging and saying hello. I was watching Charlotte greeting everyone and that made me smile. The energy at this moment was magical – friends who had not seen each other for years, people meeting new babies and toddlers for the first time, hugs, tears, more hugs, cheers, group photos, selfies and loads of hugs . . .

Pre-wedding get-togethers are a good idea if possible because, firstly, the initial excitement of having everyone together can be enjoyed earlier and, secondly, it takes the panic out of catching up with everyone in one day. Which means on the big day there is a calmness when everyone gets together . . . well, for a while anyway!

My job for the next four hours was to ensure everyone had everything they needed, including a cold local *cidre*, sun cream, games to keep the children entertained and anything else that one could think of! I have found the best way to maître-d' is to be doing something, so I always ensured I had a bottle of cider and a napkin in my hand to top people up. That way, the guests don't feel watched but I also have everything on hand to keep people supplied.

Serving any meal for eighty is all about the preparation. We had the side dishes, the spiced-apple sauce and the vegetarian option all prepared so all that was required was to get the pig out, remove it from the spit, carve and serve it. After five hours, we'd allowed the heat to die down a little but I probed the fattest part of the neck and the leg and found that our pig was cooked to perfection. It was a very dark brown due to the smoke and we'd basted the inside with cider so it was moist and lovely.

I took charge of the carving and was very pleased to see the pinky-coloured ring around the flesh that meant it was smoked exactly as I wanted it. Carving was methodical and all we added to the platters taken away for service was a healthy sprinkling of salt. Obviously we had to try it and I have to say the roaster got ten out of ten – it was yummy. There were a number of people over by the carving table chatting away and I encouraged them to taste the meat – this was a relaxed get-together and those letting others go and be served before them deserved the fun of picking some of the choice morsels, which were as diverse as the chaps and the fillet. Service was smooth, everyone was well fed and those with an appetite were encouraged to come back several times for more. The noise of lots of concurrent conversations was an indication that the aim of people meeting, mixing, catching up and getting to know each other was achieved.

As the evening came to a close, Dick and I took charge of reminding everyone that tomorrow was the big day! No one wanted it to end but we wanted everyone to be on their best form for the following day and we also had to clear down the château so it was sparkling again.

Richard and his groom's party stayed at a local hotel in Laval, twenty minutes from the château, and Charlotte and her brides-maids stayed at the house. They did not need much looking after and they could see us all clearing and preparing for the following day, so they retired quite quickly to the honeymoon suite. As the clocks hit midnight, I kissed my hubby 'happy birthday'. In the excitement of having our first wedding booked in, I may have forgotten that it was also his birthday until then, but I planned to make it up to him and I'm very pleased to say I never did that again! It was 2am when Dick and I finally hit the sack . . .

The big day had arrived and Dick was in the kitchen at 5am. I followed at 6am after getting the kids ready so that they could be taken over to my mum and dad's. I wanted to ensure that when Charlotte surfaced, I was up to welcome her. But first I drove to the bakers and collected the baguettes and breakfast patisseries.

Charlotte came wandering down, happy and calm. I was delighted that she had slept well. I took a cheeky minute to give Charlotte a vintage kimono that I had worn on the morning of our wedding. It was just her colours and she loved it. It was a special moment but I did not want to take any of her day. There was a lot to do and get on with.

Patrice arrived at the same time as the photographers. It was happening! The bubbles started early, the windows in the *chambre de honor* were open and I could hear music playing . . .

Weddings are magical and what makes them so special, aside from the people, are the steps before, during and after. Every moment is different and must be savoured and it's easy to write this, but you must be in that moment and not thinking of what's next. If you're in events, like Charlotte and myself, it's really hard not to always be two steps ahead, so I was grinning like a Cheshire cat seeing Charlotte enjoy every moment and watching the bridal party having a blast.

There was a hive of activity at the château. Chairs were being laid out, the gigantic balloons for the bridesmaids were being carefully blown up with helium in the entrance way, coffees were being made and there were the most incredible smells coming from the kitchen. It felt like something big was about to happen.

The groom's party arrived around 10.30 for photos in the salon. Dick ran upstairs and changed from his chef's blacks to a tweed suit with a yellow waistcoat. I felt incredibly proud of him. He helped all the guys put on their buttonholes and was pouring the odd morning tipple for them! It was a very special moment . . . but you could cut the nervous energy with a knife.

I was happy that the kitchen was on track and ready for the canapé service. No canapés were made and left out. We were to make them at the very last minute to ensure they were as fresh as possible. I had left myself plenty of time to go to our suite and get changed and to spend some time with Richard and the groom's party.

There is a sense of anticipation in the last period of time leading up to the ceremony and the vows. It is my job to ensure anyone who looks nervous or worried has their concerns addressed so they disappear. The placing of buttonholes is a great opportunity for the photographer but also an icebreaker for the chaps. I led the way, discussing where on the lapel, what angle, who got which button-hole. However, I seldom actually attach the buttonhole. That is the responsibility of the best man and you can see their pride as a job is well done.

By the time the coach arrived we were all ready and chilled.

I was like a yoyo in and out of the honeymoon suite. There was a hive of activity around the place and my priority was to ensure the bridal party was okay. Every mirror was occupied, every glass bubbled with champagne and everyone was sharing stories and giggling ... clothing needed ironing, nail varnish remover was called for, hair-smoothing brushes were requested. It was honestly just as I had imagined.

Then it was 11.20, ten minutes before the coach was due to arrive, so I took those ten minutes to powder my nose and just be still. In the past, I've learnt that busy mornings require you to find a moment to ground yourself as a calm and controlled host. You need to catch your breath!

When the coach arrived, it was a playground of style, colour and incredible hats. The cheesiest line, 'If you build it, they will come,' came to mind! They had arrived and everyone knew the drill – they knew where the toilets were, who to ask for some water. And our team knew many by name! This thirty minutes is always calm and gentle but with an incredible build-up underpinning everything.

I never let anyone sit down until I get the nod from Angela that the bride is actually ready as timings are there for a guide only. But it was not too long after midday that I got that nod.

Charlotte was ready. She was glowing. She looked the perfect Charlotte. But there is a different glow on your wedding day that you cannot create with make-up or curls in your hair. It's not even like the glow of being pregnant. It's the glow of feeling loved, by your husband to be and by every person present to celebrate your moment. Yes, Charlotte was glowing. I escorted Adrian, the father of the bride, to the honeymoon suite. It was their moment; Adrian was minutes away from 'giving away' his daughter. He welled up as soon as he set eyes on Charlotte and she told him off for making her make-up run. I left them to share the moment and to ensure the photographers were in position and I gave Dick the nod.

Silence covered the château like a blanket; in fact, it felt like people had stopped breathing. I stood by the double doors and watched Adrian and Charlotte arm in arm carefully take each step together down the double staircase. This moment, although minutes, rolled out in slow motion, every step was considered. I stood by the doors, ready to fling them open. There was a look and a smile with the eyes my way, a look at each other and then . . .

The cheer of celebration . . . Oh my, it was overwhelming! I used that moment to close the door softly behind them and, when everyone had settled, Dick began.

The ceremony was a celebration of Charlotte and Richard's love and the vows were the commitment they made to each other. It was a success. Everyone laughed at the right places, cried at the right places, and when they kissed at the end the cheers were heartfelt and wonderful . . . Bridesmaids and groomsmen left the stairs and, after a couple of moments, Richard led his beautiful wife down to their family and friends. I was beaming. I'd loved being there for them and, as they descended the stairs, I stepped back through the doors, ran upstairs, put on my chef's blacks and ran down to oversee the canapé service.

Dick completely plays down how amazing he is at the ceremony. His strong but calm voice hugs the crowds and his timing for jokes, loving moments and reading the couple is faultless. This was the first time I had watched him do this and I could not have been prouder.

'I now pronounce you man and wife.' Yes, that moment . . . Family together, sharing confetti, hugs, tears and happiness – it does not get any better, really. From this moment on, the atmosphere shifted into party mode. All that was left to do was to eat, drink and be merry!

We'd discussed the wedding breakfast and the fact that the afternoon was to be relaxed. Courses would appear as and when people were ready. Angela was to be the link between the front and back of house. And we were to remain flexible. The back of the orangery was our service kitchen but it was very rudimentary: there was a 'pass', a gas four-burner cooker and tables for the final food preparation. I'd tried to think of everything but the 200-metre trip back to the main kitchen was a well-trodden path by the end of the day. Food was transported in thermal boxes on a small trolley.

Charlotte & Richard's Wedding Breakfast Menu

—

Amuse-bouche
Succulent lamb bite with rose garden jelly

—

Soup
Onion and garlic soup with an egg yolk topped with a crunchy garlic crumble

—

Starter
Quinoa and roasted seeds served with beetroot and honey-mustard-dressed salad

—

Palate cleanser
Sloe gin sorbet

—

Meat
*Carpaccio of beef on a celeriac and horseradish purée served
with summer vegetables and a light broth*

—

Salad
Fresh green salad with toasted sesame seeds

—

Sweet
Caramel mess served with a poached, spiced apple and syrup

. . . .

We started to call the courses 'waves' because the meal effort-
lessly drifted in and out. Some items stay, whilst others go. We
had decided to weave the speeches in after the soup course so that
there was not a big block. It worked well and, on this occasion,
it was very emotional. Dick had three false starts on the sorbet
because of Charlotte popping back to redo her make-up! But that
is the beauty of what we had set up. We could be flexible and reac-
tive! Towards the end of the wedding breakfast, it was a delight
to see everyone had completely let their hair down. Maybe some a
little too much!

   Coffee, tea, whiskey and digestifs were served back at the
château. There was also the small detail of the orangery being
cleared down for the evening party. Charlotte and Richard were
party animals, as were many of their friends, so even though I had
given my opinion that midnight for the bus was honestly enough
after twelve hours of celebrations, they wanted a 2am finish. To
compromise, we agreed on two coaches: the first at midnight, the

second at 2am. Guests cannot call a taxi if they decide enough is enough. It seems completely crazy and I still, after all these years, do not understand the lack of taxis but they just do not exist.

When the bus arrived at midnight, everyone got on, though some looked like they may not last the bus ride! But it was all in good spirit. When Rich realised everyone had got on the bus and was ready for home, he rallied the hard-core party goers back off and they headed back to the orangery until the 2am coach.

At 2am we waved the second coach off and slowly started to walk back to the château. What a day! What a totally magical, emotional celebration of love! It was certainly going to be remembered.

By now it was 3.30am and my feet were sore – in fact, I cannot remember the last time they were so sore. We were pooped. But still Dick and I took a moment to sit and reflect on everything – what worked, what process needed improving. But most importantly, how happy Charlotte and Richard were.

Goodbyes are never easy but the guests all came by the château the next day, grabbed a coffee and shared a couple of moments with Richard and Charlotte throughout the morning. Charlotte was on fantastic form; Richard possibly a little more delicate!

Our coffee machine was maxed out! I'm not going to lie, we were completely short-staffed and had Arthur and Dorothy back in our care as well, but at moments like that you just think on your feet! Dorothy decided that she liked pressing the coffee-making button. This not only got a job done but also kept two-year-old Dorothy amused. Arthur was busy entertaining the kids in their playroom.

Then it came to our goodbyes. It's strange because with events with as much intricacy and detail as a wedding, it feels like you give a part of yourself. That is why I have always said that I must really like the people getting married. It's more than a job. We pour everything from our heads but also our hearts into it. From the moment Charlotte and Richard got in touch to the minute we said goodbye, we had spoken hundreds of times. When that is over, it's a strange feeling. Not an unhappy feeling but still the end of something incredible. As we waved goodbye, I was crying and giggling. Charlotte whispered cheekily in my ear, 'Please don't have any more weddings here. I won't be able to deal with it.' A job well done, I think.

*

Life settled down a bit after the wedding and we managed to get more time together again as a family, more time in the garden and enjoying our surroundings. Our cockerel had grown huge and was hurting the hens. Angela's mum said to me, 'Dick, I think the chickens are poorly, they are losing hair on their backs.' I took the coward's way out and didn't tell Jenny about 'treading'. Instead I said, 'Don't worry, I'll sort it.' So that evening, we ate him.

It sounds brutal but our cockerels are there to herd the girls and look after them; if they are rough or even think of attacking us (it happens and they scare adults, never mind small children, or toddlers, like Arthur and Dorothy!), they are dispatched without a second thought. When I saw that the girls were not only bald on their back but one had scratches I cornered, caught and killed the cockerel. That all sounds very cold but I am fortunate enough to know what to do and how to do it. The bird was plucked and drawn very quickly so he was barely cold when I presented Jenny with our supper. The birds you buy at a supermarket are very young and that is why they tend to be very tender – we are talking about a few months old. A bird that is months older will be tough, so we made the decision we could make Jenny's famous chicken soup.

We had to go to my kitchen to get her a pan big enough. Jenny was obviously a bit surprised to see the cockerel but it did look like any chicken you would get from the supermarket or a butchers, only a lot bigger. I reckon dressed, he was nearly 10lb!

We all love Grandma's soup that is served over two courses. First, you make the soup with onions, celery, carrots, a little bit of the chicken, noodles and '*kneydl*'. And then we have the chicken as a chicken dinner – it's served in a roasting pan full of potatoes, rice, sage and onion stuffing and the majority of the chicken that wasn't cooked in the soup. It is split and placed on top before going into the oven where it's roasted until the skin is crispy and all the flavours are melded together.

It was delicious and lasted two days, but that left us cockerel-less. A task we set Papi to resolve.

Life got back into a rhythm quickly after Richard and Charlotte's wedding. Arthur was back at school and, after we caught up on some family time and some much-needed sleep, we could not wait to get stuck into what was next. When my dad, Papi, found out that a trip to St Hilaire du Harcouët market was needed to buy a new cockerel, he jumped at the chance to see a new part of France.

St Hilaire du Harcouët is a lively market that meanders through the streets of the busy town. There is a vast selection of fresh regional produce, plus a colourful variety of other stalls, including live produce! A year earlier, Dick and I had purchased our chicken from there and we had a blast. It was a lovely reminder of how beautiful France is. When my dad arrived back, we laughed so hard: the cock was tiny! We were sure the market stall owner had taken him for a ride. But as the weeks passed, we had to eat our words as our cockerel grew and grew, and even began to cock-a-doodle-doo. It had been a summer of firsts and although busy, even chaotic at times, it had been perfect.

Magnet fishing.

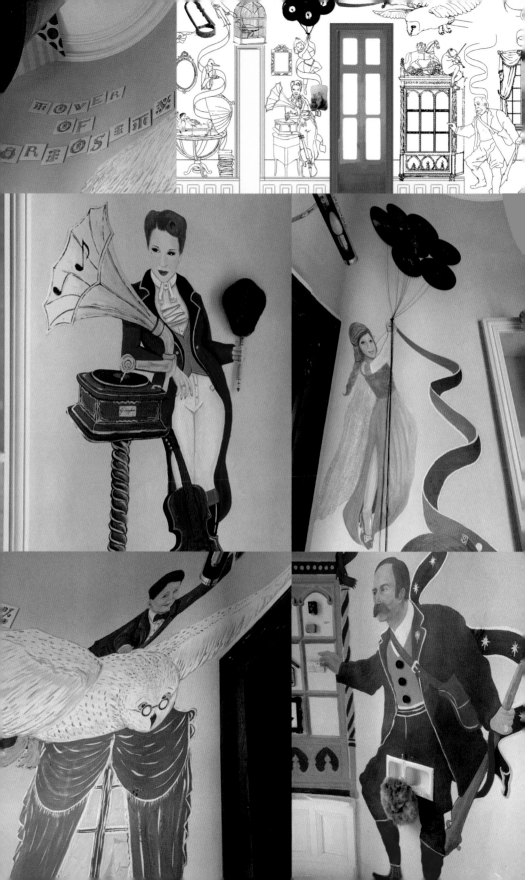

THE
BOTANICAL
SUITE

Christmas 2016.

CHAPTER 4

The Lift

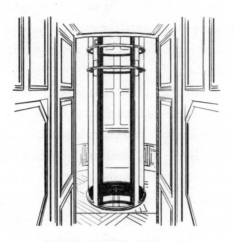

The change from summer to autumn is gentle. It does not happen overnight, unlike spring, which springs you into it. Autumn holds your hand and steps you out. First, it's a cardi, then the flowers and grass turn golden and copper, then it's a jacket . . . and woven throughout are days that still feel like summer. Just like after our wedding, I was still on a high from Charlotte and Richard's celebrations. We were looking forward to keeping our dream progressing. We were taking wedding enquiries, arranging viewings, getting ready for viewings and preparing for our remaining food lovers. Yes, it was busy, but we managed to keep the balance with the children and ensure that we had lots of family time. In fact, in many ways, the children came first and when we had a commitment, they spent the time with Grandma and Grandad, who they loved being with and vice versa. It was win-win for everyone.

The château was becoming more and more comfortable week by week and it was working as our home and our place of work. It seems a bit silly to say it but the château has a nice intimate feeling. It has never felt big and we definitely don't rattle around in it. However, no matter how you look at it, there are a lot of stairs. To get up to our guest bedroom suites is four flights of stairs and it can be testing even for the young. We were very aware that Angela's nan would struggle getting up to the ground floor and even though my mum was game, it wasn't fair to expect her to climb seventy-plus stairs to get to bed . . .

We'd been thinking about how to link the dining room to the family kitchen in the *sous sol* with a spiral staircase in the tower and it was during one of our conversations about this that the idea of a lift was mooted. It didn't take long for the idea to get traction and soon the idea of effectively turning the château into a bungalow using technology seemed a no-brainer. We didn't underestimate the cost or the scale of the job but we had a couple of wedding deposits coming in and a lift would give us more flexibility – if we could get it to work.

Even before we started talking about what was possible, I knew Angela had a vision of a vintage cage lift with concertina doors and a floor indicator with a big arrow pointing to a curved array of numbers, all in brass and burnished metal. As usual, I had to be the party pooper and explain that such systems usually have a pit below the lowest floor, but as we are surrounded by the moat, the water table would preclude such a solution! So the research started. I could never imagine a box-shaped structure in the centre of the tower and I was aware of cylindrical, pneumatic lifts so I searched out some pictures and showed them to Angela. It didn't take long before we had found something that looked like it was capable of doing what we required and looked good – all we had to do was source it and then start work . . .

The lift business must have been doing well, or there must have been a run on pneumatic lifts, as the only person we could find in the UK didn't seem that interested in selling us one and said it'd take several months to get here. Not to be put off, we tracked down the manufacturers in Florida and spoke to them. They said the other option we had was to speak to their Spanish agent and they'd let us know the quickest they could get the kit to us. We arranged a visit and within days the decision was made and the survey took place.

We were told what we had to prepare before the installation team arrived and the need for accuracy was impressed upon us. The lift was to sit on the floor in the basement, which had to be perfectly flat and horizontal; the hole had to align perfectly vertically above. I took the statement seriously and my builder mate Steve and I proceeded to prepare for installation. The first challenge was finding the centre of the floor space in the tower, which is not an exact circle and there is a slight variation between the floors! We started in the tower off the *salle à manger* on the ground floor. The first thing we had to do was take out the old bath and toilet to expose the floor. We found the centre and drilled a hole through the floorboards, the clay insulation and the plaster ceiling of the floor below. We then shone a laser vertically down through the hole and marked it on the floor in the basement. We then mounted the laser in this exact spot and shone it upwards onto the ceiling of the tower. We drilled through that ceiling, then shone the laser through the two holes onto the next ceiling above. This gave us perfectly aligned holes and, what was better, they were all approximately in the centre of the tower rooms!

I had decided that the best way to create the lift shaft was to start at the bottom. We'd make each hole and drop the mess down, then we'd start again at the bottom, putting in electrics and first fixes. When we reached the top we'd then work our way down, making good, finishing the plastering and painting, so when we got to the bottom we'd be in good order.

Our starting point was off the family kitchen and to clear that room we had to remove the old clay sewerage pipes from the bathroom above. I set Angela loose with a sledgehammer and she started to 'dismantle' the waste pipes. I went upstairs and as she broke one of the pipes, I dribbled water through the floorboards onto her. She squealed and I told her the sewerage pipes weren't empty . . . I thought it was funny but Angela was sure she'd been showered in something very unpleasant.

After a couple of weeks, it was clear our plan had worked. However, I was surprised just how scary it was looking down through the five holes from the loft . . . the hole sort of sucked you to the edge. It's a long way down!

The weeks were flying by; the lift shaft was being carefully prepared bit by bit and every week we had more wedding viewings, wedding tastings and food lovers' weekends. Every day we seemed to be deep cleaning the house to get rid of dust from the work ready for our visitors. We found ourselves very busy and did not have much time to stop. However, a visit from our friends Johnny and Nadine who live in Hollywood helped. Dick had worked with Johnny the previous year and, after a couple of visits, including for our wedding, they were hooked on France and eager to buy their own château. It was such a pleasure to have them here, not least because Arthur and Dorothy love them just as much as we do!

We knew the moat had been around for hundreds of years and had been part of an early medieval fortification. We had no details about what had happened here but we speculated that maybe the French had repelled the English, or vice versa. We'd been told by Christine, one of our neighbours, that some 500 years ago the local 'Captain'(who we assume must have been responsible for this district) used to live at their château a couple of miles away, and if the English came he'd grab his valuables, head to the fortress on our site, haul up the drawbridge and wait until they headed off, then go home, tidy up and carry on.

When our American friends Johnny and Nadine came across to see us and heard this story, there was no way they were going to be happy with anything short of a treasure hunt to see what valuables we could find. As I wasn't about to let them loose digging the place up, magnet fishing seemed the best idea. It was ridiculous and lots of fun. We started on the bank throwing in our magnets on the end of a strong rope and trawling them back. We worked our way around the château ... nothing. A phone call later and we'd borrowed a Canadian canoe. So Johnny and I headed out to the middle. The silt was deep, so we couldn't tell if we'd got to the bottom. Even though the magnets were heavy, they only sunk a bit into the silt. We tried pushing in our paddles and poles but it was nearly impossible to feel if we reached the bottom. It was very frustrating and not very satisfying. We found nothing, absolutely nothing, which led us to conclude that there must be something just out of our reach. We ended our day a bit silty and smelly but remained optimistic. We decided that it was an adventure to be continued another day, rather than written off entirely. There could be medieval armour or weaponry down there ... who knows?

That evening, we sat outside the château and talked for hours. By the time we headed for bed the sun had gone down. It was dark and we were carrying a portable spot light with us to ensure we weren't wrong-footed! To our great amusement, we realised the château had become like a puppet show, with our shadows dancing around like full-sized puppets against it. And bedtime got a little bit later. We laughed so hard and everyone

was being very silly . . . my belly hurt from laughing so much. Never underestimate the benefits of a good belly laugh; it's good for the soul!

With the lift in progress, my thoughts had moved on a couple of paces to other jobs. The elephant in the room was the fact that we needed more accommodation but were absolutely broke because of how much the lift had cost. No sympathy required. We knew how ridiculous it was to have purchased a lift when there was so much other essential work to do in the château. But the lift was part of a master plan to turn the château into a 'bungalow' and had been fuelled by the sadness that the Strawbridge ladies were coming for their third visit but were not able to stay with us because the stairs were just too much.

But the fact remained: we needed more rentable accommodation, both for food lovers' weekends and future wedding guests. We only had the honeymoon suite. The next suite that felt achievable was the botanical suite. It already had some basic stud walling, plumbing and electrics in place from when the original camera crew (which was only one person, by the way) stayed with us to film for the first series of *Escape to the Château*. At this point, though, it felt forgotten and unloved. It had been stripped of the original wallpapers and the woodwork and walls had all been covered in white paint. It was dusty. Very dusty. But at the same time, the suite had such beautiful light and so much potential.

This suite sat directly above our Strawbridge suite and had the same blueprint, with the connecting rooms separated by doors. It's a great space for a family to stay. We had named it 'the botanical suite' due to it being a calm and peaceful space. Because of how high up you are, it feels like you are engulfed by nature when you look out; everywhere is green and luscious. In the distance, you can see the beautiful orangery with its art deco windows and gorgeous structure. It's a beautiful and very special view. That, and I like the word 'botanical'.

For the most part, I believed the work it needed was mostly cosmetic. But when you break it down, our suites are all rather large. The botanical suite consisted of:

- A master bedroom
- A second bedroom
- A bathroom
- The turret
- A walk-in cupboard/storage space
- The vestibule, joining all the rooms together

We think about every space we have in the château carefully and, after much consideration, we decided it made sense to make the botanical suite into a family suite, like ours. But to achieve that it needed a bath.

'It needed a bath.' Those are words that strike fear into any man who knows that the only bath we owned was a solid cast-iron one, currently residing at ground level. I could see that getting that bath up the seventy-three stairs was going to be painful – and it was. The external stone steps are gradual and wide, like the main staircase. We had to take it slowly but there was at least space to get extra hands on it. When we reached the servants' stairs it was a different story: only two of us could get hands-on and the heavy bath had to go around the corner, vertically.

There is an old saying: 'It's better to do something than live with the fear of doing it.' Steve and I went for it and moved it up one stair at a time. We put a cloth down to protect the stairs and Steve went at the top, keeping it vertical and twisting as we went around the curve, and I was at the bottom, lifting it one step at a time. By the time we reached the level of the second floor (four floors up) we were shagged and we slid it into the botanical suite on a blanket. You can only imagine my frame of mind when Angela started wanting to see where to put the bath.

We didn't even consider the bathroom as Angela had other plans for that, so instead it was put into a small 'cupboard' . . . then in several areas of the main room, before Angela was sure it would be at the end of the bed. I must have been tired because I just accepted the decision without pointing out there was no plumbing or waste there, or anywhere in that room, for that matter.

Hot and cold water was not the issue but emptying a bath that was basically in the middle of a room was a bit of a challenge. It couldn't go straight down – that's the ceiling of our suite on the floor below and, though it may have been funny having a waste pipe sticking down into our room, it would have made more work in the long run! The answer was a plinth for the bath that was high enough for the water to flow along a pipe under the bed and through the two-feet-thick wall to join the other waste pipes in the bathroom next door. All in all, we needed at least four feet for the run to work . . .

The botanical suite was in the old servants' quarters. The rooms are spacious but the ceilings are lower than the 'high-status' rooms. The floors are not oak but still good-quality wood and the doors are panelled and similar to those in the rest of the house. All in all, I would be very happy if I stayed there and I always use my fussiness as a guide to ensure everything is up to the right standard.

Dick humoured me with the bath. I know he knew subconsciously that the bath would end up in the bedroom. I had looked at so many interiors magazines over the years and was romantically attached to the idea of having a bath at the foot of the bed.

Alongside the bath that I had purchased last year, I had several other things that would go in the suite. Taking centre stage would also be the nineteenth-century French empire bed we had purchased from Emmaus on my birthday. The bed was made from mahogany with original brass acorns and ornate details. It was stunning and felt wonderfully regal! On either side of that were two side cabinets with marble tops, purchased for €15 each at different times. They were similar in style, but different. And then we had a few lovely lights all purchased at Emmaus, each for around €5.

It felt achievable and exciting.

Alongside the work on the botanical suite, there was huge preparation happening to get the château ready for installing the lift. One of our final and unexpected jobs was to enlarge the door in the kitchen into the bottom of the tower, which is where we would receive the lift. We discovered the doorway was narrower than the one off the dining room, which annoyingly had been the one we'd measured when having discussions with Jesús, who'd come to do the survey. All the holes were perfectly aligned to within a couple of millimetres, so we were confident all would be okay. But then we remembered something else Jesús had mentioned . . .

Aligning the holes to receive the lift was undoubtedly an engineer's accomplishment; Dick's accomplishment. Although it was messy, he had worked methodically and now I could concentrate on design. And so, the tower of curiosities was born.

Surrounding the actual lift in each of the turrets was just under a metre from lift to wall, which meant we could have items in the surrounding space and on the walls. Because there had been so much happening, we had not put any thought into Jesús mentioning on his last visit that the lift is *very sensitive to dust*. It was a comment that I remember I liked hearing. In fact, it was music to my ears; I love a clean house and detest dust, so this would give us a goal to work towards. However, what didn't sink in at the time was that it also meant we couldn't go back into those turrets and re-do walls, floors or generally create any kind of builders' mess once the lift was installed. Suddenly it became a priority to make as many decisions as quickly as possible to agree on the finish of each turret in the tower, so we could get anything we needed in order. My focuses were: lights, walls, floors and decorations – for all four floors!

For the ground-floor kitchen turret, I was after a rustic look. The floor had been in a terrible state and was levelled with concrete and tiles. I chose a rustic grey floor tile. I didn't want to paint the walls but of all the turret rooms, being so close to the ground, this one was in the worst condition of them all, so, after a chat with Dick and Steve, we decided on a plaster and cement mix. It was perfect and looked lovely, curved smoothly around the turret, but with the rustic texture I was after as well . . . nearly porous looking! We returned the original cowtail pump that was in there and then cleaned up all the rustic cider pots and ceramic jugs we had found on this floor. To keep within the natural colour scheme, I put dried flowers in all the vessels. It was a lovely way to start your journey through the château!

The 'high-status' turret needed a pièce de résistance and this was inspired by a couple of unusual bits we had previously found in the château. I decided that this floor would be a showcase of some of the unusual historical items we had found that were once owned by the Baglion family. I'd become rather attached to the name 'the tower of curiosities' and, before long, that's what we started calling this turret, which gave me the perfect excuse to hunt for more treasures and antique delights to display.

There is one main place to rummage for château paraphernalia: the attic. It seems crazy to friends and family that even after six years of living here we have not looked through everything in the attic with a fine-toothed comb yet. But there are still lots of dusty corners and old baskets that have not even been touched. And I haven't even set foot in the top, top attic yet! I think deep down I'm trying to prolong the mystery of the unknown. I guess it's the same reason I have always loved going to bootfairs and charity shops, because you never know what you are going to find. Our attic gives me the same excitement every time I go looking for treasure!

So up we went to the attic looking for special new artefacts for the tower of curiosities. First, we found some lovely old postcards and little matchboxes, then a collection of phono records, which later inspired the design for another of the turrets. We also found a rather scary spiky necklace that Jacques told us used to be put on a calf to stop it going to its mum to feed. With the spiked collar on, the cow would not allow the calf near it. All rather curious and sometimes quite strange stuff.

I also had my heart set on decorating these turrets in a way that tied the present to the past and this came in the form of a playful Strawbridge portrait in the 'high-status' tower. We decided to create an image of the four of us using items of the past. The seed had been planted and I was full of visions and ideas. To help me execute them, long-term friends Sam and Sophie, and their very new daughter Lyra, were booked in for a working holiday!

While rummaging in the attic we found some old records that used to belong to the Baglionis. Angela decided the damaged ones could adorn the tower of curiosities but we were determined to hear some of them play again, so we headed off to PHONO Museum in Paris to find out more. It's only a short train trip to Paris and Angela and I treated our outing as a date. The records were not common and lots of them were in remarkably good condition. We were able to listen to one in the museum and, with a bit of assistance, we sourced our own gramophone capable of playing our format of record – the Pathé Disque was like the Betamax equivalent of video tapes: it worked but never really caught on.

It was hard for the other two tower rooms to compete with the tower of curiosities but that was okay. Our turret room, which, on the lift is the third floor, was going to be useful. We needed space for shoe and hat storage, so our family tower got a lick of paint and lots of shoe racks. I knew that, one day, this tower would need to be revisited but for now it did exactly what we needed. Saying that, I could not help hanging a few rather magical pyjamas that I found in the attic on the walls. When they were up, it really reminded me of *Alice in Wonderland* and the rabbit hole!

The final floor, which would welcome guests to the botanical suite, quite simply needed to celebrate the suite's name. I did not want to clutter up this turret and so, after chatting to Sophie and Sam about the original inspiration from the view out of the window with the orangery in the distance, we decided it would be lovely to tie this in with the design. The art deco orangery windows therefore became the focus of the design on these curved walls . . . It was all coming together beautifully!

The final task before the lift arrived was to clean, clean and clean again. With the lift on its way I had a slight niggle about the accuracy of our hole cutting; we thought it was good but we had no idea if the holes were aligned accurately enough for the installation. The lift and the installation team from PVE arrived, Jesús, plus Tomas and James, and we nervously awaited their verdict on our holes . . . Fortunately they were very complimentary and proceeded to prepare for the installation. A chain winch was set up in the attic above the tower and the top section with processors and fan mechanism was hoisted up first. I was surprised how easily it fitted.

When I commented on this to Tomas, he showed me the rings that were floor and ceiling mounted to hold the lift in place and finish it neatly. I was speechless! These rings meant there was a 20mm tolerance on each side. Our use of lasers and careful alignment meant we were within a couple of millimetres – we could have simply guessed or used a weight on a piece of string. I would have been grumpy if I wasn't so relieved!

The installation was faultless and, once it was fully commissioned, it wasn't long before we were ready to test it. Of course it was ladies first! We loaded Angela in at basement level, she pressed the button and miraculously she headed up. It was like magic and a bit of a 'beam me up' moment. To be honest, I had no idea where Angela went – she just went up, which was a result!

Tons and tons of work went into getting the turret 'lift ready'. Dick had not stopped and Steve had been busy filling and plastering walls. Sam and Sophie arrived for their working holiday and sprinkled their artist touch on the turrets – curiosities were given homes; lights had been fitted and were working. Dick had kept the holes covered with wood to ensure no accidents happened but on the eve of lift arrival, everything was uncovered for a final clean.

Arthur and Dorothy and my parents came into the kitchen and looked up. What a sight and what an achievement! It looked incredible, you could see all the way to the top, which finished with magical twinkly lights.

The lift was installed rather quickly the next day. It really was all in the preparation and Dick insisted that I went first! Because of the suction, there is a feeling like you are being blasted into space. It's so clever. We absolutely loved it! We knew that the lift was going to be a game changer. It was a huge feat – one of the biggest jobs we had taken on – and it caused us to pause and reflect on all that we had achieved since our wedding, just a year ago.

We celebrated our first wedding anniversary at the mushroom restaurant we had gone to for my birthday. We had enjoyed it so much and having a night away was really good for us both. It had been a hectic year! Since the day Arthur (and then Dorothy) was born, I have slept with one ear on alert and it's only when you leave them with grandparents do you remember what a real night's sleep is!

We spent the afternoon discussing the whirlwind of our year and, Dick being Dick, he had brought his notebook to take notes . . . but we did not need to look at our notes to remember not to have the mushroom dessert this time!

It may have been a short break but it was exactly what the doctor ordered and we came back full of energy, ideas and plans for the months ahead.

After our experiences at the Michelin-starred fungi restaurant, we decided to check out what mushrooms we had available to us, so we invited a mushroom forager to our grounds to see what we could harvest. I was very excited as I'd done a fair bit of mushroom hunting, starting by going with my mum when I was a youngster. The rules are very simple: if in doubt, don't! I had collected many varieties in the past before moving to France and had even found some field mushrooms in the grass in front of the orangery and puffballs in the back paddock area, but I was very excited about finding some *Boletus edulis*, such as ceps, penny buns or porcini, in our woods, or even chanterelles. Or maybe *trompette de la mort* . . . We owned woods and I couldn't wait to learn what we had.

Our expert was lovely and so enthusiastic. As we walked around, he pointed to every single type of fungi he found. After a long description, I would ask if it tasted good and he would answer 'not edible'. Indeed, this happened so often that Angela and I started giggling. He did explain that it had been a dry autumn but of the dozens of fungi found, not one was edible, never mind being a culinary delight!

After a busy and focused time inside the château, doing lots of renovating and decorating, we found ourselves eager to get back out to nature and to find out more about our grounds. We had seen so many mushrooms but neither of us knew if we could actually pick them. Although it was disappointing that 99 per cent were not edible, it was good to know and we laughed hard because the expert described every mushroom with so much passion. Like it was the best, the rarest and most delicious mushroom, and nearly every time, we said, 'So, can we eat it?' And he replied with a very dry, 'No.'

With a good understanding of our woodlands, our attention turned to the moat and exactly what resources we had there. We'd had lots of enquiries from people who were interested in fishing the moat but thought we should get some facts under our belt before committing to anything.

We knew we had a lot of fish in the moat – I'd seen some decent-sized fish and I'd caught a couple of varieties of carp and some roach – but we didn't know the health of our fish stock, what else was in there or indeed the size of our fish. We found our fish experts at Andrew Ellis fisheries and arranged for Andrew to come and survey the fish in our moat.

A current was passed through the water to stun the fish and they were netted and transferred into some large crates. There were hundreds and we had a good mixture of sizes. There was an abundance of small fry, of the size that were enjoyed by our king-fishers and herons, and then decreasing numbers until you got to the larger fish, the biggest at 9–10lb. The large fish were slim and athletic and all were healthy. For lots of carp fishermen, the aim is to get big fish and our moat, though there were lots of fish, was not providing enough food for the biggest to get really big.

We discussed the findings and decided we were happy with the balance of our ecosystem and we did not want to feed the fish to achieve the big weight that was possible from the amount of water we have. Something was working well as we did not suffer from lots of mosquitoes or midges. We concluded that it was all about the balance and, while undoubtedly there were eggs laid and lots of insect nymphs in the water, harmony had been achieved by the number of fish, the dragonflies and other hawkers around the moat. The swallows and other insect-eating birds and even the numerous bats contributed too. We did not have the fish to attract fishing trophy hunters but everything seemed healthy and that was most important to us.

Apart from making cups of tea and popping over every now and again to see developments, I left them to it, as surveying the moat was Dick's domain. Hearing the results was fascinating and Andrew's evident passion was lovely. But it did confirm that the moat was not – at least, not without lots of investment – going to be part of our business plan for the time being.

However, it was a fun day that ended with Arthur coming home from school and the whole family going to see the fish. Dorothy was terrified of the slippery sliders but of course Arthur got involved . . . he even kissed one and smelt like fish for the rest of the evening!

CHAPTER 5

Christmas 2016

For us, Christmas has always been about family time. Mine and Dick's families both adore Christmas. After a busy year, it is the perfect reason to come together and snuggle up. We know that it's important to also allow yourself to stop sometimes and not to have any worry or guilt about it. Let's face it, Christmas is a good time to do it, as many others will have stopped too.

Our first Christmas at the château in 2015 was a rather low-key celebration, after all the activity of our wedding the month before. This year had been busy too but in a different way. We'd had lots of firsts – lots of new business ventures, figuring things out, exploring new parts of the garden and growing on our land for the first time. It was exciting, but also tiring having so many unknowns. And we had not seen our families anywhere near as much as we would have liked, so Dick and I got on the phone and invited everyone to join us for Christmas.

My mum and dad had planned to be back in the UK visiting my grandma, who had been unwell, but they would be around until 20 December. Jenny (Dick's mum) and the sisters said 'Yes please' but wanted to be back in Northern Ireland no later than 20 December because snow was expected. My brother Paul also said 'Yes please' but he had to be back for the last week of his retail business, for obvious reasons. Dick's daughter Charlotte already had plans. Dick's son James, his wife Holly and their kids were busy for most of the month of December but free over actual Christmas. And so, just like that, a family-filled December started to take form and we were thrilled.

It meant we were going to be having two celebrations and there were no complaints from us! Family staying is not like having guests; with family, everyone mucks in, and it's all about having fun and eating and drinking too much.

When Mum and the girls had come to visit us previously, they'd stayed at a local gîtes, as our stairs are a bit of an endurance test, but this time they were to come and stay with us at the château – because we had a lift! Although there was still some work needed to get the botanical suite ready for them all.

Because a lot of the groundwork had been completed on the botanical suite, it came together rather nicely. I had the furniture and had found a charming wallpaper in a local DIY shop. It surprised me how much I loved it. It was taupe with lots of embossed ferns. It felt right for the suite. Apart from plumbing in the bath at the end of the bed, which I'm sure Dick is writing a separate book on, the bathroom was where we threw the final energy.

I was after a monochrome art deco feel but all the tiles I found that felt right were far too expensive. So I decided to use reasonably priced tiles – metro, square tiles and marble – but break them up with borders and details to give the feel of a really bespoke art deco bathroom, but at a good price.

I try to add something unique into each room and for this bathroom I had my heart set on designing a tile with some 1920s beauties diving into the moat. It tied into the era of the bathroom design perfectly and I would border the top of the white metro tiles, which were grouted with black.

The design ended up taking longer than I hoped because the château kept looking 'stumpy'! Then, one evening, I was doodling in bed and Dick looked over and said, 'Give me the notepad.' And he changed the shape of the château into something beautiful and perfect. Mr Strawbridge can be very creative if allowed!

The bathroom was finished off with a shop-bought mirror, to which I added an oriental black geometric wooden pattern to lift it into something completely unique and two Tiffany-style hanging lights. I even popped into the attic and found a fabric-covered picture that sits in pride of place by the window. The placement of the black and white tiles really elevated the bathroom and it looked quite luxurious.

And that was the suite done – on a tight budget but fabulous all the same – and it was finally ready to welcome its first very important guests!

In our first year, we were disappointed to find that turkeys in the supermarkets and butchers were all a tad small. I'd grown up with the problem of fitting the family turkey in the oven at Christmas and cooking it long enough to ensure it was cooked through. In France, the turkeys were not big enough to allow for the extra days of turkey pie, turkey on toast, turkey curry . . . So the obvious answer was to rear our own. A bit of research found us a market where we bought half a dozen poults. We repurposed a shed used as a toilet for our wedding celebrations as the turkey shed. Having erected a decent-height fence, keeping the turkeys was not onerous apart from the fact that they were never any good at going to bed by themselves. At dusk, we had to encourage them to go to bed, as they do not put themselves to bed like chickens. It involved lots of arm waving and encouraging 'go-to-bed turkey noises'. If we left it too late it was somewhat interesting doing it in the dark! As they grew and matured, we soon knew which one was going to be our Christmas lunch. He was a beauty!

When my family moved to a smallholding in Northern Ireland, my parents reared turkeys every year to fund the Christmas season. A week before they were to be collected, which was usually on Christmas Eve, the birds were all dispatched and plucked, and hung in a cool place. They were only drawn and prepared on the morning they were to be collected and each bird had the neck, heart, liver and the cleaned gizzards put in its cavity in a plastic bag. I had continued this ritual when I lived in Cornwall and the day the birds were to be killed started with those who wished to help having a glass of sherry and, if desired, a cigar.

The process must be efficient and respectful, so I would go into the shed, select a bird and carry it into a barn, where it was dispatched and bled and plucked. Depending how many people were helping, two birds could be plucked at the same time. When preparing our own birds at the château, we couldn't help but think that it must be very similar to what would have happened here over 150 years earlier, when it was first built. Angela didn't quite understand why I was happy we were preparing turkeys and not geese, as we assumed they would have done back then . . . she hadn't yet had to try and pluck the down!

Christmas doesn't seem to start in France until 1 December but then it's all systems go. We love the fact that there is a break between festivities and Christmas is not being advertised at Halloween, or even before. On our second Christmas at the château, we discovered that Laval, our local city, is very proud of its light display and is a must-see evening out for the family. As locals, we felt it was our duty to head out to enjoy the spectacle. Wrapped up warm, we headed off in good time to park up and walk into the centre. I had a feeling the traffic, and parking, was going to be difficult. After much searching, we found some parking on a back street near a little family restaurant we liked to take the children to. It was a nearly ten-minute walk but with Dorothy snuggled in her pram we headed off.

As we crossed the river under the shadow of the old town château, the streets were bustling and the atmosphere was wonderful. There were people all along the river and everyone was getting into position to see the lights coming on and the fireworks. We passed a café that had been very entrepreneurial and was selling *vin chaud* on the street, so Angela and I picked up a couple and some churros for the children. As we flowed with the people along the bank of the Mayenne we just looked at each other and smiled. Arthur got into the pram; Dorothy got on my shoulders and we just laughed and chatted until we came to a halt about a hundred metres from the main bridge crossing the river. We stopped and everyone was absorbing the lovely feeling of being out on a crisp evening with the objective of enjoying ourselves.

Just before six, at some signal we were unaware of, it went quiet. I popped Arthur on my shoulders; Angela took Dorothy and the Christmas lights burst into life. They were white, twinkling and magical, and the children's faces lit up. We joined in the cheering when the fireworks started and scared most of the children – and a fair number of the adults! The display was impressive and lasted about fifteen minutes. A round of applause ended the brief silence that followed the fireworks and everyone started moving away. We had thoroughly enjoyed ourselves and, most importantly, Christmas had started!

Visiting us from Northern Ireland is not that straightforward as there's a decent amount of sea in the way. The girls all like to drive or fly/drive to give themselves flexibility as they don't like to think they are inconveniencing their hosts. I could argue with them until I am blue in the face but I'd be wasting time – they'll always do what they think is right! This time they had sailed from Dublin to Brittany on Irish Ferries, which is our preferred crossing. We tell the children it's a cruise and always have a lovely meal in the restaurant. It's not an arduous drive at either end so, as long as the Irish Sea/Channel are behaving themselves, you arrive recharged and smiling. On the day of their arrival we had been getting texts informing us of their ETA and they are all so well organised they take a pit stop before arriving to ensure hugs and kisses are not interrupted by steam coming out of anyone's ears and rushing off to the loo.

As the girls turned the corner everyone squealed. Arthur and Dorothy ran down the stairs, eager to hug everyone. We quickly headed into the house for our first cup of tea. This may have been their third visit but it was their first time staying with us and that was so incredibly special.

I'm not sure if we were more excited to show them the lift or their new room but it was not long before we put Jenny in the lift. And then everyone else, one after the other, was sent up to be received in the botanical suite and shown around. Dick was dispatching and I was catching . . . The investment in the lift paid for itself in that precise moment. As Jenny stepped out into the botanical suite, we both had tears in our eyes. It had not sunk in that Jenny had never been to this floor *ever* and she was blown away to be up and experiencing the amazing views this floor brings. The château was always meant to be a family home, for all our family, and finally it was fully accessible to everyone. We were so happy to have them staying with us.

When we all congregated four floors up, we proudly showed them around. They had never seen around this floor and were surprised by the thirteen rooms and loved the view from every window. They'd always trusted that we'd made a good decision buying the château but now they fully understood why we had bought the decrepit building and called it home.

First thing in the morning, and every morning during their visit, Angela, Arthur, Dorothy and I would head up to join Granny on her bed, have a cup of tea and chat about what we were going to do that day. Sitting on the bed together could have been a scene from our lives fifty years earlier, only now we took up much more room and we creaked a bit, getting up and down! My mum was in her element and loved Arthur and Dorothy cuddling up to her, one on each side, and doing the thing young children do when they try to occupy your very space. She was beaming.

After lots of catching up, we needed to start preparing for the festivities. Our working partnership truly shines at moments like this. Dick was instantly working out our festive menu and I was designing the table, place settings, crackers and other gifts. The centrepiece of the dining room table was to be full of foraged foliage with exotic sugared fruits. I wanted each place setting to be a visual delight that oozed with personal touches.

I used round pieces of wood for these, each one inch thick with holes in the top for a piece of string. Dick had cut and even sanded them for me. I used the same method to transfer images onto the wood as I had for printing pictures for our Strawbridge suite and made each setting bespoke: my dad and I on our wedding day, Jenny with me and Dick, my mum with the girls. And so it went on . . . Even with a party of twelve, I still wanted everyone to know where they were sitting and feel special.

For the 'crackers' I used vintage books and hollowed out the inside. Antique books are like pieces of art to me. I particularly love the festive-looking covers with their red and gold foiling. But turning them into 'crackers' is the magical part:

....

HOW TO MAKE VINTAGE CHRISTMAS 'CRACKER' BOOKS

You will need

Newspaper
PVA glue and a container to mix it in
Beautiful hardback vintage books (you can pick these up cheaply in junk shops, charity shops or at car boot sales)
Small paintbrush
£1 coin (to use as a spacer)
Metal ruler
Pencil
Sharp scalpel or craft knife
Clear varnish (optional)

Method

Step 1:

Lay out a few sheets of newspaper to protect your work surface, then mix up a glue solution of PVA and water into a fifty-fifty ratio.

Step 2:

Flick past the book's title pages to the second page of full text – this is where you will start cutting. Hold the bulk of the book together and brush the outside edges of all the pages from the second page to the end with the glue solution. Use enough to stick them together – you may need two coats.

Step 3:

Put the £1 coin into the book between the first text page and the now-glued second page to make sure they don't stick together. Close the book and allow it to dry. Remove the coin. Stick the back cover to the glued pages and allow to dry again.

Step 4:

Open your book to the first glued page (i.e. the second text page) and, using a metal ruler, draw a rectangular border 2.5cm (1in) from the edges of the page. Carefully and slowly cut along the lines using the scalpel or craft knife, resting the blade against the metal ruler as you cut. Keep the blade vertical or the hole will slope as you cut deeper into the book. Continue cutting until you have cut through down to the last page.

Step 5:

Remove the cut-out paper, then brush the PVA solution inside the hollow and on the top of the first glued page. Now turn over the first text page onto the glue – this will stick it to the glued and cut-out section of the book. Close the book and leave to dry thoroughly.

Step 6:

Open the book to the first text page which is intact and is before the cut-out section, which is now glued to the cut-out section. Carefully cut out the shape of the rectangular hollow beneath this page using the scalpel or craft knife – this covers your earlier pencil markings and creates a neat finish on your top page. As an optional extra, you can now brush the entire inside hollow with a coat of clear varnish, so that you can wipe it clean after storing sweeties inside! And then you're done and ready to fill your hollow book with secret sweet treats.

Step 7:

I love to add lots of personal touches and so I put an antique perfume bottle inside for Dick's mum, little gloves for Dorothy and pictures of our wedding on a memory stick for my dad. All little touches that I thought everyone would like – and that would fit inside a hollowed-out book!

· ·

The following day, my nan and my brother Paul arrived. They were the missing pieces and now that they were here safe and sound we could all relax and start the food preparations. My brother drove them over from the UK and they arrived late in the evening so it

would be a big surprise for Arthur and Dorothy to see them the next morning. It was quickly turning into a rather special occasion!

Our turkey was 'oven ready' before mum and the girls arrived. They would have happily helped with this but instead we had time together in the kitchen preparing for the meal. Our bird was a respectable 20lb and looked good. As I brought it out, I saw knowing eyes looking it over for any quills or ripped skin. There were no blemishes and it promised to be perfect. Family Christmas lunch seldom involved a starter and we followed the tradition on this occasion. The main course, followed by an abundance of Christmas pudding, was more than enough. Our meal was the following:

- Roast turkey with a forcemeat stuffing
- Bread sauce
- White wine gravy
- Roast potatoes and parsnips
- Carrots and peas
- Lemony, buttery leeks
- Puréed cauliflower with white pepper
- Brussels sprouts, sweet chestnuts, lardons and shallots
- Savoy cabbage

It involves a lot of dishes for service but with a bit of planning it all appears at once and there is a flurry of everyone passing everything to everyone else and helping serve each other.

The preparation can be done in advance. As always in our house, everyone free came and sat around the table and joined in. Arthur even peeled his first Brussels sprouts and watched a cross being cut into the stalk end. It's to help it cook more evenly and by the time he's my age hopefully he will have watched it, or done it, at least another fifty-nine times. I see no reason for Christmas to change too much! We were all chatting and in next to no time everything was sorted. Vegetables were ready to cook and the bird was ready to go in the oven.

I always leave the neck skin on the turkey long, as it allows for more stuffing and can be tucked under the bird and sealed with a single skewer. Charlotte, my eldest daughter, has always loved my turkey, stuffing, bread sauce and gravy, but on Christmas day she has to have at least a morsel of each of the other dishes on her plate as part of her five-a-day. If you'd like to try a Strawbridge family Christmas, here's a little more guidance:

....

ROAST TURKEY WITH A FORCEMEAT STUFFING

For the stuffing:

1.5kg sausage meat
1 large onion, finely diced
2 eggs, beaten
4–6 slices of bread, crumbed
Good handful of chopped parsley
Zest and juice of a lemon
The turkey liver, finely chopped if you have it
6 slices of streaky bacon, chopped

Method

Mix together all the ingredients well. Stuff the neck end of the bird and push the first handfuls of the stuffing up under the skin to sit on top of the meat. Cover with foil and go through your ritual cooking. Know the bird can sit for a good forty-five minutes when it comes out, so only put your roasties in once it's out. I put tinfoil on the bird and put a couple of tea towels over the foil while it sits.

. . . .

BREAD SAUCE

(This can be made as thick or as thin as you like)

Put eight cloves in half an onion and place, along with a bay leaf, in 500ml of milk. Bring to a gentle simmer, add 50g of butter and then turn off the heat. When cool, fish out the onion and bay leaf, then add four to six slices of bread, crumbed. Heat gently before service.

WHITE WINE GRAVY

Save the juices from the bird in the roasting tin, put them into a jug and pour the fat back into the roasting pan. Add six tablespoons of plain flour to this fat and stir well. Cook the flour for two minutes, then add 250ml white wine. Stir to make a paste, then add in the rest of the juices, stirring to minimise the lumps. It'll be too thick so add some of the cabbage water to thin it to perfection. Strain if you wish.

ROAST POTATOES AND PARSNIPS

Parboil and bash around the peeled, chopped spuds and 'snips and add to a super-hot roasting tin containing a good amount of duck or goose fat. Shake it all together with more salt than you think you should use and roast in a 220°C oven. Shake it again after fifteen minutes, reduce to 200°C and cook for a further twenty minutes.

CARROTS AND PEAS

Cook your carrots in butter for three or four minutes. Add stock to cover, then add the peas and cook for another three or four minutes. Turn off the heat. This can sit while you finish everything else.

LEMONY, BUTTERY LEEKS

Cook the leeks in butter until soft, then, before service, add the juice of half a lemon and stir well. Turn off the heat. This can sit too.

PURÉED CAULIFLOWER WITH WHITE PEPPER

Boil florets until soft, strain, add some milk, salt and white pepper and purée. This can sit.

BRUSSELS SPROUTS, SWEET CHESTNUTS, LARDONS AND SHALLOTS

Cook the chopped bacon in a pan with one tablespoon of olive oil. When some of the fat has rendered out add the whole small shallots and cook for another three or four minutes. Add in the peeled chestnuts and cook for another couple of minutes. Add the Brussels sprouts and 100ml vegetable water or stock. Cover the pan with a lid and cook until the sprouts are 'al dente', or four or five minutes, depending on their size. Turn off the heat. This can sit.

SAVOY CABBAGE

Cut the cabbage in half and slice (starting at the stalk end; it's easier to cut that thinly). Put it in a pan and add an inch of water and a sprinkling of salt, then cook for a couple of minutes from the time the water boils. Turn off the heat – this can also sit. Strain and serve.

You'll note that most of the elements of this can sit in their pans while they wait for you to finish everything else, so don't fret about timings. Taste everything and adjust the seasoning, and have at least one glass of sherry or a G&T. Smile – it's Christmas!

....

Earlier on the day of our Christmas feast, I went foraging for greenery for our decorations with my mum and Dorothy. It was a first together and unbeknown to us it was the start of a new tradition. Dorothy wore a tartan jacket that my mum had purchased the year before and it had a matching hat. She's always known how to melt our hearts! We picked lots of evergreen for the table and I later laid it out like a very simple table runner. It's a very quick and easy thing to create Christmas magic: bring the outside in! Then it was time for final table prep. The books and decorations were carefully placed, with balloons everywhere. We were ready!

Then everyone entered and we had a quick family picture before everyone saw their table setting for the first time. They loved the books. Although it took everyone a few moments to realise they were hollowed out! I'm pretty sure there were tears at this point. Arthur loved the policeman's whistle he received in his – a little too much, perhaps.

I made sure the wine was being passed around and, before we knew it, we were all seated and glasses were raised to 'families',

with lots of cheersing. We may have sat down hungry but, by the end, we had had our fill and were ready for a pre-pudding nap!

We'd been manic preparing for the big family feast and, with Arthur and Dorothy in safe hands, as the evening approached, Angel and I headed across to the orangery. I had a surprise for my wife. It was a lovely, romantic moment, just us and the twinkly lights of the orangery – our gramophone had arrived so we could finally enjoy our old records.

Having wound up the gramophone and worked out how to start it, I asked Angela for a dance. We were giggling like school children but it turned into full belly laughs as we realised Angela was not prepared for being led. Our moments alone turned into a very special dance to remember, and eventually my size, and strength, brought me victory as I led my beautiful wife, dancing to music that had probably not been played at the château for over a century.

When life is as busy as it had been for us this year, you must savour every romantic moment. This one was filled with a lot of laughter, then love and then just being in that exact moment together.

We could have been forgiven for thinking our Christmas would get quieter once our guests started to leave but almost immediately we started getting ready for the next Christmas celebration with James, Holly and my gorgeous grandchildren Indiana, Pippin and Arrietty. With Uncle Arthur and Auntie Dorothy, that meant we had a one-, two-, three-, four- and five-year-old – all the makings for a wonderful Christmas. Our time was definitely child-centric and we had lots of fun just playing. Indie was into LEGO that was so complex that I found it challenging, but the girls loved dancing, which was lucky because we had the most amazing *maître de ballet* visiting: my big boy James! He'd done ballet until he was old enough to start playing rugby and he still had all the moves and looked amazing in a tutu that magically appeared. (I think he brought it with him . . .)

We mostly stayed at home with our visitors; however, we wanted to take the children to visit the Christmas decorations in Laval. In addition to the lights, the square in front of the château always has a Christmas-themed display. We hadn't seen it yet but off we went. It was a bit odd but the children loved it. On top of obvious Christmassy things, imagine any mundane domestic act and then add Father Christmas or elves . . . there was a scene with elves doing Father Christmas's laundry (we now know what his boxers look like); a kitchen scene with lots of food preparation; mechanics were fixing the sleigh; cobblers were mending boots . . . There was a surprise around every corner and the children ran around as a gang and smiled and laughed.

We had no fixed agenda for the visit, but on Christmas Eve we baked and roasted the ham for Christmas breakfast and made mince pies to ensure there were some to put out for Père Nöel. A shocking fact that not a lot of people know is that the French don't make mince pies or sell the mince! Luckily James had brought a supply with him so making mince pies involved the children rolling and cutting pastry, putting in the filling and glazing them before they were popped into the oven. Another little-known fact is that when you allow children to help you with pastry their hands end up looking cleaner at the end and the pastry has a slight grey hue. To be clear, that is even if you wash their hands before you start. It's a mystery.

After baths, we had the most adorable group of angels, all dressed in their PJs and discussing what to put where for Father Christmas and all the reindeer. There were mince pies, port and carrots on little plates around the fire in the salon. Our over-excited but tired children went to sleep surprisingly quickly and when we congregated in the salon for some adult time, I couldn't help but notice that Father Christmas Junior had been at Père Nöel Senior's port and mince pies. A diplomatic incident was avoided by getting some more out but FCJ was on a warning that PNS may not leave a pressie for naughty boys! We all have to get older but there is absolutely no reason to grow up!

A ridiculously early start was followed by present opening and slices of ham and chutney or mustard on toast and our morning disappeared. Christmas lunch was the way it should be – relaxed. Too often, people stress about getting it right as it's a big family celebration. I firmly believe we eat when it's ready and everyone will love it. James and I thoroughly enjoyed time together in the kitchen with a glass of Christmas cheer, chatting as we prepared the Christmas meal I'd grown up with, which was the same Christmas meal he'd grown up with. We savoured the time and I love the idea that someday we'll have Arthur and Dorothy, or their grandchildren, helping and making their own memories in the same way.

Boxing Day had a completely different vibe. It was a little more relaxed but magical all the same. You can imagine the excitement and anticipation of the arrival of Father Christmas the previous day. Once he had been and delivered wonderful gifts, the children were calmer, as were the adults, and everyone was very happy playing with their new toys. Especially the adults!

James, Holly and the children left the morning of 28 December. The house felt very quiet and we slept deep that evening. What a Christmas! With just a couple of days left of the year, we planned to rest, reflect on all we had achieved and move down a notch or ten!

On 29 December we all had a lazy morning. We got up slowly and had a family breakfast of dippy eggs, ham and toast, and then sat in the salon playing with Arthur and Dorothy. The phone rang. It was my grandma, who had been poorly on and off for over a decade, but batted it off, not allowing it to set in. She had never

been to the château but was stupidly proud of everything we had achieved. The call was short and sweet, and these were her words: 'Darlin', I'm going to die soon, any chance you can come and see me? I'd especially love to see Arthur and Dorothy. No offence.' With that, we packed our bags, booked the tunnel and headed off back to England in our rather rickety old Mercedes.

We stayed in Southend that evening and visited a favourite restaurant of ours. It was originally a quirky tearoom called San Fairie Ann. They did great British food and were especially family friendly – in fact, the owner had a basket of kids' toys behind the bar and she always used to give the children a pressie, which made them very happy! Arthur had 'Essex boys' beer-battered fish, chips, mushy peas and tartar sauce while Dorothy had spaghetti Bolognese. I had their classic burger and twice-baked chunky chips and Dick had sticky pork belly, potato and leek cake, apple purée and cider jus. They also did a mean cocktail and as we did not need to drive anywhere, we took advantage and had a couple of their espresso martinis! It was 4pm, the restaurant was very quiet but cosy and the staff were very attentive. In fact, I would go so far as to say my memory of it was magical, completely perfect, as we sat there chatting about going to see Great-grandma, ensuring Arthur and Dorothy knew this was *not* a sad moment. It was the first time they were to visit a hospital in these circumstances and we had done our best to make sure they were prepared. Dorothy had her doctor's kit and Arthur had his box of plasters that he carried everywhere with him just in case anyone got hurt.

After the meal, we walked along Southend's seafront. There is nothing like the sea air to clear away any cobwebs, or a cocktail or two!

The following morning, we set off to London to visit my grandma, Enid. On arrival, it was mayhem. My uncle had installed a ticket system to ensure everyone got twenty minutes with her. They say life is what you make of it and my grandma had lived her entire life for her family. With seven children, ten grandchildren and eight great-grandchildren, many who were married and had partners with them, the hospital was bursting!

Our ticket was called . . . My grandma had this wonderful ability to make you feel like the most important person in the world to her. She did it for everyone, and she oozed happiness and cheekiness, and loved a giggle. Arthur put a plaster on her arm. Dorothy used every item in her doctor's kit and tested it out. Even the hammer thing. And then Dick took them away, so we got a few minutes alone together. We held hands and talked for a couple of moments. She told me how proud she was of us all. I thanked her for being such an incredible grandma and we spent the last bit of the visit chatting about current affairs and how cute the kids were. I gave her a gentle kiss on the forehead and left. There was no time for tears; the whole family was outside and all eager to say hello and goodbye.

The car was full of fuel and ladened as we crossed on the evening train to Calais. Funnily enough, the tunnel wasn't busy on New Year's Eve. There was not a soul on the roads. The car heating was not set too warm but Angela, Arthur and Dorothy were all snuggly, so as we left the port all three drifted off to sleep. The trip had been very last minute but so necessary for Angela to say goodbye to her very special grandma. I'd reckoned on five hours to get home, plus maybe one pee stop.

Driving through the night, it didn't take long before it got a bit spooky. The *péage* was deserted and the fog appeared in patches. The road markings are not great in France, as they get obscured by dirt, and there are no cat's eyes. To be honest, it was a hard drive. I had to reduce speed and I was still north of Rouen as the new year arrived. I smiled, looked around, and smiled some more. I had the most valuable cargo imaginable on board and all of them were fast asleep. We are very lucky but we also live life to the full and really believe in sucking the marrow out of the bones. Our beaten old car did us proud and, as we headed south, I thought through all that had happened, as we completed our first full year living in France.

It had been a year of many firsts and the foundations for our business were well established. Our to-do list was not getting smaller, it was growing, but that was probably because we were no longer scared to write it all down. The balance in our bank account remained worryingly low but we had an impressive order book and we were optimistic about the year ahead.

It was just after 3am by the time we got home. There was no reason to empty the car, so we took a cuddly, warm, duvet-wrapped child each and headed upstairs. There were trips to the loo and very quickly we all settled in our massive bed and slept.

I think 2017 started properly with Arthur's foot in my face; he's always been a wriggler.

That morning we introduced the children to the concept of a New Year's resolution. They found it funny and, to be honest, when you try to explain it to a child, it does make you wonder why we don't just take charge and change things straight away if we're not happy with how they're going. But a new year always feels like a new beginning, or a new cycle to me, something that motivates us to 'be better'.

Our life was evolving at an all-time crazy pace. Arthur was at school; Dorothy was to start school this year and we had a wedding and hospitality business! It was still early days, but January 2017 brought change – and lots of new interest. The word was out and now we'd had Charlotte's wedding and added her beautiful photos to our website, things went up a notch.

Enquiry after enquiry came in. For every enquiry, I would call the couple. Ninety-five per cent of the enquiries came from brides and on the odd occasion it would be a groom. I like to have a call because you get a real feel for their personality. I am a businesswoman but when we do weddings it's more than a business transaction and we give it everything. For it to not feel like a job and for us to be able to keep the magic alive we need to really like the couple, and for the most part it was fine. But as I said, that first phone call is always very important . . .

CHAPTER 6

Arthur's First Birthday Party!

No matter how manic our lives are, the children come first. Arthur and Dorothy know exactly how much they are loved because we tell them and show them at every opportunity. They were growing up fast and as Arthur had started school four months ago and had made lots of new friends, this had to be celebrated.

January is a grey month – living in London, the streets were always grey at this time of year and at the château it feels the same. But since Arthur was born on the 29 January 2013, the month has had a purpose for me and it's not just the grey time of the year when I get organised! We have had a few family parties for Arthur, but never a true birthday party. For his first birthday we had a party in Southend; it was minus five and we all decided

to get an ice cream on the beach . . . I can still remember how cold it was! His second was the day before we moved to France and that was more for me, so I felt I was being a good mum. And his last birthday was very quiet with just the four of us at Center Parcs. So this would be Arthur's first birthday party with his friends!

I was excited and nervous. You just want your babies to have a wonderful time. I guess I'm a romantic because I have no real memories of being four years old, so it didn't matter, but we were also opening our home to the locals and that was a big deal.

The theme for the party was superheroes: Captain America, Spiderman, Superman, Thor, Iron Man – all the characters you'd expect a four-year-old boy to be into. I had purchased on the internet some rather brilliant hoodies – the kind you might wear on a normal day and not only if you were going to a fancy-dress party. I still wasn't really sure how many friends would turn up, so I ordered ten. I also made some masks and capes and other superhero stuff. I'd even managed to find Dorothy a wonderful silky (but not tacky) dusty-pink spider-girl cape and mask. When we were back in the UK I had bought some vintage Spiderman wallpaper that I knew Arthur would love. At £12 it was a bargain and perfect to use as a table runner and wrapping paper for his presents.

Superheroes need sustenance, so in addition to the party food we decided to provide some proper food that both the parents and the children would eat. As we didn't know what French families would expect, we agreed that we'd do spaghetti and meatballs, one of Arthur's favourites at the time.

....

TURKEY MEATBALLS AND TOMATO SAUCE

This is a meal for all the family and is a light, and child-friendly, alternative to beef meatballs. Children who are not averse to anything green (the herbs!) tend to love it.

Ingredients (for four)

Olive oil
400g spaghetti

For the sauce:
1 onion, finely diced
4 cloves of garlic, crushed
750ml passata
1 tbsp sugar
1 tbsp red wine vinegar
Salt and black pepper

For the meatballs:
400g turkey or chicken breast meat, minced
2 slices of bread, crumbed
Zest of 1 lemon and juice of ½ lemon
Small handful of chopped green herbs (whatever you have to hand – for example, parsley, coriander, basil . . .)
1 beaten egg

Method

Put half of the chopped onion into a large frying pan and soften but don't colour. When nearly cooked, add the garlic for the last minute. Then add in the passata, sugar and vinegar, and bring to a simmer. Taste and season.

Make the meatballs by mixing all the ingredients in a bowl. Season generously and form into meatballs about the size of a walnut. When you've got them ready to go, gently set them in the pan of sauce. By moving the pan in a circular motion every minute or so the meatballs will be coated in the sauce and should be cooked all over in about ten minutes. You can cut one open to test as a chef's perk . . .

Cook the spaghetti, drain and add to the sauce. Do your cheffy thing of tossing so the spaghetti is covered in the sauce. Tip into a large bowl to serve.

The meatballs should be soft and light, and you'll taste the lemon and herbs.

. . . .

On the morning of the party, I had six confirmed guests but I set a few extra places at the table just in case. We knew that if six guests came, it would be a brilliant party. The excitement levels were high and games were at the ready – pass the parcel, pin the tail on the donkey, treasure hunting. We even put a few beers in the fridge.

We had no idea what the French expected from a kid's birthday party and whether children would be dropped off or the parents would stay, so we covered all eventualities, which was just as well.

Zellie, Arthur's 'girlfriend' at the time, arrived first. Arthur is a big-hearted, gentle soul and at the time was not embarrassed by having girlfriends. Elouan, Nicole, Lini, Lola, Tom, Gabrielle and Luca followed close behind. First note to self: parties in France start punctually. Not knowing the tradition, we asked everyone who arrived if they wanted a beverage. Before we knew it, there were nearly thirty-five people here, kids running everywhere, parents drinking beer and coffee. All having a lovely catch-up and looking around and taking in the château. And no one left! All the parents stayed until the end!

I had been living under the belief that everyone just stayed of their own accord until I read Angela's paragraph above! It makes sense that she invited everyone to stay and have a drink and, as they thought it was what the British did, they all felt they should stay! This means we will now never know what the French practice is, as at every party and gathering since we have been asked to stay . . . but was that because they thought it was the British thing to do?

Shortly after the food, we started the games. The children loved pass the parcel and Dick was incredible at engaging the children and making them laugh. It could have been his witty jokes but most likely it was just his Irishman-being-French accent and fabricated words!

It was a huge success; Arthur was smiling and having a great time. And, as everyone was leaving, we received many compliments that 'the English' know how to put on a party. When we shut the door on the final guest, we laughed so hard at just how crazy it had all been!

When Arthur went back into school for the beginning of the second term, all the children were asking to come to his next party, so we must have done something right!

*

Dorothy had a complete blast at Arthur's birthday party. I remember thinking that it felt like her party too and some of the parents even brought little gifts for her. It then occurred to me that she could be ready to start school, but I pushed that to the side because I was not ready yet for that! But it was just a few short weeks later, at the end of January, that we received a letter saying that because Dorothy's third birthday fell before the next half term she would start going. This was a bit of a shock and I must admit I cried. But I also felt excited for her because I really thought she was ready and she is such a bright cookie (says the biased mummy).

Angela could not come to terms with Dorothy going to school full time even though it was quite the norm. Our little girl wasn't yet three though, so we decided that she would go three mornings a week, from 8.45am to midday. A gentle start for Angela – oh, and for Dorothy! In France, school has an important role providing childcare. There is a nursery attached to the primary school and parents can arrange for their children to be dropped off early and collected after hours at the *garderie*. The school day for Dorothy could have been from 8.45am to 4.30pm with a two-hour lunch break that included a three-course meal, a nap and play time. For reception classes it is very flexible and we felt that three mornings was the way to start.

Dorothy was due to start after the next half term, which was in early March. Just before that date, I was called to a meeting at the school to be attended by all parents of the under-threes. Even though I realised I would be out of my depth, I went along. Even with a lot of *bonsoirs* and smiling, I detected an atmosphere. Apparently, there was not space in the reception class for all the little ones in the village to start that term, so they would have to wait until the following term and some mums were not happy. I was noticeably silent, particularly when I realised the cut-off date was done by age and our little Dorothy got the last-but-one place.

When Dick arrived home that evening, we discussed Dorothy not starting until September. But I had seen how she loved interacting with the other children and it was only a few mornings per week. It would be a gentle ease into school. I knew it was the right thing to do. But that did not make it any easier.

It felt like 2017 was going to be a big year of evolution for us and one of our resolutions was to try to do a few more things for ourselves. At the top of the list was the Strawbridge suite. Our suite consists of five areas: the turret, luckily redecorated recently when we installed the lift; our main bedroom; the kids' bedroom; our shared bathroom and the vestibule that joins them all together. We had never given it a second thought that our suite be left until now to 'make-nice'. We still had no electricity in the suite, apart from extensions from the kids' room, which had had a little more TLC when we first moved in. Basically, we had not done anything beyond the initial work to make it liveable. It was comfy because we had a very comfy bed and I had grown rather attached to the stud wall in the bathroom and the wallpaper hanging off the ceiling, but it's fair to say it left a bit to be desired.

We always tried to ensure that we put the infrastructure in place as early as possible and our suite had a junction box in the bottom of the cupboard in our room, an electrical spur in the bathroom for heating and a cunning plan . . . It just hadn't had any work put into it yet.

Firstly, we had to move into the honeymoon suite. I can think of worse places to stay! The two children's beds fitted nicely in the *chambre d'honour* and we had the main bedroom. It was rather

fabulous and bath times were brilliant! It was like being on holiday! Moving out, even though it was only from our room, gave me a great excuse to have a clear-out too and rationalise the kids' clothes, drinking cups, baby monitors and to find many items that had got hidden over the last couple of years.

I truly believe that a child's material surroundings do not shape them. Arthur and Dorothy would have the same love, values and work ethic wherever we lived. We would have made sure of this. So I had not thought for one moment the fact that our suite was slightly dilapidated even registered with either of them but one evening, at bath time, Arthur asked if we could stay in the HMS because it was shiny and the wallpaper was not falling off! After the shock had worn off, I laughed and explained that was why we were in the suite – so we could 'polish' ours.

We knew where our electricity was going to start in our room, but then came the debate as to where it would end . . . Where were the plugs, lights and switches going to be? I knew the answer and I also knew that it is always best not to ask a question you don't want to know the answer to! But I had to ask Angela those painful questions. Guess what? The lights and sockets were going on all the walls miles away from their starting point and all the wires were to be hidden. To coin an old phrase – bugger!

There were no options. The lights had to be on both sides of the room, as did the sockets, and the light switch was to be near the door. When connecting power to the chandelier in the dining room below, I'd discovered some boards that were not screwed down and that allowed access to the chandelier anchor point, so I started there, right in the middle of the empty room. I had to get to the four light locations that we had decided looked nice and would provide good illumination (these were wall mounted, as it made no sense to hang anything from the wonderful ceiling). They all had to be chased in (a groove chiselled into the wall to hide the cable and conduit) enough for the necessary ducting and cable, then all we had to do was to pass cables under our beautiful wooden floor. I had purchased a couple of sets of fibreglass wire pull rods that were made up of a number of sections that could be screwed together and used to probe under boards between beams to find a way through. Once through, you attach an electrical cable to one end and pull it through. They were a godsend but only worked if there was a clear path for them.

The job went relatively smoothly but I couldn't chase in the lights we planned to put next to the bed as the walls on either side of the chimney breast were made of cheese – or rather, a single layer of thin bricks. The first hole I tapped with the cold chisel took out half a brick. I would have been worried if I hadn't been so excited by seeing a void in the wall. I peaked in and found a wallpapered cavity. The walls had been rearranged. My first thought was of 'priest holes'* but I discounted that as the château is nowhere near old enough at a mere 150 years. I called Angela and we looked in. I shone a torch but it was hard to make out the dimensions. We decided it was only a couple of feet square and floor to ceiling. We said it could make a possible built-in wardrobe or change the shape of the room in an interesting way but as we were on a tight schedule, we decided to note it and come back to it when it came to remodelling in the future.

Dick's first answer to everything is 'no'. Most people believe he says yes all the time but, boy, do I have to work hard at getting him to agree to anything! He always comes up with a list of why not to do things. A couple of heated chats later and we normally meet in the middle. I love him to bits and he keeps my ideas achievable in the often tight timescales we are working to. On this occasion,

---

* Hiding places in old houses to conceal priests when they were outlawed – part of our Protestant history!

my requests were simple: I was after a bright room with lights and lots of electric sockets. We needed to be moved out of the HMS and back into our suite in March, in time for our first food lovers' weekend, so the pressure was on.

With electric sockets and lights in our bedroom sorted, builder mate Steve was set to plaster. The next task was our bathroom. We'd used a sink that we had found in the château. It was stunning but the glaze had blown and there was staining under the white topcoat that had turned it a sad blue so there was no way it had a place in our revamped bathroom. I told Angela that the bath was to stay where it was as, apart from being heavy, it was plumbed in and working. It was hard to believe we had showered in the bath with a Frankenstein curtain around us for over two years. I couldn't wait to have our own walk-in shower. But before we could go any further, I needed details of what was going where and how it was going to be heated.

I wanted to keep the design gentle and fun. I knew that this was probably the only time I would be able to have complete control over the kids' bedroom without too many 'cooks'. The next time we redecorate their room, I will most likely simply be manpower. But for the moment, they were four and *nearly* three years old so it was my playground and that was sort of my theme.

Arthur and Dorothy's bedroom had had some very early work before we even moved in. The windows and the paint had been stripped, the walls had some plaster thrown at them and we had painted the room before we allowed either of them to sleep in there. There were even two lights dangling in the correct place! However, if we were doing up the Strawbridge suite, I wanted to take the kids' base and make it better, more playful and more personal. And, as I like the circus and love a safari print with palm trees, I had found my twist . . . I found some charming safari material, which was printed onto a canvas; it felt child-like yet would not look out of place in our room either and so I bought about thirty metres of it.

The colour of the walls was something I had made up a couple of years earlier from white emulsion and dye, and was a lilac-grey colour. I knew I fancied painting stripes on a number of things and so I chose my complementary grey paint and stocked up on lots of Frogtape.*

Our main bedroom already had a French-style rattan bed. It was a reproduction made in the UK but the reasoning behind why we didn't choose an original French bed, which is a fraction of the price, was due to size. On a daily basis, there are four in a bed and French beds are tiny. Say no more! Dick and I also talked a lot about how we wanted to use the room. Our current routine was that we went down to the *salle à manger* for breakfast with the children. But when we have food lovers staying, sometimes the kids have breakfast in 'bed' whilst I lay the table in the dining room. But I'm literally a hater of crumbs in bed, so the decision was made to have a table and chairs in the suite where they could have breakfast. In the winter, this made complete sense too because our suite is generally the warmest place in the château.

I decided we needed 'something' at the end of the bed as well but all the ottomans we considered looked tiny because of our large bed, so instead we decided to re-upholster a €50 sofa I had picked up in Emmaus. Dick agreed (finally) to chase the electrics into the back wall. Looking back, this is something we could not have lived without. Although, to be honest, to begin with, just making the walls, ceiling and floors nice and not having cables everywhere was enough to make me overjoyed! I chose a dusky-pink lustre wallpaper for the sides of the room and my favourite sage green for

---

* A type of masking tape that doesn't peel off paint when you remove it and gives you a lovely crisp edge when painting.

the front and back walls – calm and attractive. I then tied in the sofa and pelmets with the safari material chosen for the children.

The bathroom was the place that I knew would make the biggest difference – mainly because we had an unfinished stud wall dividing the kids' room and the bathroom. Currently we had a very clever circular shower rail that Dick had made, which hung over the bath where we showered. It did a job but in winter when you got in the shower the cold synthetic shower curtain stuck to you and was horrid! We had an inherited sink and an old toilet. I was definitely looking forward to this being 'polished'. To keep things moving, Dick always had a list of things I needed to choose and buy. Of course, I'd already chosen some of the easy things like wallpaper and our bedroom had a lot of stuff in it. However, in the bathroom the list was long and full of items that were not easy to source:

- Wall lights above the sink
- The sink(s) – I always fancied a double sink like the one in the HMS
- Heating, plus a decision about where it would go
- Floor tiles
- Wall tiles
- Shower fittings and screens, plus a decision about where they would go

Dick and I spent several late evenings in our horizontal office, looking at pictures and deciding what would work where.

I have to say, the only curve ball I got on the bathroom makeover was being asked to install underfloor heating. It had never crossed my mind but Angela had heard good things about it, so why not? It was easy and effective so that was a win-win. Between us, somehow the lights for the small entrance to our suite became three hanging world globes with lights in them and, to make it interesting, we drilled little holes in the places we had been. Angela and I shared one, and the children each had one. It was very effective and just went to show how big the world is and how much we still had to see. The light diffusing through the globes was not very bright but it was the perfect night light for the children

I had picked up three globes at Emmaus. I chose three because things look good hanging in threes, so Dick and I shared a globe and the kids had one each. I'm soppy and hope that one day if the light design is changed in the vestibule the children might want to keep their globes and carry on drilling holes in them! Like most globes, they came spinning on axes and when those are taken off, there is a hole in the top just big enough to fit a lightbulb in. I chose a red cable I picked up in IKEA and it really worked well with the colour of the globes and the sage green ceiling.

Alongside the growth of the family was growth and understanding of our business. This year saw our first full calendar of wedding book-ings, so we spent the beginning of it working out our wedding cycle and what needed to happen when. What became obvious early on was that the start of the year, from 2 January onwards, was busy with new enquiries and current couples wanting to get organised. January was historically a quiet month for us, but not anymore.

It was fascinating finding out all our couples' wishes and require-ments. In fact, even for me, someone who is rather seasoned in events, it was a learning experience. Half of the couples wanted to see the château before making any commitment, which was completely understandable, and many also requested a tasting before committing (not quite as doable). And then we had some couples that requested 'refundable deposits'. We even had one couple request to reduce the bill for a guest who didn't eat very much! The requests were varied and all manageable with an honest 'yes' or 'no'. I hate saying 'no' to anything, but with time I got better because I had to – this was our livelihood now. Learning our flow had started, and processes and 'rules' came together quickly, and ensured that, by the time we signed a contract with our couples, we were all on the same page.

We had eight weddings in the diary for 2017. That was a huge jump from the single wedding we had the year before and we knew it was going to be a challenge. At moments, we did feel the responsibility, but mostly it felt exciting and really motivating. We felt blessed to have been asked to host these weddings and I was looking forward to diving into the planning still to do: the hotels, logistics, coaches, flowers, confetti and other decorations – and that's without even mentioning the food, drink and ceremony, all of which Dick would lead on. It was going to be a busy year and nearly every third thought to myself was about getting organised!

As February rolled around, it was time to batten down the hatches. With high winds and the Pays de la Loire on orange alert, we just had to hope our roof would survive the storm unscathed. We didn't do so badly. The château seemed to groan a bit and there were more bangs than normal in the night but an inspection in the morning revealed only a couple of dislodged slates, which we combated by strategically placed buckets in the attic. Thankfully we were all but dry inside. That said, it was clear that we needed to think carefully about getting started on the restoration of the roof. After some research, we found Ian, who had been a roofer man and boy. We called him in to report on how bad it was going to be. Every château owner knows the roof can be the most expensive and time-consuming part of any renovation, so we needed to know what we were dealing with – and then to start saving!

Ian came along and, instead of the usual French process of looking, providing a quote and then returning sometime in the future, Ian surveyed from the inside, checked out the access windows and pronounced we still had life in our roof – but we needed to do some patching ASAP. We negotiated on prices, then I asked when he was available and he said 'now' and, grabbing his tool belt and some old slates from an outbuilding, he headed up to the attic. I led the way up and Ian pointed to a very old wooden roof ladder and asked if he could use it. I thought he was joking but he wasn't . . . We struggled to get it out of a tiny access window and then he hooked it over one of the ladder hooks, clipped himself on and headed out. I looked out of the window and just like that he was up on the ridge, removing damaged slates and inserting whole ones. Within a couple of hours, he had patched us up and no sunlight was coming through the roof.

We chatted afterwards and Ian felt that with some preventative maintenance we should get another five to ten years from our roof. That was music to our ears and gave us some time to build up the roof fund!

Although we did not set up an official bank account, Dick and I started talking about our 'roof fund'. We also put into this mental pot the fact that the windows needed doing. Some jobs around the château can be done with a bit of elbow grease. Others need a bit of that, plus a few thousand pounds thrown at them. Some, like the lift, cost tens of thousands of pounds. But the roof and the windows were eventually going to need hundreds of thousands of pounds spent on them. Once done, they would last our lifetime, for sure, and hopefully the children's too, but building up that sort of money at this stage seemed impossible, and, to be very honest, it kept me awake at night. It also kept us very motivated to make the business work. We knew keeping the balance of family and work was going to be tricky but we were doing everything we could and gave our all to them both because the business was in fact for the future of the children.

*

After months of work, our Strawbridge suite was coming together. The back wall in Arthur and Dorothy's room had been painted with thick, rich grey stripes. I had planned to do more on the ceiling but one wall looked great and it was very time consuming! I'd also decorated their drawers with the same grey stripe. I'd made their initials – A and D – from a lightweight board and threaded circus lights into them (which were just string lights you can buy in any store!) and everything had been scrubbed, filled and polished before we put the room back together. An old chair that Dick and I had bought in Battlesbridge, Essex, was the first safari upholstery project; it had mint green piping, which really brought out the monochrome tones in the fabric.

The bathroom was sparkling. I had managed to convince Dick that because this was our forever bathroom, having my dream double sink – which was the same Arcade sink as in the honeymoon suite – was a good move. I loved it so much that I decided we then needed to get a matching shower, bath taps and cubicle – which was not cheap. But I planned and sort of promised not to change the design for many years! The shiny Parisian curved bathroom was set on Bert & May encaustic cement tiles. The company is based in London and their founders were inspired by Spanish encaustic tiles. Reproductions of this style of tile are very popular now but the real deal will always be the best in my eyes. Ours were white and grey stripes, gentle chalky colours, and, because of the way they are made and fired, every tile is unique. I was charmed and knew I could not put our gorgeous bathroom suite on anything other than something I adored. I finished the bathroom off with 1950s opal glass hanging lights. It was fresh and clean. I honestly knew bath time was going to be such a pleasure from now on!

The vestibule that joins all three rooms together had been papered with the safari print that I had picked up in the UK and Dick finally got to hang the globe lights! The children were going to love them. And finally, our room: the blush wallpaper was not working so I used the same technique to paint stripes in the sage green I had used on the walls. Although a lucky accident, it tied our room into the kids' room and looked fantastic. It had a nod to the 'circus' theme but in a really grown-up way!

Upholstery project number two was the French sofa I purchased for €50 using the safari fabric, which sat proudly at the end of our bed. And upholstery project number three was the pelmets in the same material. We had no intention of adding curtains but I thought it really finished off the windows in a lovely way. Then Dick and I put the finishing touches in place: the table that was picked up for €20 and painted with a petrol chalk paint and the amazing quilt that Dick's sister had made for us for our wedding.

Angela had kept the handmade patchwork quilt that Bunny, my big sister, had made for us in a safe place. She had thought over every detail and each section told a little of our story. In fact, unbeknown to us, she'd even drawn around the kids' hands when she'd seen them last and included the hand prints on one of the patches. There was a mixture of symbols and motifs from moustaches to teapots and, unbelievably, the colour palette fitted into the bedroom that Angela had designed. We laid it on the end of the bed together . . . the quilt had been patient and now was placed in its forever home.

As soon as the finishing touches were in place, we brought Arthur and Dorothy to see their new suite. They squealed at all the details. And they loved the globes! Dorothy sat on my shoulders and looked at the world and I thought to myself, I can't wait to put more holes in it, as a family.

CHAPTER 7

Wedding Season Preparation

Nature has a clock that ticks relentlessly. As we come out of winter and into spring, any dormancy is replaced by sap rising and vigour. Right from moving to France in January 2015, the start of each year here at the château has been about planning and understanding the year ahead. The days are short and the long evenings encourage thinking. Our first winter was slightly chaotic as the château was not habitable, but still had that element of understanding what the year had in store for us, and making decisions about how we were going to execute our plans. In addition to planning, there are some tasks that can only be done when nature is sleeping.

Compared to some of the châteaus we had seen, Château-de-la-Motte Husson had not been badly neglected. However, it's fair to say there had been minimal effort put into some areas.

Compared to the UK, France has a positive love affair with pollarding their trees, which involves pruning them back, every couple of years, to a main trunk or branch and allowing new growth to start from there. Our trees were in desperate need of a haircut. Angela loved the beautiful old lime trees as they were. However, the tree trunks were all but hollow and had been formed to support relatively light growths of branches. Some of the 'new growth' was more than fifteen years old and as thick as a healthy tree. It was quite possible that a summer storm, when all the leaves were caught by strong winds, would split the trunks apart. Indeed, one of our trees had a thick metal band around it, which had been partly grown over now but had definitely been put on to save the tree.

Logic is all well and good but when I got a local tree surgeon in and Angela saw what was meant by pollarding, I was seriously in the poop, and what's more, there was nothing that we could do. Pollarding is a one-way activity! Angela considered my 'act of vandalism' unforgivable and insisted that I promise they would grow back before the first wedding in two months as their shade was essential. I couldn't, so I didn't. Instead I went out and bought some very large umbrellas. Pollarding is officially a dirty word in our home!

I did understand the concept of pollarding but as we were to have our first full year of weddings and the trees were visually beautiful, as well as offering incredible shade, I was reluctant to give them a structure with no shape, so we compromised and I know we did because *I was there* with Dick and the French 'pollarders'. We discussed that most of the weight would be taken away but they would leave a small number of branches in a sympathetic shape, so they looked like trees. My worst nightmare was that they looked like tree stumps.

You can imagine my genuine shock and surprise when I walked out with Dick and the trees no longer resembled trees. It was *a moment*, I must tell you. They were the nightmare stumps that I had visions of. I'm a trouble shooter, I fix problems with solutions and where there is a will there's a way . . . but I don't think my head could cope with what I saw. There was no solution, no fix, no fast track. They just had to grow back in their own time. My heart sank.

Dick has spent years justifying that he had to save the trees. I have never denied that . . . I do, however, believe they would have still lived if we had given them a tiny bit of shape.

I may have been in a 'naughty' mood after the tree-pollarding incident but one evening when Dick was away for work I was trying to find solutions to make our weddings as smooth as possible. Our main 'problem area' was the bar and the challenge of serving cold drinks and ice. It had caused lots of behind-the-scenes problems at Charlotte's wedding and with eight weddings in the diary this year, I knew a solution to this issue was an investment that would pay dividends.

Initially we were looking at old Citroën H vans we could turn into a mobile bar, our very own 'van de vin'. But the truth of the matter is that, although they are a beautiful shape, they have become very popular and are hard to get hold of for a bargain. Dick suggested we look for an old horse box. I loved the idea and found some rather nice ones but the amount of work needed to turn them into a bar was probably too much and we only had a few months. One evening, after the kids were in bed, I started looking at options on eBay, especially anything that was unusually shaped. A monster van popped up! I was not sure if I loved or hated it! There are moments when you believe you are meant to have something and I was undecided if this was one. Was it ugly or uniquely stunning? I couldn't decide. What I did know was that it was in France, being sold by an English person in euros and was French registered. It was also dirt cheap: under €3,000 for everything. It came with a *carte grise*[*] and also a working permit if you wanted to drive it to a market and sell 'stuff'!

The van was white and blue and about thirty feet long. It was made in 1978, my birth year, which I took as another sign, and it had six pull-up sides that when down protected the vans belongings and when up allowed you to serve. Once all the sides were up, there was a gangway in the middle and the surrounding area was shelf after shelf of storage as every part of the van has been designed cleverly to transport goods. The top of the van had storage; the bottom of the van pulled out. It was meant for just this: serving the public! At this stage, I have to admit, it was ugly (I might have mentioned that!), but the potential for a bar, which we would need to store glasses, ice, etc., was phenomenal and I knew I could make it attractive – well, sort of – and very functional. I also love a challenge.

I was eager to find out more about it and in a panic, I called the English telephone number on the advert. A lovely lady called Jacquie answered. She spoke beautifully and we ended up being on the phone for over an hour. The van had lived a full life but now it was a little old and needed some mechanical work to get it working well. Jacquie told me that it belonged to her friend who lived in France. He could not bear the thought of it going as scrap metal so he was trying to sell it very cheaply so it would have a home. Many people had visited and some had made offers but they kept falling through because they were worried about driving it. I mean, it was a beast. When Jacquie's friend told her of his sadness, she said, 'Let me put it on eBay in the UK for you, it's a whole new market.'

---

[*]   The official vehicle registration document in France.

We also talked about Jacquie and her story. She was the sort of crazy that I love – completely into old cars, a member of the classic automobile club and had a house in France and England. In fact, she told me on the phone that she re-built an old Morgan in her living room. At that moment, I just loved her and told her we would buy the van and we would give it a new lease of life. I also let her know that I had a very clever husband who was going to be in for a shock but would help turn it into a bar.

Dick called me shortly after. He was back in the UK doing voiceover work and was tired. I was slightly hyper and not finishing any of my sentences properly but I think he got the gist that I had found a van. And that I loved Jacquie!

Angela is nearly perfect but she'll admit she doesn't do geography. Now, France is a big place, so if I'm honest we were lucky the trip to the van, and back, could be done in a day.

It's true that geography is not really my thing and when buying things on eBay, I never check the location properly. To be fair, I've looked at maps many times and I drove in the days when you could only use paper maps to find new locations, but I'm the sort of person who will come out of a shop and walk the direction I have just come from. I once (twice, actually) was convinced my car had been stolen because it was not where I had parked it. Yes, that was a bit embarrassing. At first, I'm sure Dick thought it was an endearing trait. I mean, we had a great time driving up to Birmingham to collect a Victorian taxidermy case. But maybe I need to look at where things are located a little more carefully. I knew the van was based in France. But, like everything, I tried to make a positive out of the situation and treat it like a holiday. I dressed up our visit to view the van as 'a day at the seaside'.

We had a lovely trip up to the Somme region; the children were perfect and slept for a large part of the drive. We'd decided to go straight to see Jacquie and then on to the coast for a play on what would be a chilly beach. There were some amazing old vehicles about the 'yard' as we arrived and I was a bit concerned Angela would get distracted and we'd leave with the old Fairway taxi we saw there, as well as the van. The vehicle was not for driving around the country-side, it was to be our bar, so I was not worried about it passing the *contrôle technique* tests to be roadworthy; I just wanted to know it was sound. Up close it was huge. It extended out to the length of an articulated lorry and the aluminium-on-steel frame construction was pretty well bombproof. Driving it would be another problem, so it was going to have to be brought to us on a low loader. But the deal was done, as I'd known it was going to be from the moment Angela told me about the 'amazing van' she'd found at such a good price.

To turn our outing into fun for all the family, we then went to the nearest seaside town and had a lovely lunch in a crêperie over-looking the windy beach. Rather than going for a set menu, as we tend to, we had a simple main course each and decided to head to an ice-cream parlour where the children were allowed whatever flavour they wanted. To no one's surprise, they ended up with double *boules* of the most garish colours there were, which may have been a mix of bubblegum and unicorn berries, all covered with rainbow sprinkles. To get any unwanted E-numbers out of their system we had a lovely hour charging around the beach collecting shells and pretty pebbles. The seaside was out of season and the weather was windy but visiting the beach always has two magical effects: the children always get wet (so we always have a change of clothes) and they sleep on the journey home.

The man transporting our enormous van was Casper. Jacquie helped arrange it. He was well known around France for transporting old

vehicles. Dick happened to be working away again, which was just bad timing, but with the clock ticking for the first wedding, we needed the van to arrive as quickly as possible. I had my instructions of where to ask Casper to park the van.

Casper turned up, which was a great start, and on time, which was even better. I showed him where Dick had requested he park the van. Because of the size of the truck and van together, there was only one direction he could unload the vehicle, so he told me, once the van was off, he would drive it into place. He was very confident and his transporter vehicle looked the part. I'm sure I saw him attach . . . 'things'. But I also remember telling the cameraman to move out of the way, which must have been a sixth sense because the next part happened very quickly.

Casper started the transport vehicle winch, which was slow and steady. The van started to move. A good sign. But then it started to move very quickly. And then, bang! Within a second or two it had rolled into one of our outbuildings. Two thoughts jumped out: firstly, was Casper okay? Because he was trying to hold onto the pulleys to stop the van from crashing. And he was tiny. I mean, in hindsight, that was completely mental. Once he confirmed in an out-of-breath voice that he was, it was time to see the damage.

Thank goodness for those outbuildings being built to last! The corner of the van made first contact with the top of the door, where the lintels were. This must have taken the impact. I'm assuming that had the van not been as tall and had fallen off a slope into a wall, the whole wall would have been taken out.

Casper then shakily drove it into position. And I shakily called Dick.

Once I heard everyone was safe, my first thought was, 'What a plonker!' Followed by, 'What about the van?' And third, 'What about our outbuildings?' To summarise: yes, cosmetic damage to the van that was not really visible from ground level, and a chipped stone above the doorway that would always be a reminder of Casper the vehicle delivery man.

I had not slept well the evening before Dorothy started school. It may have been partly because of the rather ugly van outside our château, but most probably because I was having annoying anxious dreams all night about her first day. There was a small part of me that felt happy because she was over the moon to be starting and, I'm not going to lie, the fact that I would have three mornings a week to get real work done was a positive. The wedding side of the business alone would eat up that time. But I felt empty. She was my little angel who still slept in our bed (lots). But knowing kids can pick up on any sadness, I overcompensated in the car, making lots of jokes about pee pee. Arthur was bubbly and great fun, and he told us he was there to look after her. I smiled all the way to the door, hugged them both goodbye and, as I turned around and left the school, I was in floods of tears. I'm sure it's meant to be the other way around! Dick was fantastic and very loving. He joked that we could go for a coffee and have a date. But when your last baby goes to school, the house feels quiet and empty and you suddenly don't know what to do with yourself. I was not used to not thinking, where are the children?

Our little 'Dodo' was tiny. She had the smallest schoolbag in the world and it looked huge on her. Angela was obviously devastated but Dorothy had seen her big brother going off to school to make friends and she was ready for it. So we were all smiles and excitement. We have got used to the fact that both Arthur and Dorothy are very tall compared to the other children in the class but in the early days we kept thinking there had been a mistake. All the children were even smaller than Dorothy! We found her peg, hung up her coat and bag and put on her indoor slippers and, with a perfunctory hug and kiss each, she headed in to play. We were happy it had all gone so easily but were also gutted . . .

When the clock struck twelve (*midi*), Dick and I were there, ready to pick up Arthur and Dorothy. (Actually, we'd been there for ten minutes in case the gate opened early.) We made our way to their classroom and they both ran out smiling and very happy to see us. Dorothy ran into my arms and everything was great. She had had a ball. And so, it had started . . . Dorothy was now at school and we had moved into a different stage of childhood.

Even with our three mornings of four hours to be completely focused, we were most certainly being kept busy still, as our business was growing fast. But we could only fulfil so many events as we had a few restrictions to work within: firstly, the number of finished rooms in the château; secondly, the number of weekends in the year and thirdly, the decision that we made early on that we would personally host everything.

We were still only hosting one couple per weekend for our food lovers' weekends but had made the decision that as soon as we got a third suite finished, we would increase the capacity for the weekend to three couples. Although that was in the future, all bookings were made at least one year in advance, so at the start of 2017 we had to let the people on the waiting list know. At this point, we had around 2,500 couples on the waiting list, all in order of when they enquired as we have always tried to be strict about first come, first served . . . I had assumed that many of these would not turn into actual bookings, something I may have naively underestimated.

We had hosted nine single-couple food lovers' weekends in 2016, so we had our groove, and already had a further thirteen couples booked in for 2017. The food lovers' single-couple crew, in order of date booked, were: David and Helen, Bob and Angela, Ian and Jennifer, Alison and Millie, Christine and Pete, Daniel and Nikki, Claire and Simon, Cheryl and Dennis, Michelle and Andrew, Tara and Jordan, Melanie and Clive, John and Dan, Michael and Nathan, Lesley and Graham, David and Sue, Sherraine and Adam, Eileen and William, Sarah and Simon, Steve and Marjorie, Katherine and Matt and Mark and Lynn.

Angela and I don't compromise easily and our FLW were all about doing something special for our guests. Menus varied and our Saturday cooking sessions meant we seldom did the same thing twice. It was fun and challenging too.

We know what it is to earn our keep and that £1,000 for a weekend is a lot of money. But, despite our working hard, and the popularity of the events, having one couple at a time was not a viable way to pay for the château upkeep or to build up our roof fund. We did not spare expenses when it came to the food and drink but we were charging £1,000 per couple, VAT inclusive, which meant we had just over £800 to play with. We'd spend around £300 on food and drink, allowing another £100 for getting the rooms ready and turned around after each visit. That meant there was around £400 to split between Angela and myself for three days, two of which were fifteen-to-eighteen-hour days. When you do the sums it's below minimum wage ... However, in the early days, every penny counted, it was all part of a bigger plan and we completely loved how special the weekends were. But, and it's a big 'but', we are a business and so are always reviewing what we are doing and trying to do it better to stay viable. The idea of offering less for the money never even crossed our minds.

I've got such fond memories of every couple and wonderful stories. And there are many that we still keep in contact with. It was mid-March 2017 when Nathan and Michael were booked in. Two weeks beforehand, Michael messaged us and asked for permission to propose to his partner Nathan. Not only was it a yes but it was a dream come true. The château was rapidly becoming a place where joyous memories are made.

When they arrived, the first thing I noticed, apart from how stylish, handsome and well put together they both were, was their matching haircuts! They got out of the car and gave Dick and I a big warm hug. It was going to be a wonderful weekend.

I had to keep the dining room doors closed because earlier that day I had been out collecting blossoms. It was spring outside and the trees were bursting with cherry blossoms. My all-time favourite. A delicate, fleeting flower that transforms into delicious fruits. I could not think of anything more romantic to dress the dining room with for the special evening. As I was dressing the room that day, my heart kept racing with excitement, so I could only imagine how Michael felt! I wanted it to be perfect for them and so I ensured every candle, every piece of blossom looked on point. I can only judge if it looked magical enough on what I would be happy with and, when I was happy, I closed the doors . . .

Angela and I had settled into a gentle harmony in the kitchen for food lovers'. I had done all the food preparation and would send it up in the dumb waiter so it was a matter of finishing as necessary and then I would 'call' service or, if Angela was hosting, I'd ping the very old bell we'd bought. I'm not the sort of chap you'd allow to carry four soup plates at once or to do silver service. We always believe in giving our guests time together and it is a fine line between the right amount of chatting and being intrusive, so we err on the side of caution and find we have a lovely evening in the service kitchen catching up and talking. I always cook extra food to cover any disasters, which are rare, but mainly so I can give Angela a lovely meal as well as our guests. However, this evening there was nervousness and anticipation behind the scenes. I reckon Angela was more nervous than Michael but we'd done all we could to prepare for the moment. Michael would be on his own.

We like to start the evening with an aperitif in the salon. I think I was sharing Michael's nerves and when Nathan popped back to their room to get something we had a quick chat. We wanted to ensure we gave him enough time to propose. It was such an intimate setting and neither Dick nor I wanted to burst in at the wrong moment. We were all planned and on the same page and knew exactly when to bring in the champagne!

The proposal was to happen straight after the soup course, so Angela had planned to clear the bowls, top up the drinks and then give them space. We stayed very quiet and kept giving each other the knowing look that something very special was happening.

Then it happened. We knew because of the obvious happiness and tears but we had no idea how long to give them before bringing in the champagne. Michael and Nathan needed to savour that moment together, so we were highly sensitive to not interrupting their moment. We were next door in the service kitchen, with glasses and champagne all ready, but when would be the right time to go in? You can't listen at the door but you need to know when they are 'ready' for visitors. It was a problem with no perfect solution, so we gave them a couple of minutes before nodding to each other, knocking on the door loudly and joining them.

It might have been a couple of minutes but it felt like an hour . . . We entered together and congratulated them both. The room was charged, lit only by candlelight, the table bursting with delicate flowers filling the room with their perfume. Nathan and

Michael both had a happy tear in their eyes. Nathan showed me his engagement bracelet. It was Cartier from the Love collection. It had a small white-gold ring interlocking a black ceramic ring. I remember thinking how lovely it was and how different not to have a conventional ring. It was so them!

With thirteen food lovers' weekends, eight weddings to plan, twenty wedding viewings and eight wedding tastings to be done before the start of the wedding season in the summer, we were busy and the only way to ensure things ran smoothly was to be organised. Time was ticking before our first wedding of the season and I had not seen my girlfriends for some time, so I came up with the idea that they come for a visit and help paint the van. It was a huge job, so the phrase 'more hands make for less work' came to mind.

Let's be blunt – the van was big and ugly. Because of its size I knew I could see it working but I had no idea how Angela was going to make it look nice! I was also about to head off to film the series *Cabins in the Wild* for Channel 4, leaving the van in the hands of Angela and her London girlfriends. I knew there were copious quantities of gin and tonic in the *cave* and the fridges were stocked, so what could possibly go wrong!

It was terrible timing, not planning, that meant that Dick was going to be away when my girlfriends arrived. But we would make the most of the weekend, and April always seems to be full of unexpected sunshine. I'd been getting all the rooms ready, making sure everyone was comfortable for our busy time ahead. I gathered together all the overalls I could find, as I knew no one would come dressed appropriately – in fact, I would have been disappointed if they did! It had been a hectic time but there was lots of excitement around the place. Arthur and Dorothy were also very happy because they love Sara, Kate, Andrea and Louise. They came by Eurostar and then a taxi and, as the taxi came around the corner, I ran out ... Yes, London was in town! The door opened and the most stylish yellow boot appeared, then my girls swaggered out of the taxi, sunglasses, hats and *all style*. For a brief moment I felt completely underdressed. It was only for a millisecond, then we all screamed and hugged and it did not matter what we were wearing. We were still the same and so happy to see each other. When you have been friends for so long with people, you don't often get the chance to reminisce about how you became friends, and when you do it's always a lovely trip down memory lane.

Sarah and Kate are sisters. I met Sarah in Shoreditch, east London, about fifteen years ago. We hit it off and I invited her to a vintage night I used to hold in my flat. And the rest is history! We met Louise through our friend Young, who was in a band with some of her friends. And Andrea I met via the Red Bull Music Academy through a mutual friend, who had also been picked to take part. Andrea has an amazing voice – husky, soulful, folk-like, full of emotion – *and* she's gorgeous and a wonderful person. I used to take my girlfriends to see her gigs and then we became friends and have been so proud watching her career grow. There are of course more in our circle from the old days when we used to run around east London without a care in the world and I was so lucky to have had them all together at my wedding!

The sun was shining, it was hot, and it had been a while since we'd seen each other, so we cracked open a bottle, turned the tunes on and danced at the front of the château with Mum, Dad, Arthur and Dorothy. We ate and caught up, chatting non-stop, until, one by one, people needed to sleep.

The following morning, I put on a brunch: kedgeree, eggs, bacon, tomatoes and, of course, fresh baguettes and fresh orange juice. It felt like old times . . . but in a castle, with two kids. It was one of those 'how did *this* happen?' moments! I remember Sarah saying, 'Well, Angie did say she was going to buy a castle in France! And what Angie says, she does!'

I had never really put any thought into being that person who does what they say but, looking back, I have heard many people I have known talking about a dream, a business, changing their life, but they haven't done it. There is always a reason not to, often excuses. Not the right time, maybe next year; no money; not the right skill set. If I have an idea, I go for it. And I've always done everything on a shoestring because I've worked hard for every penny I've earned and understand its value. When I met Dick, his can-do personality was so refreshing. I'd met my match and the love of my life, and nothing could stand in our way.

*

As a professional 'telly tart' I took jobs to keep the money coming in but I also love promoting engineering and sustainability on the television. Don't tell anyone, but our love of all things vintage and old, and my passion for gardening and cooking, is a covert way of promoting awareness of sustainability. When I was offered a series with the working title 'Cabin Fever', which later became *Cabins in the Wild with Dick Strawbridge*, I jumped at it. The timing was not great because Angela had arranged for a group of her girlfriends to come that weekend but we both understood that we still needed to keep the funds coming in.

The concept was simple: build a camping 'cabin' that fitted on the back of a trailer (sizes specified) so the finalists could be transported around to form a moveable hotel. The finale was to be in Wales but I was working with Will Hardy and our cabin was to be made in Essex, though visiting the other entrants meant trips around the UK. Dovetailing dates into the diary was an interesting exercise but we managed.

One of the things I loved most about the series was the fact that Angela had never been camping, so I set our test criteria for our glamping ('glamorous camping') cabin as somewhere Angela would love to stay . . . There's nothing like a challenge. Our first problem was that the cabin footprint was too small for all the facilities we needed, so we made it extendable. When parked up, you tugged here and tugged there and it grew to more than twice the size with a lovely outdoor patio area. I blame living in a château . . .

I visited a number of ingenious locations from tree houses to forts in the English Channel. The series was probably the reason why, when Angela mentioned glamping at the château some time later, I didn't immediately say 'no'.

While Dick was hard at work, so were we. Well, sort of . . . we may have had little hangovers, we may have just eaten a rather substantial brunch and, to top it all off, it was raining, but nonetheless, a couple of coffees later and with a 'Dickie' jumpsuit on, the girls were ready to go. Though I think the amount that needed to be

done was not the most motivating sight. But after a prep-and-plan chat, we put some music on and all got our heads down to work.

That was until I went to get everyone a drink and Lou's favourite song came on. When I came back everyone was dancing on the van ... Yes, on the van roof, and it was rather raunchy dancing. After a mini heart attack (health and safety), I got my phone out and filmed it! We giggled that we could never show the video to anyone but – sorry, girls! – I never said I wouldn't write about it!

When Dick got home, we knew we needed to start talking about our third suite. We agreed that the two rooms directly above the *chambre d'honor* in the honeymoon suite, overlooking the driveway, would be our next project. They needed to be ready for November when Sheelagh and Les, Graham and Jane and Dave and Jane were due to come for our new food lovers' trio weekend. If we left it too late, the wedding season would start and we wouldn't have enough time to finish it.

The rooms on the 'second floor" (actually four floors up) had historically been for children and the staff and could be described as lower-status rooms, but the only difference between them and the higher-status rooms was the fact that the ceilings were normal height and not ridiculously high. Access was up a set of elegant oak stairs, hidden by double doors from the top landing of the main staircase. These stairs take you up past somewhat shabby walls to the next two floors.

The rooms that were to be converted into a suite had a single doorway that went into a corridor with two doors off it at the end,

---

* The *sous sol* is at ground level, the *rez de chaussée* (the ground floor) is one level up, followed by the first floor that's on the third level, the second floor on the fourth level and the *grenier* (the attic) on the fifth level, with another attic above that.

angled and coming to a point, one to the left and one to the right. If you want a single room, you knock down the corridor and then think about what to do with the total space, but Angela loved the choice of entering on the left or right into the same room, even though the corridor down the middle meant the light from the double windows didn't penetrate into the room in the same way, so the far ends of the room away from the windows felt quite dark. The windows had already been replaced with aluminium double-glazing but we basically had to remove some of the studding and get back to an empty shell, which was to be 'U' shaped, with a simple marble fireplace on each side, to get the light in. We had run waste pipes and vents down the corner of the room into the HMS below so that dictated which side the bathroom was to be placed. As we stripped out the wooden structure of what had been a small wash-room (the jug and ewer type with no plumbing), we found the built-in cupboard had the simplest, and most interesting, lining.

I'm pretty used to having heated chats with Dick on what goes where in a room. Normally I'm trying to convince him about the best place for the bathroom, and he's complaining that the waste pipes need gravity! In this instance, we had already agreed where the bathroom and the lights were going (roughly) but we had not chatted about the corridor that opened into two rooms. I had assumed it would stay as it was, as I loved the idea of something different and I think it gave the room real character. Dick had assumed it would be ripped out. Luckily, we finally had the chat before it was too late! Of course, I managed to convince him that on this occasion I was right and every time I enter that suite, I still love the detail!

I had spent a number of days in this room renovating a bath for the botanical suite but I had not looked deeply into every crevice. It was not until this point that we decided together to explore,

because ... well, we needed to rip out everything that wasn't needed (which was not the corridor!). As we bent down to go into what must have been the servants' under-stairs wardrobe, we saw it had been lined with newspaper. Dick got out his phone because it was very hard to see in there and then we saw that it was pages from an 1880 copy of the *Paris Journal* – just a couple of years after the château was completed. It was amazing to see. Someone had lined their wardrobe with an antique. Although obviously at the time they were simply being resourceful with their daily paper, which would otherwise have been used to start a fire.

The newspaper had been very well preserved, and it was floor to ceiling across the width of the cupboard and came across the ceiling of the structure. The colour was that orangey brown of age and just looking at it took us back to the life that must have been led at the time. The advertisements and the articles were all really interesting. In addition to an article on oriental fashion – something close to Angela's heart – I even found a couple of recipes. Chicken Royale could have come straight out of *Pulp Fiction* and there was a macaroni dish done the way Parisiennes like it ... '*La timbale de macaroni à la parisienne*'. I would never have thought that the French were eating macaroni in the nineteenth century ...

Now this was something fabulous that we both agreed we would preserve in this suite, and although we knew we would keep it, we were not sure how best to showcase it. We also both liked the name 'boudoir', which Dick initially thought meant something else ... maybe that is why he liked it. The rooms were always dark, though. I must admit I wasn't sure why until I just read Dick's comments above! All I knew was that the room felt moody and atmospheric and that's what inspired the colour palette of black, gold, red and green, which also fitted in with the name boudoir.

The perfect place to sulk! I have tried to keep several plants in there over the years since we decorated the rooms but they have all withered. At one point, we even ended up with a 'plant hospital', trying to nurse poorly plants, all from this suite.

We were still ensuring we had revenue streams to provide the income to build our dream and so I had been having discussions about building a model railway across the UK. The debate was about whether or not it could be done. My answer was a definite yes but with some caveats, all to do with resources and time . . . When we worked out the detail I said I'd be involved and Angela and I agreed that it could be considered my R&R, rest and relaxation, before the summer ramped up. It was a very silly idea but what a couple of weeks!

For what became known as the Biggest Little Railway in the World, we built a temporary 71-mile, 1.25-inch-high model railway that ran from Fort William to the City of Inverness, the two largest settlements in the Scottish Highlands. It has also been described as 'a crackpot project by an army of madcap enthusiasts, geeks and engineers in the best spirit of eccentric Britishness'. I had the honour of leading this merry band of very special model railway enthusiasts.

It was seriously gruelling and after the first couple of days saw our model steam engine derail hundreds of times, even ending up in a canal, I was party to a discussion with the production team about how we were to spin this glorious failure. The answer was: we could not fail. Instead, we had to dig deeper, and up our game, which involved everyone working shifts and through the night. At one stage, it was decided we had to let our team rest and, as we'd used all the hours available to every member of the camera crews, the three of us who were on-screen talent and the executives from the television production team took the night shift and laid track and babysat our engine through the night!

It was all very British and when our engine, *Silver Lady*, puffed up the hill to Inverness Castle there were more than a few of the fifty-six volunteers, three presenters and thirty-odd crew who had a tear in their eye. They say a change is as good as a rest; now, it definitely wasn't a rest but it did give the restoration fund an injection of cash! I didn't know it at the time but the château had now reached the stage where it could stand on its own two feet and this project was the last time I *had* to go away to keep our bank account topped up.

We always agreed that until the château could fund itself, Dick would carry on working away as a TV presenter. Although we missed him, absence makes the heart grow fonder and every time Dick returned it would feel like a special occasion. I knew this particular project was hard work but he loved it and when we watched it on TV I cried because all the train enthusiasts were so wonderful. We were so proud of Dick.

Getting back to some normality at the château, after several projects that had taken me away, my focus changed to the walled garden. In the early part of 2016, we were having to be very frugal as the château hadn't started to produce any income, so we had to occupy ourselves doing projects that did not cost a lot, hence we did some work in the walled garden. This year was very different; we wanted to continue to make progress but with only so many hours in a day, it was a little challenging getting enough time in the garden. That said, it was easier to do some weeding than it was to let nature take back what we had fought to conquer. Angela was taking more interest, as was the whole family, and we loved time out in the fresh air.

I had never really given Angela a lot of flowers when we first started courting. If she needed, or wanted, flowers she would go and buy them. Or I could turn up with a bunch to discover she had half a dozen bunches left from an event. It was very hit or miss. However, in France, it all changed. Instead of giving my gorgeous wife a bunch of flowers, I gave her a cutting garden so she could have flowers and foliage for most of the year. I willingly admit I don't know as much about flowers as I do about edibles but I had more than enough knowledge to get started. It is usual to have a four-crop rotation system – I'd always assumed that's why most walled gardens had four quadrants. But flowers tend to be perennials and so I decided to give over the quadrant closest to the main entrance. It would be convenient for Angela getting flowers but it would also look good as you enter the walled garden. Beds were rotovated and some essential plants were put in immediately, including scabias for me, roses for the scent, lavender for the buttonholes and eucalyptus for the bouquets.

The 'van de vin' also needed attention. The engine was tired and didn't want to start. Luckily it was a wonderfully simple old petrol engine with a distributor and a single carb. Angela didn't know what I was talking about but Dorothy spent ages with me, sitting in the passenger seat, passing tools and talking away – it was lovely and, to top it off, a couple of attempts later, with clean points and spark plugs (I had to borrow a very long plug spanner; they are about eight inches down in the engine!) and a squirt of WD-40 in the air intake (I had no idea where to buy 'easy start' and I knew the carb needed cleaning), we had life and Dorothy was impressed!

To be honest, the engine was a nicety, as we could always treat the van like a trailer and tow it from place to place, though that would have been a bit undignified. However, for our van to be a bar we needed somewhere to keep the cool drinks. This is not trivial if you have sparkling wines, white and rosé, *cidre*, beer and soft drinks for eighty people. The volume is significant. We determined that the

VdV would be pointed towards the château when at the orangery, so the back of the bar was to be on the left. That's what I had to work with and, as there was a significant space between the rear wheel hub and the front seat, my measurements were done for me. The internet provided me with a cooler powerful enough to chill a small walk-in cold room and I set about building my drinks cooler.

Like lots of things, the principles are simple but there are pooh traps. An A+ fridge has more insulation than a D-rated one so I had to make my box as big as possible but lose as little heat as possible. The final design criteria were that the bar staff had to be able to reach the beers at the bottom. I did have to be liberal with the nine-inch grinder to cut out the racking from that side but soon the space was cleared. The solution was a big wooden chest with a cooler at one end and insulated on all sides, including the lids and floor. The four lift-up doors gave access to all the different drinks and it proved effective even on the hottest days. The only slight downside is that it looked like somewhere you could store half a dozen bodies.

Once Dick had the cooler box in place, there was still quite a bit of 'prettying' to be done. It did not matter how much we painted it, the end was never in sight . . . it seemed to go on forever! So we called in Denise, builder mate Steve's wife, for some extra power. After a full week of painting, even Denise was punch drunk but this time the end *was* in sight and it was just a matter of elevating the design and organising it. My favourite bit!

I started off by rummaging in my old Vintage Patisserie kit. I found letters from old shop signs that spelt 'London' and I also dug out lots of old wooden fairground signs because the van reminded me of trailers that you played games on at the funfair. The ones with lots of teddy prizes hanging at the back! The back of the van was painted using chalk-board paint. Using a tracing

technique, I managed to do some rather good chalk-board menus on them!

Our dear friend Sam came for a working man's holiday – he loved the change of scenery from London and we looked after him well on all levels. He painted on the front of the van snippets from our wedding invitation and the all-important words 'Vin de Van'. All that was left was to stock the bar. We'd had our delivery of drinks already, which was being stored in our *cave*, and, as always, Dick complained that I had bought too much! But I took great pride in filling the fridge and adding the racks of glasses. It looked great and the best bit about this was how organised it was. We had a bar. Not just any bar: a bar that allowed us to serve cold drinks at the château and then move across and serve all the drinks needed for the wedding breakfast and evening party. I literally could not wait to serve a selection of perfectly chilled drinks from it!

Before . . .

LOVE Laughter AND HAPPILY·EVER·AFTER Helena & Owen 28·5·17

CHATEAU DE LA MOTTE HUSSON

DV·764·JW

After.

Our measuring wall.

Resurrecting the greenhouse.

Constructing 'château under the stars'.

CHAPTER 8

Summer 2017

Summer officially starts with the longest day, the summer solstice, but it feels like summer has arrived once all the trees and hedgerows are fully in leaf, from about mid-May. With all the foliage, the land around the château takes on a different feel. You cannot see into the woods or through the hedges and shrubs, so wildlife hides away from us. The red squirrels are hardly ever seen and the deer and boar have so much cover and so much daylight that it is only early in the morning as the sun comes up that you can rely on catching glimpses. The exception is the coypu (*ragondin* in French) that seem to love the warming waters of the moat and come out earlier so are easy to watch. I have never been able to work out the name for a baby coypu, it feels like it should be a 'kit' like a beaver of even a 'pup'? However, the young are evident and as they are precocial, born fully furred with open eyes, they can eat vegetation with their parents within hours of birth.

With the arrival of summer comes our urge/ability to work longer hours and I had convinced myself we needed a tractor. There was lots to be moved back and forth around the grounds and rather than hiring something, we felt we needed to invest in our own tractor. In addition, if the VdV did not start, I could tow it! As always in the early days, funds were limited and we wanted the best buy. The first question was whether to go for a large, relatively old tractor or a compact, slightly newer tractor. We decided, if it could get into the walled garden, a compact tractor would be great, so our criteria was to find as big a compact one as we could, which still went through the gate on the side of the walled garden.

I was searching for a second-hand Kubota, or something similar, when I found the Kioti. The reviews for the two were much on a par; however, there was a significant price difference – I could buy a new Kioti for the price of a reconditioned Kubota.

It was like Dick's birthday when his new tractor arrived.

Fair enough, when the tractor arrived, I was like a big kid. I had my very own tractor! It's in the 25-horsepower bracket so is not huge but we don't have a large estate and it fitted through the gates into the walled garden, which was a result. I was ready to tow anything, dig anywhere or even have a go at cutting any grass or brambles!

Whilst the grounds were receiving much-needed love in preparation for the wedding season, work was also progressing on the boudoir. Once decisions are made, it's easy for me to take a project forward. Dick and I had agreed that the sleeping area would be on the left-hand side of the double doors, as it felt quite cosy because it was tucked away. On the right-hand side, at the back, we put up a stud wall, behind which we were to put in a toilet and shower cubicle, but I had made the decision to keep the sink and the bath

just outside so they were part of the room. Dick shook his head, not understanding, but for me it worked and ensured that this room felt open. It also meant that from the doors to the double windows the entire width was free and that, of course, meant space for seating, the bar, the coffee machine, etc.

I have loved the combination of black and gold forever. It's classic, but, in the last decade, it's become a 'fashion' with the popularity of *The Great Gatsby*. Some may get frustrated when the things they love come into vogue and are suddenly everywhere but there are always different ways to perceive change. One year art deco is popular, the next eclectic is popular, then tropical prints are popular . . . It meant that I could take advantage of the trend for art deco designs and buy some more affordable items. First, I bagged some black and gold fern wallpaper, an art deco style trolley, black metro tiles, a second-hand cast-iron bath – which I promised Dick would be the last bath I asked him to bring up the stairs. Then I found some stunning art deco taps for the sink and the bath, a 1950s light that I painted, some mosaic tiles and some red and gold art deco fan material – the same that I had used on Richard and Charlotte's chairs. Who says fashion is a bad thing?

We had a plan . . .

I didn't really have to come to terms with Angela wanting a bath in the boudoir itself, all I had to do was sort the plumbing! I'd actually put in 'T' junctions to the sewerage and hot- and cold-water supplies that fed the loo in the HMS salon. We did that work two years earlier, so it was a matter of getting the local connections right. We have stayed in some hotels with a bath in the main bedroom and it's different to have a 'sociable' bath with your partner sitting in a comfy chair chatting to you. The only issue we would have was emptying the bath. No one really wants to see the waste pipe carrying cold bath water across the room.

The bath was an Angela special: it was a refurbished cast-iron bath with an amazing external paint job that was going to be in keeping with the black tiles and gold grout. Once we had confirmed the location, I managed to route the waste pipe – gently sloping of course – through the yet-to-be-built shower and toilet wall, there to be joined into the shower, then passing into the void between the boudoir and the ceiling of the floor below and finally descending gently to the waiting connection. The lights were to be routed through the floor of the as-yet-unused room above and then chased down the walls into position. The HMS was directly below so I wasn't brave enough to do anything that could cause a problem in the ceiling of the floor below. There's a place for cowardice!

Whilst Angela was hard at work on finishing touches inside, I was enjoying the opportunity to spend more time working outside. I had discovered that there were the remains of an old glasshouse in the walled garden. It would have been an important part of the garden but there was only a vague outline of what was once there left. To get more information we had to dig away stones, metal, broken glass and lots of vegetation that was trying to hide it. I was very excited to start the restoration, as a greenhouse can really extend your growing season and the diversity of what you can grow.

After a good day's work, we knew what we had. It was really impressive – the floor of the building was a pathway that ran the length of it, against the wall, where the sloping glass was at its highest. There was a large bed at the far end and, along the right-hand side, there were four more beds that stretched over a metre to the front of the building. Between each of these side beds was a potting station. The whole greenhouse was about ten metres long.

I was really pleased with the design. The wall faced south-west so it would warm up well and retain heat in the winter and would also absorb heat and help stop the greenhouse overheating in the summer. I particularly liked the fact that you stepped down into the greenhouse and the areas under the potting stations were voids with outlets to the front of the beds, all of which would help reduce frost issues. The wall acts as a heat sink and, on clear winter days, any sun will be captured and heat the walls. They will then give out their heat as the temperature falls. If you think about it, cold air sinks down and, in the greenhouse, that means into the path footwell. This falling air will displace the slightly warmer air there, which will be pushed up. As it's under the potting stations, it would be pushed through the outlets onto the beds, helping to keep the frost off them. It was ingenious – all we had to do was bring it back to life.

From the remnants of the metal window frames we had found, we knew the front of the building had glass panels. The remaining walls gave us the dimensions and the slopes of the original building. We needed to rebuild the arched doorway and the sloping walls at the other end. We'd found the keystone for the arch, so Steve and I built a 'former', a wooden arch that fitted into the elements that were still standing and that we then rebuilt the stonework on top of.

On the rough wall there was evidence of metal spikes having been driven in to support a beam that would have been where the window frames were attached. The original frames to support the glaze had obviously been metal but we rebuilt in wood, which we routed to hold the glass panes. Our materials may have been slightly different but the shape and function of our glasshouse must have been very similar to the original that would have been there. I loved it, and now it was restored, it was time to get it productive!

First, I lined the potting areas, which had a raised brick wall, with plastic that I then filled with gravel. This allowed me to nestle pots of compost into the gravel, so they had a ready supply of moisture. A dozen bags of compost filled the beds and we planted heritage tomatoes, chillies, peppers, cucumbers and aubergines. And then I used the potting trays to bring on salad and beans. There is no doubt about it, a greenhouse is a great place to go to if you want to garden but it's too cold or wet. You can potter around and somehow the world is peaceful.

When we were searching for the château, we visited a very large town house that was for sale. One of the outbuildings had been used as a notaire's office and it had a huge conservatory. I was particularly taken by the magnificent vine that was growing there and had noted that it had been planted outside and the stem came through a hole in the wall, so it grew in the heat of the conservatory whilst being watered and growing naturally outside. I'd said to myself, 'I'll do that one day.' And guess what? That day had arrived.

I bought a muscat grape and knocked a three-inch diameter hole through the base of my new wall. Then I dug a large hole to give it a good start and fed the roots out and planted it. The vine loved it and has gone from strength to strength as it has reached the back wall and spread along it.

I was buzzing off Dick's passion for the newly reconstructed greenhouse in the walled garden. I'll never be a land girl, but I have changed, and this was undoubtedly the start. I was understanding nature first hand and was trying to absorb as much as possible.

Dick had finally allowed himself to get in the garden. I think he always thought of gardening as his hobby and therefore, until the château was comfortable for the family, he simply never allowed himself to indulge in it. However, at this point, with the Strawbridge suite now very comfortable, Dick allowed himself to get stuck in, guilt free – and rightly so. Because he is the most romantic man in the world (in my eyes), he made me a cutting garden. We joke that he never buys me flowers but, boy, did he make up for it with this! I would have never dreamt that I would have my own cutting garden and I got to work straight away, sowing wildflower seeds, lavender and an entire row of purple flowers for a wedding later in the year.

Doing the flowers for a wedding felt quite grown-up. During my Vintage Patisserie years, I always did the flowers as part of the setting and table displays. After quite a pressured set-up, due to never having enough time (because I couldn't get into venues until two hours before the start or because of the short turn-around between events), I used sorting the flowers as my moment to breathe and relax, as they were always the finishing magic.

Weddings are different because you lead with the flower designs and it's often the first thing, even before dates, that brides wish to talk about! Making the bouquets on the day is nearly a formality because by that point the bouquet, the wedding flowers, button-holes, selection, form, wrapping, etc., must already be agreed. As this was all new to me, I wanted to get guidance from someone who was at the top of his game.

Château de Chenonceau, often referred to as the 'ladies' château' due to its substantial influence on prominent women in history, is one of the most famous châteaus in the Loire Valley. It's about two and a quarter hours from our château and is completely magical with its symmetrical turrets and well-manicured grounds. It boasts an amazing in-house florist, which very few châteaus have. They fund him by holding floristry courses. I would not normally take a visit like this alone but I had managed to get a lesson with Jean-François Boucher (the master floral designer). It was quite an honour and I was very excited.

I'll never forget the time I spent in the gardens waiting for Jean-François and Nicolas, the château's botanist. It was mind-blowing – the rows of blossoming flowers, bushes, the greenhouses, the orangery, the *potagerie*. The beautiful vibrant colours and the amazing aromas and smells. I could not take it all in and I felt sad that Dick was not with me. This sort of thing needs to be shared and I made a mental note that we would come back together because the millions of pictures I took did not do it justice!

I didn't realise at that point that the true beauty had not even begun. Jean-François and Nicolas arrived and started talking about their flowers, their vegetables, their grounds and the passion they shared. The way that they touched everything like they were butterflies, and the stories they told about each of the plants and flowers – everything had a reason for being there; be it visual or for the health of the gardens. It's the same passion that Dick has; he speaks in the same way about produce and lovingly touches our flowers. It was a magical hour as we walked and talked . . .

Part of the experience was being allowed to pick blooms. I could not get over the peonies – delicate pinks, white with freckles or fuchsia . . . To this day, I'm not sure I have ever seen such beautiful peony bushes. Jean-François was also very passionate about his foliage and showed me bed after bed of different varieties. One felt like velvet, similar to angel wings, and was called lamb's ears; I guess because it was so soft and very cheap, apparently! It really inspired me to get more variety in our walled garden. I have always loved eucalyptus and most brides do too, but seeing their foliage really opened up my mind to other styles . . .

Holding a huge French wicker basket full of stems to play with, we ventured into Jean-François's workshop. It was a stand-alone little cottage with thick wooden beams, stone and lime plaster. As you would expect, it was bursting with flowers, plants in pots, hanging plants, plants growing out of the walls. The smell was floral heaven and I could not help getting lost for a moment. The next thing that struck me was how well organised he was. Attractive wooden drawers and glass jars lined the walls with all the materials he used: wires, string, decorations. The centre of his workshop was the pièce de résistance: an island where he worked and where we would work together. He kept his picking flowers there, in lovely pots, jars and buckets. It was amazing.

We both had our vessels. To begin, Jean-François showed me how you start to build up your display. He placed everything symmetrically – if he had one rose on the left, there would be one on the right, and if he used a peony at the back, he had one at the front. I think he was a bit put out when I didn't copy him but he did tell me I should follow my instincts and I love my flowers to be asymmetric, with wild grasses, and basically to look like the most amazing collection of wildflowers that you have just picked from your garden! I used mainly roses, peonies and lots of stunning ornamental grasses. I absolutely loved it! At the end, I told him how lovely his display was but he didn't repay the compliment. Mine was clearly wonky! But his passion and workshop inspired me so much and it was a real treat to be there. And the trip gave me great confidence as well; I could not wait to go back and show Dick all the pictures.

Angela's trip to Château de Chenonceau ignited a fire in her for our own flower garden. We had not yet finished shaping our beds to make them neat and formal but we had strips of flowers that would bloom at different times and give variety for Angela to go and pick. Wildflower mixes are a wonderful way to see what you like and they are fairly bombproof when it comes to growing them . . . they are weeds after all, aren't they? The local bees were loving this area of the beds as much as Angela. They worked the lavender and spent a long time going from flower to flower. There was an abundance of bumble bees and solitary bees but not many honey-bees, so I made a note to myself to raise 'getting my hives' up the priority list.

We were being treated to a mild spring and the garden was showing its potential. We have two areas of wild strawberries: the first is on the wall of potager above the moat and the second is on the top of the wall by the north-west of the château. They mature much later than cultivated strawberries and are much smaller and less juicy but, boy, do they have flavour. It is like little concentrated strawberries that have been dipped in perfume.

Dick was planning his garden for the future and although this was his passion, his inspiration was the children and the family, as we all love strawberries. Dick planted the strawberry plants with Arthur and Dorothy so that they would understand exactly where the strawberry came from and we both could not wait to watch them pick their first fruit. It was going to be a very special day.

We planted half a dozen cultivated strawberry plants to start our soft-fruits area, knowing that the shoots they would produce would allow us to go into massive strawberry production next year.

It was a pleasure to pop into the garden. There were courgette plants that were trying to produce more than we could eat, rows of spinach, beetroot and salad leaves, and herbs, plus our glasshouse was paying back all that effort we had invested. As the beds were filled with compost and the space was well tended, somehow the weeds that try to reclaim the garden at every opportunity don't get a hold in there, so it's a little 'we've tamed nature' oasis.

Our tomatoes had started to provide the wonderful fruit that smells of tomatoes. That may seem an odd thing to say, however, all through the winter months you struggle to buy tomatoes that have any smell or indeed taste. There is a list of things that when home-grown will spoil you forever. Being Northern Irish, I'll start with potatoes, then strawberries, then tomatoes, then everything else!

The walled garden wasn't yet the place to come and sit and chill out. There wasn't a groomed area with table and chairs that felt comfortable but it was somewhere peaceful to come and potter or harvest and take things back to the château.

When we sat down to an al fresco lunch it would be outside the château, surrounded by the moat and looking down the driveway. Our first task was to go into the garden and see what was mature and ready to eat. Even though we had not yet set out our raised-bed system, we did have to walk around a number of areas to harvest what was available. Arthur and Dorothy were a great help as they would invariably spot things they thought should be eaten. No ripe strawberry (or, indeed, some green ones) ever escaped and mangetout were shared between the large colander and which-ever child found them. Funnily enough, Angela or I were usually responsible for picking the leaves off the salad bowl lettuce, the rocket or the spinach. Despite tales of Popeye, spinach was only really eaten by the kids if we turned it into soup. And they did love it with gnocchi. I loved the fact that the cherry tomatoes were nibbled like sweets but the large *tomate Marmande* or *coeur de boeuf* were treated with reverence and placed gently down. After our harvest we'd head off to the family kitchen and, if it was a warm day, we'd let the children rinse the leaves with all the carnage associated with running cold water and a job to be done.

Lunch would involve a tray or two of the contents of the fridge and fresh baguettes being brought to the table. We'd add some chopping boards, a bottle of cold *cidre* or a carafe of syrup and sparkling water and some tumblers and plates, bowls and napkins, and everyone helped to lay the table. Often we'd include a fresh soup, made with produce from the garden. When we had spinach to harvest we'd knock up a quick and easy spinach soup as the children loved it and it was so good for them.

....

CREAM OF SPINACH SOUP

Ingredients

1 onion, roughly chopped
50g butter
2 cloves of garlic, chopped
A colander full of roughly chopped spinach leaves (the old
gnarly ones are fine but add more)
100g crème fraîche (and a bit extra to serve)
750ml semi-skimmed milk
1 stock cube
Half a nutmeg, grated
Salt

Method

Soften the onion in the butter, then add the garlic. After two minutes add the spinach.

When the spinach has wilted, add the crème fraîche, the milk, the stock cube and the nutmeg.

Simmer for five minutes, then take off the heat and attack with a stick blender until smooth. If you have a weedy stick blender, put the soup through a sieve to ensure there are no stringy bits of spinach. Test and season (we don't use pepper as its mainly for the children). Serve with a dollop of crème fraîche.

....

On the table, as well as any cold meats or tempting cheeses, we loved having smoked chicken. A green salad with a vinaigrette is essential, as is a platter of thinly sliced, room-temperature tomatoes arranged one slice thick and with a sprinkling of salt. Of course, you can add basil, mozzarella and a drizzle of olive oil, though as our tomato crop is so beautiful I usually wouldn't bother! There is nothing quite so satisfying as watching Arthur and Dorothy mopping up the tomato juice and seeds with a bit of baguette. It's worth noting that the meal could be a wonderful mix of culinary delights but the stars of the show will always be anything from the garden. So speaks a proud gardener!

Not all the produce from the garden had been lovingly tended. There is a period of a couple of weeks from the end of May to the beginning of June when the walled garden holds the sweet fragrance of the elder-flowers. The elder trees around the walls were undoubtedly weeds but we pruned them back to control their spread and the result is masses of the large cloud-like flowers that we can reach. We pick our annual elderflower harvest in the walled garden to make elderflower fizz, elderflower syrup and elderflower fritters. The day has to be warm and dry so the fragrance of the flowers is at its most intense.

We start with making the champagne as it takes a bit of time to ferment before you can enjoy it.

ELDERFLOWER CHAMPAGNE

This champagne is a light, mildly alcoholic drink that is perfect for the warm summer's evenings.

Ingredients

750ml compressed flowers
750g sugar
Zest and juice of 2 lemons
2 tbsp white wine vinegar

You'll also need a five-litre container – we use a massive stainless-steel jug – and plastic carbonated soft drinks bottles and lids.

Method

Mix the freshly picked flowers with five litres of water and stir well. Don't think of washing them as you'll lose all the fragrance.

Stir in and dissolve the sugar. Add the lemon zest and juice and the vinegar. Keep stirring until you're sure the sugar has dissolved and everything is well mixed. Leave in a warm place for twenty-four hours. Strain the mixture into a jug, then pour it into bottles. Screw the cap on well. Leave for at least two weeks and drink within months – this is a real summer treat.

. . . .

ELDERFLOWER FRITTERS

*While you wait for the champagne to go fizzy, it's worth
making another very seasonal treat: elderflower fritters,
which are great served with aperitifs.*

Ingredients

2 elderflower blossoms per person
1 tsp cornflour
50g rice flour
Pinch of salt
100ml fizzy water
Vegetable oil, for frying
Salt and sugar, for sprinkling over

Method

*Tap the blossoms to remove any little insects. Make a simple
tempura batter from the flours, salt and fizzy water (don't
add all the water at once; it just needs to be a thin batter
consistency) and dip the blossoms in the mix. Fry for twenty
or thirty seconds on a high heat and drain on kitchen roll.
Sprinkle with a salt/sugar mix to your liking and garnish with
extra flowers.*

. . . .

Since our first wedding, held here at the château the previous
September, we had been exploring our grounds and improving
our home and our facilities. In fact, although we had put effort
into our Strawbridge suite this year, all decisions outside of this
were to improve our home for celebrations. May had come around

so quickly and I really felt well prepared. The van, of course, was a huge deal but we also had the new botanical suite, which meant that the bride and groom could have their parents or bridesmaids stay on site. There was excitement and buzz and the team, which we were also growing, was ready for the hard work and the pure joy that hosting a wedding brings. We had eight weddings that year between May and September and all the couples were special in different ways.

Helena and Owen were a youthful couple with busy lives, and a love for France and food. Helena was the sweetest and I still remember our very first phone call. She told me that her father had recently passed away and she was keen for all the family to have something to focus on. I was in tears during the call, although I tried to stay professional!

Then came Annie and Trev. Annie was so beautiful and creative – her father Roger initially contacted me and we never looked back. After that was Cheyenne and Martyn. Cheyenne was shy and delightful with a sweet and gentle nature. I wanted her wedding to be just right for her and always kept checking that we were doing what she wanted.

Kate and Phil were next. They visited a number of times and we became close before the wedding even started. They were real grafters and Phil had lots of input and involvement . . . They were wonderful and I was counting down the days to their wedding!

Then there was Sue and Graham. Sue was a six-foot stunner, full of confidence and personality. Graham was shorter than Sue and on our first meeting we heard that they met on a dating site and Graham had lied about his height because Sue had specified that she wanted to meet someone taller than her! They were second timers in the wedding world and had a slightly different outlook on life. We loved them and Dick really had a soft spot for Graham and his grumpy (actually very kind) nature.

Then it was Pete and Emma. Pete and Emma were both very busy with their careers and Emma started a new job just as we started to talk about their wedding, so Pete and I did most of the preparation together. Pete had said to me that he wanted purple flowers at his wedding and so I planted lots of purple flowers in the hope that they would be in bloom in time for their wedding.

Next were Jack and Simon, who wanted a high tea wedding. Well, that was completely up our street and it was nice to do something different. They were so fabulous, as were their family, and they chose Dick's daughter Charlotte to do the photography.

Ian and Janine were the last wedding of the year and they were delightful. Ian was very tall and Janine was a pint-sized beauty. Dick nearly spat out his coffee one morning when Ian told him that he would have paid double for their wedding!

The wedding season had been a joy and the van had paid for itself on the first wedding . . . in fact, I don't know how we coped before it! I was always the last one in the van serving drinks until midnight as most of the staff had done a long day and often needed to work on the Sunday. I loved it; it became a focus point for chatting. I even made Dick agree how *great* the van was.

We also got into a flow. I found a new supplier of flowers; Tina was making the wedding cakes and we were finding our team. We kissed a few frogs but found some princes and, at the end of the season, we felt sad that it was over. But that sadness did not last for long because our list of things to get finished before the end of the year was still long – including the boudoir, the back staircase and phase one of the old stables. Mum and Dad needed to be here, on the island with us, and we would do everything we could to make that happen.

My mum and dad had been simply epic during the wedding season. Their selflessness during the summer to allow us to host these weddings will never be forgotten – they planned all their holidays around it. It was done with a loving and willing heart and, although I knew we would do the same for Arthur and Dorothy, it's still a sacrifice and we appreciate it so much. But they loved it and took the kids away on a few beach holidays for our busiest weekends.

It is very easy to feel a sadness as the summer comes to an end. August sees the end of the holiday season; school starts and the routine returns. By the end of September, it is truly autumn and leaves are starting to make more regular appearances on the ground. The flowers and grasses of the meadow are all but spent and appear to be lying down, getting ready to weather the seasons ahead. However, the end of our wedding season, as well as a time to reflect, is a time to celebrate. We'd done it! We had helped all our couples to have the celebrations they had dreamt of and both our home and our business were going from strength to strength. We had learnt so much and our team was getting stronger.

CHAPTER 9

A Family Trip to Paris

As if in recognition of our achievements over the summer, autumn was heralded by the trees around the château starting to display their most vibrant golds and reds, and unbelievably quickly the season of mists and mysterious beauty was upon us. There may be a simple explanation for the mists of autumn (warm moat, cool air) but that doesn't make it any less surreal as you watch the mist forming on the moat and gently swirling up onto the banks and settling all around us. The trees are not bare in a matter of days or even weeks. It does take a couple of months, with some of them stubbornly hanging on. At least the slow release of leaves allows us to get used to the fact that the year is coming to an end.

With the wedding season behind us, we turned our attention to the work being done on the coach house, which had actually commenced earlier in the year and quietly continued throughout the summer, but not when there was a wedding on. This was to be Jenny and Steve's home. Once the clear-out of the old stables had taken place, we intended to fix it up as a self-contained flat that would eventually be a granny flat attached to the fully converted building. When it was finished, this first stage would be about the same size as the flat Jenny and Steve were currently renting in the village.

The clear-out also involved demolishing the stalls and saving the materials. There was the most amazing floor that was made of granite setts, or blocks, varying in size and depth. They were between six inches and two feet square and about eight to twelve inches deep. Sadly, the floor was sloping and very uneven – definitely not right for anyone's granny – so we had a choice to cover it or take it out. The answer was to take it out and preserve it, so it could be re-laid, more evenly, somewhere else.

To progress the conversion of the coach house, we needed a mains water connection and a septic tank, which in turn all needed to be connected to the filter bed behind the walled garden. It's fair to say Angela was a bit worried. She knew this meant that lots of holes and trenches would have to be dug, in the height of our wedding season! The work to be conducted on the island also needed heavy machinery, and when Bertrand and his nephew Jean-Bertrand told us they were only available on a date between two of our weddings we didn't really have a choice. Angela nearly had a heart attack when she looked out the window. Wedding guests were due to arrive the next day and the front of the château looked like a building site ... But, as I told Angela, it was all carefully planned and Jean-Bertrand promised me he would come back very early the next morning to fill the holes back in, so I had everything crossed that nothing cropped up to distract him.

To say I was worried is an understatement but Dick had promised it would all be all right, so I just had to breathe deeply and wait. To be honest, I was surprised at just how quickly their team put things back together in the morning. The gravel was raked back in position and hosed down so there was no mud evident – I could have hugged them all if they weren't so messy. All the machines were gone before the first guests arrived but it was very close. In fact, I think Jean-Bertrand might have waved to them as he left the château!

In the lead-up to the first wedding, we had done lots of the dog work in the boudoir suite but we'd had to put a stop to this over the summer due to the grime generated whilst renovating. No matter how hard we tried, the dust would be walked through the house and it was a never-ending problem trying to stay on top of it. The second, equally important reason for pausing work on the suite was that I was short of time during the summer and any spare was spent as a family. However, with autumn arriving, and the weddings now completed, it was nice to change the focus back to the boudoir and to get it over the line. We had around six weeks before our first trio-couple food lovers' weekend – and it's always the final part of the work that takes a while to get right.

After a huge push the boudoir – our third suite – was finally complete. Right then, it was my favourite. When the walls had been stripped of the wallpaper it left a stunning patina that I did not want to cover over with paint or wallpaper, so I painted *nearly* everything with a see-through lustre paint that allowed the story to show through. It elegantly sparkled like a pearl. On the back walls, I used the gold and black fern paper – it was meant for that room. Wallpapering the door to get into the bathroom cubicle meant it looked like a hidden/secret door. There was a strange element of surprise that felt nice! On the left, where the bed was, there was a stunning piece of wallpaper hidden under an original old mirror. I left that in place to keep its history and next to it we also retained the original 1880 Paris wallpaper – I mean newspaper! – which had a couple of coats of varnish. Once you take something away, it does not take long to forget it was ever there.

The space for the bed area was small, but a French mahogany antique bed that I had picked up in Emmaus fitted perfectly and left just enough room to walk down comfortably on either side.

The bathroom and toilet were compact and perfect but outside of the cubicle was where the real magic was. I used mosaics on the outer wall around the sink . . . it was a thing of beauty. Originally, I had planned to do so much more but it took so much time; each mosaic was placed individually and then grouted. The finish was an art deco pattern in green and black – it set off that area and made it feel gloriously luxurious.

Opposite the sink was the bath. It was second-hand but I had re-painted the outside gold, then used a pebbled black to finish, which meant the gold colour broke through. It surprised me at the time how good it was! But the black metro tiles covering the entire wall next to the bath along the edge of the vestibule possibly won the prize. After six attempts to get the right gold, in brightness and colour, I found something called 'Goldfinger'. It was perfect and when watered down with some white spirit, it went on very easily. However, it still needed to be hand-painted, grout line by grout line.

Every time I go into that suite, I smile. It's moody and it's different to anything else we have in the château. The red and gold velvet curtains are the first thing you see when you open the double doors, then the art deco bar, and if you decide to swing a right you can't help but clap at the tile work – or maybe that's just me because it still surprises me that we actually finished the job in time! But we did.

By the week of our first triple food lovers' weekend, the boudoir was finished. Cutting it fine, or just on time! Our guests loved it and were thrilled to be the first to stay in the suite. The château was changing before our eyes, and it still felt exciting every day!

But then it dawned on me that for our guests to reach our stunning new shiny boudoir they would need to walk up the back stairs. The honeymoon suite was entered via the grand staircase; the botanical suite was now serviced by the lift, but the boudoir had no other options but to walk up the old servants' staircase. I mean, looking back, it was no big deal. We were renovating an entire château; I'm sure no one would have judged us for having to walk through a few dusty corridors on the way to their beautifully decorated suite. But at the time, I remember thinking how terrible it looked and that we had to do something.

At some point, there had been an old woodburner chimney that went through the walls and the stairs into the main staircase entrance and it had caused such tar damage. I thought plastering it would be a nightmare and was not sure Dick would buy into the expense. So, inspired by what many old French properties do, I had the idea to line the walls with material. From the Middle Ages all the way through to the eighteenth century, tapestries were hung on walls to stop the draughts. They were effective and breathable. My idea was a modern version of this.

I always like things to have meaning, to be connected in some way, and I loved the idea of reproducing the wallpaper museum design onto fabric that could be mounted on the wall here. I photographed every different individual design and pieced it together digitally, similar to the museum style. Unlike the real museum, I needed to create a repeat pattern to print thirty metres' worth. A repeat pattern is easier than it sounds: you just need to ensure that when you join the top to the bottom, and the side to the side, it matches. When you buy patterned wallpaper you should always look to see what the repeat length is, as long repeats end up with lots of wastage.

To repeat a pattern, you cut in down the middle or somewhere lengthways and crossways, if you are matching top and bottom. Then you put the top part of the pattern at the bottom, and the bottom of the pattern at the top. You could replicate this for the side. I must have got carried away, wanting too many designs to be included, because my repeat was 2.3 metres. Once finished, I ordered thirty metres from a company called Contrado. Technology is so advanced nowadays; you can upload any design and choose to repeat it, the size of your pattern and so many other details.

Angela had a vision that I knew would be lovely. When I suggested painting the walls with emulsion, she gave me that look that wives give silly husbands. It's well known that I don't do wallpapering or decorating, so I dodged the bullet on putting the wall coverings up, though I did help erect platforms to try to make the job easier. Our small scaffold platform was perfect for the area at the bottom of the stairs and I managed to lash a step ladder and some scaffolding planks together to work above the steps as the work continued up the stairs. It all got progressively easier as the next floor up had a ceiling that was verging on normal.

Dick and I are a good team for lots of reasons. Partly because we have different skills and partly because we remind each other to take time out. We are doers and it's in our nature to want to get things finished, especially with so much still to do. But we still made the time to go on walks around the château grounds. I'm in awe of Dick's knowledge. He is an encyclopaedia about many things, especially things that interest him, like history, the garden, wildlife, trees and everything, in fact! The kids love the great outdoors because of Dick. I take no credit for it whatsoever. I do, however, make the hot chocolate that we take for our walks. It makes the walk feel like a treat for everyone.

There was something eating our orchard. The trees were having the bark stripped off them and the ground was being turned over. We hadn't lost any trees, yet, so we rushed out and bought the spiral protectors to go around the trunks. However, in addition, we decided to find out what was prowling our grounds, so I bought a very simple little trail camera capable of being triggered by an animal and then filming it. That night, Arthur, Dorothy and I set up a camera and we didn't have long to wait.

We all sat in the salon and I played the card through the computer. The pictures were very eerie initially; all that could be seen was swaying grass, which I assumed must have triggered the camera, but no. Seconds later, there was a pair of eyes shining out of the darkness, illuminated by the infrared bulb that had been activated by the movement. Dorothy was having none of it and did that thing that children can do – from sitting on my knee, she had climbed up and over my body to be behind me in a matter of seconds. Arthur was very brave but managed to get closer to me, which was no mean feat considering we were touching to begin with . . .

The eyes moved out of the gloom and we saw a very large wild boar. The shape of the boar wasn't pig-like – it was all legs, snout and powerful shoulders. We've anthropomorphised pigs so much that to us they are cuddly and nice but the feral nature of a boar is undeniable. The excitement of seeing it rooting around was such that all fear was banished and the children started asking rapid-fire questions. We were over the moon at having filmed the boar but, as if that wasn't enough, the next time the camera was triggered a deer was captured eating our trees! Our woodland never fails to amaze us . . .

*

Life is for living and for a quick break from all the renovations, and a change of scenery, we headed off to Paris for an overnight trip. We couldn't wait to get to know Paris better and felt the children would benefit from a bit of 'culture'. Angela was seeking some advice on restoring/refreshing Howard, the stuffed mallard drake (in France a mallard is called a '*col vert*' – literally a green neck) we'd picked up at a *brocante* to put in the back hallway that we were renovating. So we headed to Maison Deyrolle, a true cabinet of curiosities, full of the most incredible taxidermy. The children and I had a ball looking around the most bizarre collections of insects, beetles, butterflies, whole stuffed animals and taxidermy birds and bits of animals. They were fascinated and Arthur loved the colours and sheens of all the creepy crawlies. I had to remind myself that this was a shop as it could have been a pay-to-get-in museum of curiosities. When Angela had received her advice we walked around as a family. The displays were set up in many rooms over several floors and we marvelled at everything in every cabinet.

Our trip to Paris was a mixture of fancying a change of scenery and a getaway from renovations, so I used Howard, the duck, as the reason to pack our bags. I'll happily use any excuse for a celebration, a trip away or anything miscellaneous to have fun and make memories.

I am a city girl and lived in London for fifteen years. I considered it home and, as both my parents are from the East End, I was virtually a Londoner. When we first found the château, we were delighted to find out that there was a direct train from Laval (twenty minutes from here and somewhere we go to frequently) to Paris and it only takes an hour and a half. Dick and I talked about exploring Paris together – walking the streets hand in hand, finding new places to eat, special places to watch the world go by and enjoy a coffee . . . It's on our list still but in the meantime we were giving Arthur and Dorothy their first ever trip to Paris and it was a delight, made even better by a visit to Maison Deyrolle. The look on Arthur's face when he was standing in front of a real, if very old, lion and Dorothy's delight

when she saw her first unicorn was worth the trip alone. But I also got to find out how to give my taxidermy duck Howard some TLC!

There was so much to buy but we left with just a couple of books to add to our growing collection. One day, we definitely need a library . . .

One of the things we miss from our previous lives is the diversity of food available when you decide to eat out. Near us, we had only found a selection of Chinese restaurants, several pizzerias and one Indian restaurant that would have struggled to survive back in the UK. Paris offered us the variety we had been missing and I think Angela and I surprised ourselves when we found a lovely little Thai noodle restaurant very near the hotel and knew it was right. It was packed and the tables were crammed in. We asked if there was a table for four just as four people stood up and within seconds we were seated and enjoying the atmosphere. We must have been hungry as we ordered enough dishes to cause the lovely, smiley young lass to raise her eyebrows.

We had a bottle of fizzy water and 'cocktails' for the children, which was a multi juice with a splash of grenadine so it looked like a tequila sunrise – very 1970s, I thought, then realised Angela probably wouldn't get it. We had asked for the food to come as it was ready rather than in courses as Dorothy was starting to gnaw her arm. We shared the first dish between us and it was devoured – it may have been chicken but we'll never know as it was gone too quickly. The individual dishes were not large but they all tasted different, which was wonderful. We'd ordered some gently spicy tom yum soup that balanced the lime, the sweetness of the tomatoes and the chilli. We also enjoyed:

- Honey-marinated pork skewers
- Sweetcorn cakes

- Crispy spring rolls – for dipping
- Crispy prawns – four portions!
- Pad thai
- Flat-noodle vegetable dish
- Beef stir-fry with Thai basil

We had all had an elegant sufficiency so had no room for pudding but we promised the children an ice cream the next day. Twenty metres down the road and we were in our hotel. We arranged ourselves in our family room and, after quick showers, we cuddled up with the children for our night-time story (usually made-up adventures of two wonderful children, Arthur and Dorothy, who are so good and brave and do nice things . . .). Twenty-five minutes later, every Strawbridge in Paris was asleep.

Returning to the château, we were soon busy sorting out not only the back staircase, but what would be Angela's parents' – Jenny and Steve's – new home. The old stable was just the first phase of the coach house conversion but it required all the infrastructure for the coach house to be in place.

Having stripped everything out, it was time to build a complete flat in the void we'd created. There was to be a bedroom with en-suite shower room, a separate loo accessible from the main room and the bedroom en suite and a large open-plan sitting room kitchen-diner that might become a utility area when the rest of the building was finished. There were many discussions about where the walls were to go. The only restrictions we had were that the windows and external doors had to stay as they were.

When the decisions were made, it was time to erect stud walls and insulate anything that didn't move. It's not very glamorous but insulating your property is one of the most important eco-projects you can do and, as Papi Steve likes to live in a hot house, it is financially important too! We had insulation under the damp-proofed floor, insulation behind the studding on the walls and a very large amount over our heads.

We were making good progress when I discovered that Jenny and Steve really, really wanted a large walk-in wardrobe. I tried convincing them that their bedroom suite in phase three would have a walk-in wardrobe to throw parties in but they needed one now, so the problem was how to make it happen.

We designed it on the back of a piece of plywood. There were four simple rules:

- Big enough
- Dry and airtight
- Good 'sealable' doors
- All material to be reusable after it was taken down

The walk-in wardrobe was built, lined and insulated over a period of two days. Another half day saw lights and sockets in there. It was temporary but would be good for several years – it was also to be a spare room should Arthur and Dorothy come and stay with their grandparents. The structure was sawn four-by-two; we didn't even cut the four-metre lengths but left them sticking up and into the old void at the end of the building that would eventually become home to their heating system.

Being practical about it, we decided we had to order all the windows and doors we were going to need in one go so that they matched and were available as and when we required them. Enquiries in France were not promising; everyone we spoke to said they would take at least three months and the prices were eye-watering. In the end, we ordered from Essex. Delivery was three weeks and the cost, including getting them to us, was about half of the three local quotes we'd had.

Builder mate Steve was busy plastering anything that looked smooth enough and with the studding, insulation and then plasterboard on, you could see exactly what the flat would look like. Everyone was impatient for it to be finished but we still had all the electrics and plumbing to get in, as well as sourcing the bathroom suites and kitchen surfaces and cupboards. It was relentless but with the knowledge that decisions had to be made and everything had to turn up, be installed and tested or our schedule would slip, everyone somehow kept things coming and every week there was a massive step forward! Our ability to work on lots of tasks simultaneously never fails to surprise me. What it does mean is that there is always something for our team to do rather than having to down tools and wait.

Meanwhile, back in the château, the back staircase was being finished in time for our guests. At first, it was a fairly simple job and lots got done very quickly. We made the wall panels the width of the fabric, which was stapled, over Dacron, to the walls. The edges were covered over with nicely painted batons. With thirty metres of fabric, two panels even matched sideways on the repeats. This soon stopped when we realised there was nowhere near enough fabric to repeat-match. But luckily, because the panels were separated by the batons and the material was busy, it worked out fine in the end.

The tricky bit, which took about three times as long as everything else, was the unusual architecture of the walls. There was lots of cutting and tucking and I had no chance on the high bits. I was just that little bit too small! Once it was done it looked rather special though. Then it was coated with a fire retardant and given a 3D shape with hundreds of upholstery tacks, which took forever. But it was worth it. Because of the Dacron underneath, it gave the walls an incredible shape. Dick named it 'the padded staircase' and it is a joy to behold.

The year was progressing rather quickly and for my birthday this year Angela had a very special plan. I think she was trying to impress me after booking a wedding on my birthday last year. She tried to keep it a surprise but the hot air balloon that was outside our house was sort of a giveaway ... I'd been fortunate enough to ride in a balloon before and knew how wonderfully sedate and peaceful the trip was and how stunning the views would be. What would be even more special was to look at the setting of our château from above and have an opportunity to appreciate the countryside around us from a bird's-eye perspective.

When I saw the balloon out in front of our château I was so excited that I didn't think to warn Angela that getting into the basket could not be done elegantly; that the duration of the flight would be determined by the elements and that no one actually knew where we would land ... they'd follow and then try to get to us.

I was completely terrified about going up in the balloon but I could not think of anything more magical. The morning was interesting. It was on and off for two hours because of fog. I could hardly cope with the stress! When we got the all-clear, there was still the remains of a tiny amount of mist, which made it look like Narnia. The take-off was quite sudden; as we were getting in, there was a blast from the burners and it only took a couple of seconds to be above the château, rising and heading off towards the village. The smile on Dick's face made it all worthwhile – we were beaming.

I was struggling to take everything in as we took off. We didn't say much other than pointing and going, 'Look, look!' I remember registering that the far side of the roof looked a bit tired, then thinking, 'It doesn't matter! It's beautiful.' The countryside around us was slightly foggy but as you looked back to the River Mayenne, it was covered in a strip of mist that looked as if someone had stretched a cloud and placed it on the river. As we climbed, Mayenne became clear back to our right and the gently rolling countryside had many more trees and patches of woodland than either of us expected.

The flight was all too soon coming to a close and, as the pilots started to descend, we startled some deer and wild boar with a blast of the burner. They galloped away and it was hard to believe any balloon flight anywhere could have been better. A point reinforced when we made the most delicate of landings in a field by a road.

*

On one of our family walks around the grounds we stopped by a rather full tree that seemed to 'just appear'. I have no idea how it happens but sometimes we just discover that a tree is full of fruit and we have a glut from a source we were unaware of. Which is exactly what happened with a plum tree on the way to the orangery in September. I only noticed it when the tree was ladened with dark violet-blue plums. There were hundreds of them, so I immediately declared it to be a Plum Jam Day and we set about collecting as many as we could. They were so sweet and everyone was allowed to eat as much as they wanted; Arthur and Dorothy had a ball. It was a whole family outing and to the plums we found on the way to the orangery we added those on an old tree in the walled garden. We needed the garden trolley to take our booty back to the kitchen.

I'm a sucker for a plum chutney but I knew we would be having a 'glutney' before the end of the season so there would be no shortage. So plum jam was the order of the day.

The family kitchen.

The boudoir.

The padded staircase.

Hot air balloon.

Easter 2017.

The *tresoire*.

Special memories.

Château under the stars – the beginning.

I don't use recipes for jam and believe in keeping it simple. Equal quantities of fruit to sugar gives you a 50 per cent fruit jam. Commercial jams are anywhere between 25–50 per cent fruit but half and half is easy to remember and fruity! The only thing you have to know is that pectin in the fruit makes jam with a spreadable consistency but if you are short of pectin then you have to increase it by adding actual processed pectin or some citrus fruit like lemons to beef up the pectin levels. It was a revelation that *sucre pour confiture* is available in every supermarket when homegrown fruits are abundant, as are slabs of a dozen jam jars. You are expected to make jam here!

Plums have a high pectin level so it couldn't be easier. Out came our copper jam pan. This can cause all sorts of debate. Is an unlined copper jam pan bad for you? From my perspective, it appears that cooking something with a high sugar content in an unlined pan has been declared not to be dangerous. It's what jam was traditionally cooked in as the even heat distribution allows you to get up to temperature quickly, ensuring a fruitier taste, and, finally and most importantly, it's part of our jam-making ritual.

Start by putting a side plate in the freezer. Once the plums are washed and the excess water has been shaken off, they go into the pan with an equal weight of sugar poured on top. We heat and stir continuously until the plums are cooked – they don't take long. Then pass them through a sieve or colander to catch all the stones – or you can set about fishing stones out. Or you could destone before you start – the choice is yours!

Now put the mixture back in the pan and continue to heat, stirring all the time. When you are making jam it's usually ready when your mix reaches 104°C, so you'll need a jam thermometer to hand. Then you are ready for your set test to see if the jam has the right jammy/jelly consistency:

- Get your plate out of the freezer
- Spread a teaspoon of jam on the plate
- The jam will cool immediately. Push your finger through the jam and it should form a bow wave in front of your finger . . .
- Lick your finger

Make sure you sterilise your jam jars. Ten minutes in an 80°C oven on a baking tray will be enough. And if you lift the whole tray out you can fill directly into the jars using a jam funnel so you'll make less mess.

Screw the lids on when it's hot, then double check the seal is tight before it cools too much. Let the children lick out the pan and utensils – you'll convert them to jam making and have less to wash off. There is always a not-quite-full jam jar – it's the law. So, as a family, we sit around the kitchen table with fresh bread, cold butter and warm jam and play pass the yummy jam on bread until it's all gone, or you feel sick.

When we first dreamt of a new life in France, the foundations always involved multi-generational living. We even asked my nan to move with us, which would have meant four generations together, but she had lived in the East End for too long and was too stubborn to move. Families supporting each other works but everyone must have their space and their independence. Right at the top of the list way back in 2015 was getting our planning permission for the coach house so it could become a proper home for my parents.

We had to get the sewerage report done first but as soon as we were good to go the work on the roof of their outbuilding started. This was a project needing investment and time and we had to spread the load over phases. We would have done anything to get Mum and Dad here quicker but it was simply not possible with so many big projects needing attention. Most of the building was

a shell but we were here to stay and, bit by bit, we would build their dream home.

Phase one was undoubtedly the biggest phase. It included getting permission, putting foundations in for the floor, re-doing the entire roof, ordering all the windows and starting the infra-structure of the electrics. The flat that took shape in the old coach house was small but perfectly formed and had all their home comforts. It was modern, light and, best of all, near to us. Putting pictures up of family was the best part. It was the start of their forever home and was a real moment.

Making the transformation from derelict outbuilding to a comfy granny flat may just have been stage one but it was undoubtedly the biggest step upwards. Even after we'd got to the point where there was no sign of the stables and we had double-glazed glass doors leading into a large living space (complete with windows with more double glazing and doors leading off to the suite with a shower, toilet and walk-in wardrobe that could only be described as a great big room), we had a lot of cosmetics to do, including plenty of painting, tiling and cupboards and work surfaces to put in. It was busy but everyone could see we were so close, so it was just a matter of putting the hours in.

We finally got the flat finished in time for winter. It was well insulated and modern on the inside but the coach house retained all of its original character on the outside. And, most importantly, Jenny and Steve had electricity in all the right places, hot and cold running water (out of actual taps) and a fully functioning sewerage system. The coach house had jumped from the nineteenth to the twenty-first century!

Mum and Dad's style has changed from when my brother and I were growing up. These days, it's ultra-modern, but they do live in France, so using second-hand French linen, I made some soft furnishings to add a touch of French chic to their new home. I cracked up when Mum gave me the bedding back. She loved it but they knew they would not use it! However, they kept the cushions, made from old French linen tea towels, and my dad adored the lights that Dorothy and I made from old negatives. When Mum made a cup of tea to celebrate, it was the best bloody cup of tea ever and I could even see the vision of Arthur and Dorothy running over in the morning to them and leaving Dick and I to have a lie-in. We just needed the kids to be a bit older, but the principle still made us all smile.

Moments like this made me realise that even though we were busy and hadn't yet managed to achieve the two-hour French-style lunches, we were living our dream.

CHAPTER 10

Winter and Family Fun

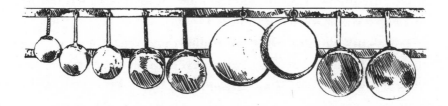

Autumn at the château is stunning. The trees slowly start to lose their leaves and the tips of the branches turn soft hues of orange. Then the rest of the leaves fall and turn copper and mustard, and our walks around the grounds start to sound crispy. There is a moment in autumn when you start to feel excited for Christmas and getting your winter wardrobe out ... and then you tell yourself off for wishing your life away! But there was a real comfort this autumn that we hadn't had before. For the first time, we had enough cash to pay the heating bills in the château without fretting, and Mum and Dad were finally living on the island. It felt like the plan we had talked about years ago had finally been accomplished and having us all together made everything feel easier. Their support meant the world to us and after such a busy year and wedding season, we really felt we wanted to change our focus. Well, for the time being, at least, while we could.

There is always so much on our to-do list that is linked to the business and obviously we have to do the urgent and important tasks first. This can lead to many things that we *want* to do dropping off the end or being so far down the list that they are hard to see. But as winter arrives and the temperature drops, we have fewer visitors that must be looked after and can think more about ourselves and what we want to do a little more. So we check out the less important, less urgent tasks that we want to do because we want to do them!

I was in complete agreement with Dick on this. Our dream was not all work and no play. Although there was still work to do, we were on a mission to change the balance.

One such task was sorting out our copper pan collection. Copper pans are undoubtedly a very effective way to cook. My eldest son, James, had bought me a large Mauviel steel-lined copper sauté pan when I was doing *MasterChef* and I loved it and had used it for many different recipes. Copper also looks wonderful arrayed in the kitchen, which I know helped make Angela a copper pan convert. For me, there is also something special about using a material that conducts heat so efficiently and is meant to last several lifetimes. In France, they have a pan for every purpose but, after a little investigation, you will find buying a copper pan is not as straightforward as choosing one that is meant for the task you have in mind.

We've done a fair amount of research and have now agreed there are a number of copper pan pooh traps:

- Lots of modern pans have an exterior 'copper lining' for the look – but it may not even be copper. 'All fur coat and no knickers' is the phrase that comes to mind. These pans have the thermal characteristics of the main material they are made of.

- When you see an old set of copper pans for sale on the internet, the photos seldom show the interior – that's often because they're worn or tarnished, which is hard to refurbish, by the way.
- The thickness of the pan also makes a difference. My main sets tend to be 3mm but if I find an unusual pan, like our egg poacher, I'll buy it no matter what the thickness.
  - Thin pans (i.e. those less than 2mm) don't hold the heat and, though not fragile, aren't as robust.
  - Anything thicker than 3mm means it takes longer to heat up and is not as responsive.
  - You may argue that 7 or 8mm of aluminium heats up as evenly as 3mm of copper, but it's not as responsive.
- The lining on modern pans tends to be stainless steel. It is durable and doesn't react to the contents.
- Don't buy old pans with the idea of re-tinning them unless you know how to do it or where to get it done. Otherwise, your pans will just be ornaments.
- Don't clean tinned pans with abrasive scourers. Obvious, but . . .
- Be careful what you wish for. Large, thick copper pans are also very heavy.
- If you have OCD, be aware that copper pans need lots of shining . . .
- Bear in mind that tinned pans can't be used at temperatures above about 240°C as the tin lining melts, so they are not well suited to high heats for searing.

We've collected sets of pans for as little as €20 at a *vide grenier* and even picked up a lovely copper fish kettle in great condition with a liner for €12 at a charity shop. On the internet or at *brocantes*, we have also bought the most unusual-shaped pans, from a deep, rectangular *daubière* to a diamond-shaped *turbotière*, and we love them, but they needed some attention and so we decided it was time to take a batch to be renewed.

A bit of research found us a workshop in Villedieu-les-Poêles, in Normandy. It was only an hour and a half north and they said they would do any pans we wished to bring along. In the past, it was not unusual for artisans to congregate in certain geographical locations and Villedieu-les-Poêles was the chosen home for the *chaudronniers*, or coppersmiths. It was a very interesting trip and we should have realised the town was going to be full of shops selling copperware.

Our chosen workshop had a small visitors' centre and it was possible to watch re-tinning taking place. As with all professionals, they made it look easy. The pans were put over a fierce heat and some form of natural rag-like a bundle of cotton was used to wipe out the very hot, melted old tin lining. Once the inside of the pan was rubbed, it seemed miraculously to look like new. Then some new tin was put in, melted and swished around. The excess was emptied and the pan was 'polished'. It only took moments and brought the pan back to life. The final flourish was to wipe the outside of the pans with their special copper polish – 'available at the gift shop' – to make it gleam like new. It was done like a show and the artisan was obviously full of French banter as everyone laughed and smiled along. Even Arthur and Dorothy clapped at the end.

The cost of tinning a pan was calculated by multiplying the diameter by the diagonal height from the inside bottom to the top of the opposite side, then multiplying that number by a number of euros. The multiplying factors seemed to vary ... The bottom line was, they made up a price and we paid it. It was a good deal though, as we had sourced our pans cheaply, so paying €15–20 each still gave us reasonably priced, good-as-new, professional-quality copper pans.

The first set of copper pans I ever bought was for Dick. I had done lots of research so I knew that the inside needed to be in good condition. I got them on eBay and, although at the time I did not think they were cheap at £175 for the set, I remember him mentioning how much the single pan had set James back, so in actual fact these appeared to be a bargain! It was complete luck that they were 3mm copper pans and although I may have taken the credit for pretending that was on purpose, it was a lucky accident. Dick loved them, the weight of them, he loved using them and they looked great in our kitchen!

It started a bit of a love affair for us both and buying copper pans as bargains off the internet or from charity shops was a frequent activity. In the early days, we were always looking out for pans at boot fairs but it was not until we moved to France that we found any magnificent deals. Over the years, we had purchased lots of pans that needed re-tinning. Dick's proudest pan was his 80cm roasting pan. These cost thousands to purchase shiny and new. We also found a very rare egg poacher and a number of 'loved' pans and lids where the tinning had simply come off from use. But without the tinning, they are no use, so this trip was not only fascinating and quite romantic, it was essential to get our pans back into working order.

The workshop was very charming; in fact, it felt like you were visiting a re-enactment of the way people lived in the eighteenth century, or even earlier. It was very enchanting as well and planted the seed for the idea of having a copper bath. They were making a commissioned copper bath and it was honestly one of the most stunning and elegant pieces of workmanship I have ever seen.

Arthur and Dorothy had been so well behaved, so we popped into Bar de Dinandier as they were serving lunch and we promised them a treat. It was on the main street and was just so French, with rattan café chairs, old pictures on the wall, chandeliers and lots of dark wood panelling. After having confit duck, which Dorothy became possessed eating as it was that good, we spotted someone else having a café gourmand, an espresso on a plate full of patisseries, and it looked so good we had a couple of those and shared them with the children – the puds, not the coffees!

We talked all the way home about the day and all the pans we had seen that were on our wish list. It was lovely and peaceful, the roads were windy and the kids fell fast asleep. I felt very lucky and blessed and giggled to myself that I actually thought that tinning copper pans was romantic!

Back at the château, a couple of days later, I must have been feeling romantic too because after all the pans were tidied away, I invited my wife to join me for a drink on a recent purchase of mine.

We have lots of alders around the moat to keep in check and to cut down, moat walls to look after, etc., and although I could have bought a barque – a robust dinghy – I thought a sturdier working platform was the way to go . . . so when I found one which could hold a boat, I was excited. After it was assembled, I did some great 'pruning' and it felt completely stable to work from, to the extent that I was using a chainsaw whilst I was standing on it.

The idea of having a drink together on the platform was not so random – as we often have a glass of port on the steps outside the château in the evening as it's within earshot of the children but allows us to soak up the last golden moments of the day. These moments are precious and we savour them when given the chance, even though our lives are ridiculously busy and most of our spare energy is spent on the children. Papi was babysitting that particular evening, so I fetched a decanter and some glasses, laid rugs and cushions down, and, very unlike me, I even got some twinkly lights. The night was still, unbelievably still, and the moon shone on the moat, as did the reflections of the lights from the château's windows. The moat was twinkling, the lights on the pontoon were twinkling and the stars in the sky were crystal clear. It was lovely. So lovely that it all backfired because Angela came up with an idea . . .

And, as a result, you could say 'château under the stars' is my fault!

The floating romantic platform was genius. Firstly, I expected the platform to at least tip a little when I stood on it, but nothing, not even a wobble. It was as solid as stepping onto dry ground. Dick had pushed the boat out and it looked stunning.

What Dick may not have realised was that I was looking into our next revenue-earning project. I had been looking at geodesic domes, the luxurious ones you stay in when you go to the North Pole! They are very cosy and have windows at the top, which are excellent for looking out at the stars. Originally I thought we could have one on the other side of the walled garden in a charming area that is private but looks onto the side of the château. But sitting there, with Dick, having a glass of port, gave me shivers and, although I was loving our romantic moment, I was also thinking, 'This is it!' It was my eureka moment for our next project: the dome should be floating, looking out at the château, under the stars. And that's how 'château under the stars' was born.

*

Another task on our 'not urgent but would like to do' list was capturing how much Arthur and Dorothy had grown. 'Where does the time go?' is something we all say and hear on a regular basis. But where does it go?! The year had flown by. It's actually such a privilege to write about our journey in this book and to share it with you because the details and the nuances of everyday life can become a bit blurry unless you sit and think about them, so we try to capture them when we can. I'm all for writing a diary again!

In the playroom wall, we have 'Arthur & Dorothy's Playroom' painted in a green fairground font and just next to this is where we record their heights. We had last measured the kids in January and now, in October 2017, we were about to measure them again to see if they had been eating their greens!

They most certainly had. Both Arthur and Dorothy had grown around three inches. Dorothy explained it was due to eating all the spinach that we had grown that year. Case rests – all the effort put into the walled garden had paid off!

We always have quite a giggle measuring the children, and you know what is going to happen before they do it but the jokes never wear thin. Arthur stands on tiptoes. Having been caught out before, he changed his tactics, so when I checked his feet they were perfectly flat on the ground but, during the small amount of time it takes to move up to his head with the ruler, you can feel him levitate. This happens a couple of times but eventually we get an approximately accurate reading.

Dorothy has a different approach; somehow the shoes worn with her ensemble are the highest heels she has and fashion dictates that she wears her ponytail at the top of her head. After lots of incredulous comments, we cotton on to her ruse and our bare-footed, flat-headed gorgeous daughter is measured. It's my job to pretend Mummy has shrunk and I have grown by using the old 'not horizontal' ruler trick! Let's hope we don't shrink during our measuring years because I'm sure the children will think I'm cheating.

*

With romance in the air, we were on a mission to carry on sucking the marrow out of the bones of life. I'm sure I could count how many times I have had truffles and they have all been with Dick. In fact, the first time I had truffles was on 14 November 2010 when Dick did a pop-up restaurant in south London. It was the night we officially met, or officially fell in love at least, and is how we chose our wedding day, so I'll never forget it. Dick cooked pigeon and accompanied it with a risotto, which had shavings of truffle on top. I remember thinking the taste had spoiled me forever and that I needed to have this flavour with everything from now on: eggs, toast, burgers, steak, pasta … Okay, I won't list everything, but you get the idea; it was delicious.

Since then, although we had the pleasure of having them on special occasions, I had always wanted to visit a truffle hunt. However, on visits to France in the past, every time we found a 'farm' it was closed or out of season. Dick had talked about how truffles could be cultivated and had regularly investigated to see what was happening in our vicinity. When he discovered a château-owning truffle farmer within day-trip distance of us he got our outing organised. This was a date, an honour and a complete education. I even wore my green Hunters Dick bought me when we first got together and, to complete my outfit, Dick's dad's hat that we keep in our turret. It was a special occasion.

Truffles are popular in lots of dishes and we love them, so when we heard that it may be possible to grow truffles we thought it warranted investigation. For the techies, truffles thrive on alkaline soils with a pH of 7.5–8.5, but before we tested to see if we could match that, we headed south to a truffle farmer, a *truffière*, whose family had a major business growing truffles and selling them in Paris. Patrick's family cultivated truffles to help finance their ancestral château, which was two and a half hours south-east of us on the edge of the Loire-Anjou-Touraine national park.

The visit was inspirational. The trees that had truffle spores in their root system were mainly holm oak, and each tree had a circle of lightly tilled and raked soil under its canopy. Groups of trees were parcelled together and surrounded by a locked fence and gate. The whole estate was neat and our truffle-hunting expert was a lovely and very handsome little dachshund. Apparently, pigs aren't used as they eat too many before you can stop them. It wasn't long before we were on our hands and knees digging where the dog indicated and, lo and behold, we found a truffle about the size of a decent conker, to be told it was worth €50–100! Our search continued and we were finding truffles every couple of minutes! It was amazing, but what was even more fascinating was that, if you put your nose on the ground where the dog started scratching, you could actually smell the truffles in the earth. It was like searching for treasure that continuously regenerated.

It brought back childhood memories of going to visit my grandparents. At the bottom of their long terrace garden was a neatly trimmed 'money bank'. The bank was a seat where we would have a cup of tea but, miraculously, when the children searched in the roots of the grass we would always find coins. Pennies, ha'pennies, farthings, the occasional twelve-side thruppence and the very rare sixpence. It took quite some time for us to realise this was our grandparents' way of giving us children pocket money without actually giving it to us . . . Patrick's bounty was all generated by mother nature but the thrill of searching to see what could be found was not unlike us youngsters being allowed to visit the 'money bank'.

Just before we left, we popped into the kitchen to view the 'harvest' and to buy some truffles. We were offered a small slice of a homemade truffle tart, which was very rich and very tasty. We were far too polite to stare at what was left in an 'I would love more' way but I did ask for the recipe. It was either a family secret or no one knew, but I felt I had enough knowledge to go and make our own version . . .

Patrick's passion was contagious and his commitment to their family estate was extraordinary. He was extremely proud of it and we could see why. He talked about every vineyard section with deep understanding and a true gentleness. In fact, he was a complete gentleman. I took my hat off to him that he worked in Paris full-time in the corporate world and in his lunchtime he would sell the truffles to the most exclusive and high-end establishments. His drive to make it work poured out of him and we could relate to this.

Watching the truffles being dug up was also everything I had hoped it would be. I had fantasised about how exciting it would be, finding a truffle in the ground. And not only did it not let me down, it exceeded all expectations. I felt addicted and when Patrick said it was time to go back to the house, I was disappointed. But I put a big smile on and said okay, when in actual fact I wanted to say, 'Just one more!' Back at the house the tart made up for it. It was one of the best I had ever had. I'm sure the generous amount of truffle shavings on top helped, or maybe it was because we had not eaten all day, but I dreamed about the tart for weeks after . . .

We left having bought a couple of small truffles, determined to see if we could become *truffières*. Not for business purposes, because Patrick had proved to us it was a full-time commitment, but for personal use and enjoyment.

On our return, I was straight on the internet and bought a soil-testing kit and a pH tester. The big question was: could we grow our own? The results when they came in were a little low but that was not enough to put me off. We went ahead and bought some agricultural chalk and started preparing some areas of the front paddock for our special trees.

The truffles we had brought home went a long way: one was vacuum packed and frozen, and we put four slices of the other into a bottle of cognac and left it to infuse. After two weeks, I could use that bottle to make very quick sauces. All it takes is for thick cream to be heated up until it bubbles, then it's taken off the heat and a good splash of the truffle cognac and a little salt is added – amazing! But especially good with chargrilled, griddled steak.

We set about perfecting our own truffle tart and, without being too modest, the first attempt was bloody good.

....

TRUFFLE TART

Ingredients

For the filling:
3 eggs plus 2 extra yolks
Truffle shavings – as much as you wish to use
300ml double cream
White pepper

For the pastry:
100g chilled butter, cubed
200g plain flour

And you'll need an eight-inch loose-bottom tart tin and
some baking beans

Method

Beat the eggs and yolks, add in the truffle shavings, the cream and white pepper and beat a little more. Set aside while you make the pastry.

Rub the butter into the flour with your fingertips until it takes the form of crumbs. Then add two or three tablespoons of cold water and knead into a single lump. Wrap it in clingfilm and chill for at least thirty minutes.

Roll out the pastry and line the tin with it, then chill it for another twenty minutes to reduce shrinkage. Prick the base with a fork, then put baking paper in the tin and your baking beans on top and bake blind at 170°C for fifteen minutes. Remove the parchment and beans and return to the oven for a further five minutes. Turn the oven down to 140°C.

Give your egg mix a quick stir – you should be able to smell the truffles! Pour it into the case and bake for approximately thirty minutes. There should be a slight wobble in the middle when you bring it out.

Allow the tart to cool before removing from the tin and cutting into slices. It's lovely with a simple green salad, lightly dressed.

. . . .

Of course, Dick's truffle tart was the best I've ever had! I'd highly recommend trying it.

If you think about it, fruit and nut trees are the least amount of work for the highest yields. They may have been neglected here but, spread around our land, we have inherited walnut, sweet chestnuts, cobnuts, sloes, cherry, cherry plum, quince and pear trees and every year they produce an abundance.

It took us a couple of years to realise we also had a perry pear tree. I had no idea what the French was for the little hard pears, as they just called it *poiré*. Perry, the pear equivalent of cider, is nowhere near as common as cider and the reason appears very simple. I was told perry pears are hard to wash and prepare. The dense little pears sink and don't float, like apples do, which makes the washing process more complicated.

There were thousands of pears on the estate that could only be used to make perry. An idea started to take shape. We had a *cave*, yet to be filled with alcohol, so why not make our own *eau de vie*, or 'water of life' – basically high-octane fire water? We had been given some at different times by neighbours, the most lethal being made from mirabelle, which are small, fragrant plums, and, when you had a drink, your sinuses were cleared and your nose began to run.

We started by collecting all the pears and then I headed off to our local distiller to get some advice. The process is relatively simple: you ferment your fruit until you get an alcoholic mush. That is then strained and put into a still to be distilled and then you capture the resulting clear spirits, which are very alcoholic. The family-run operation was about thirty minutes from the château and everyone in the family seemed to be involved. It was like a well-oiled machine. Having said it was simple, the eighty-seven-year-old grandmother who was preparing some of their fruit told me off for not having pulled out all the stalks of the pears before I turned up. I didn't know! Apparently, the extra tannin in the stalk has an adverse taste, so I set about de-stalking masses of pears (another reason perry pear preparation is problematic) before they were processed through an industrial-size masher and put back into my large plastic bins.

When we make cider or country wines, it is all about harvesting the juices and saving the flavours. Then it is the juice that is fermented. As the fermented liquid was not the final product, no one seemed to care too much that it looked like a vat of sick. I was told to add some sugar, put an air lock on it and come back when it stopped bubbling. So that is exactly what I did.

It took the best part of six weeks before I determined the fermentation was over. I'd explained to Arthur and Dorothy that the yeast, which was naturally on the pears, would eat the sugar in the fruit, pee alcohol and fart the CO_2 bubbles. They loved it and understood the principles!

When I arrived back at the still, I took my precious mash into the building and it was poured into a big vat, which was sealed and a fire was lit under it. There were a selection of pipes and coils and cooling liquids but at the end was a copper pipe where our *eau de vie* would come out.

The initial distillate was around 70 per cent proof but it reduced as the alcohol was diluted with more water. You don't just drink it to see if it's good – you take a drop onto your hands and rub them together (killing all germs?), then you cup your hands over your nose and mouth and breathe in. It was amazing – you get the essence of your fruit along with a good clearing of your nasal passages. It smelled great to me and when I questioned the experts, they all nodded sagely and said it was good! Our *eau de vie* was delivered to me in big glass flagons and was 45 per cent alcohol, which I felt was strong enough, and so it was time to do the paperwork.

Just to be very clear, this was not moonshine. There are strict rules and duties to be paid. We paid by the litre and it was cheaper than buying whiskey, and as it was ours it was so much more special. With a bit of magic our pears had been tuned into the 'water of life'. As I was leaving, I was told the paperwork meant I had two hours to transport the flagons home or I could be fined by the *gendarme*.

Then, as a parting comment, I was told we should wait three years before we bottle and drink it . . . three years?! He must have seen that I was crestfallen so he showed me his supply of bottles and I promptly bought some pear and some raspberry. A small but tasty consolation.

One of the things we love most about living at the château is that we are surrounded by history but we are also always planning for the future as we simply cannot see ourselves living anywhere else. Every time we invest in the place, from our heating to our windows to the garden, we are thinking of making sure it's the best it can possibly be for Arthur, Dorothy and the next generations.

We inherited two quince trees that have been prolific and that we have harvested from every year, but they are very old. We have planted some fruit trees in the walled garden but we can picture a time in the not-too-distant future when we have fruit trees producing more than we can use. As part of that image, there is an orchard with geese or pigs roaming around it. Only problem is that for such a vision we need an orchard, so we decided to bite the bullet and buy twenty fruit trees of varying types so we would have a mixed orchard of quinces, apples, pears, cherries, plums, damsons and even mulberries.

We'd sourced the trees from a lovely chap who sold *les arbres fruitiers* and, as a sideline – drum roll, please – truffle-impregnated trees! The truffle trees that we bought were impregnated cobnuts as, the way I looked at it, if the truffle experiment failed, at least we'd have nuts!

There is a fair amount of work in laying out an orchard. I cut the paddock with the tractor and proceeded to mark out a grid for our trees using big posts for the ends of the rows and a bamboo support for the individual trees. It was then a matter of everyone grabbing a spade and starting to dig. Dorothy and Arthur helped us to plant the orchard and we really hope they have some memory of the laughter and mess we made when they tell their grandchildren how the orchard came to be. Arthur even dug up a long, pointed stone that he insisted was a dinosaur tooth and, as we had obviously found a dinosaur graveyard, digging became frantic and rather random.

Somehow, after a physical couple of hours, we had planted all the fruit trees and our nut trees with the truffle-inoculated (that's the same as impregnated, isn't it?) root systems. We were told five years for the truffles but the fruit trees started to show their promise much quicker . . .

Dick has a saying that it is a rich society that plants trees they may never sit under for the benefit of future generations. I always get a bit choked when he says this because you can't help but be reminded that life is fleeting and we must enjoy every second. I had the vision that it would be twenty or thirty years before our orchard was fully grown and our grandchildren would be enjoying the fruits of our labours. It may have only been planting trees but I felt we were putting down our roots for future generations and it made me feel soppy and a bit teary watching Arthur and Dorothy climb all over Dick whilst he was trying to bed in a tree!

We had been having a blast and exploring France like never before but some jobs seem to jump up the priority list completely out of the blue. One such example was the wall at the back of the château that overlooks the moat and faces north-east, which had always looked very tired. Lots of the render had blown (i.e. had come away from the wall and was no longer stuck to it) and some lumps had come off, probably because it was north facing and subject to terrible weather. Falling render was not something we could ignore and there was no doubt about it: the château needed to be rendered.

We put a complete re-render to the back of our minds as it is a huge and expensive job and, despite the state of the back wall, was not quite urgent enough for us to divert resources to it. The short-term answer was to hire a cherry picker and patch the terrible parts that would soon be letting water in. There is a limited amount of space on the pathway that goes around the château, so we had to go for a spider cherry picker – when in position it had legs that extended out to stabilise it.

I have to say, the first thing I noticed about it was that it looked rather flimsy. I'm not small and the walls are very high. We'd come up with a plan as builder Steve was not keen on working at heights (that's code for he shat himself when we tried putting him up at the maximum elevation!) and I am not bad at heights, but when our delicate machine was at maximum elevation it positively swayed and, guess what . . I was shitting myself too. We were considering leaving the top bit and not telling anyone when we remembered we knew a roofer who loved being on roofs so must be happy up there, so we called in Ian to do the very top. I did the next layer and Steve did the bottom half – which was still 'very high', he said.

Normally, to render, you take your mix on a hawk, push it firmly against the wall with your trowel and then spread it flat. I'm not exaggerating when I tell you pushing against the wall caused the basket I was in to move away from the wall and when I started to spread, the wind caused me to move back and forth so much all I had to do was hold the trowel still. There was a slight positive. I didn't have to hold on because my butt cheeks had clamped me into position!

We patched in a rather Frankenstein way but it made things weatherproof. Just as we were finishing, Angela asked if we could use the machine to clean the windows. Of course we could but I thought it only fair that she pop on the harness and head up there. I thought Angela was going to lose her nerve or at least be a little worried, so I arranged some chairs for us to watch Mummy, way up in the air. But she didn't flinch as she headed up. Angela could have been on the ground as she washed the windows! I had completely forgotten that she and Dorothy share the same gene that loves roller coasters and scary rides, whereas Arthur and I understand gravity and the repercussions.

Whilst the cherry picker was here, I took advantage to clean the large window above the wolf on the grand stairs that I normally cannot get to from either the inside or the outside! Most of the year, it does not bother me at all, but during the wedding season I would secretly hope for a little rain the day before to clean the window. I have no problem with heights – in fact, as a teenager I would go on the type of rides that make many grown-ups' stomachs churn just looking at them! Of course, Dick made it more interesting by being in charge of the controls and having a bit of fun but I can safely say that this was the most satisfying window-cleaning experience of my life!

Arthur, Dorothy, Dick and Steve the builder all took a seat. My little man Arthur was worried about me being so high and that upset me a little. So I needed to get it finished as quickly as possible so I could get down and let him know I was safe. However, Dick thought it was a good idea to leave me up there. My threat to call a good-looking fireman to rescue me got him back pretty quickly and he lowered me down to the ground safe and sound. Job done.

It really surprised me how intense the rendering week had been. We had planned to get a number of small jobs ticked off our list but Dick spent every moment with Steve on the cherry picker and when Steve left, Dick carried on rendering to fill as many gaps as possible before the winter fell. At bedtime, I would play a game with Arthur and Dorothy to see if we could find Daddy! It was rather sweet ... And as soon as the cherry picker was collected, Dorothy, Mum and I went out to pick the harvest of her Bramleys. It was a big occasion as the trees had been on quite some journey.

Small everyday things remind you that you are living your dream, even if it hasn't all yet come to fruition. During our trip to Ireland earlier in the year, my mum took a five-hour round trip to get Angela's mum, Jenny, her Bramley apple trees. They had a passport to get into the county and we took lots of care planting them.

When they finally bore fruit, it was a big deal and Grandma took pride in picking them with Dorothy and Angela. Of course, there is only one thing to do with lovely home-grown apples – it had to be Grandma's apple pie. But not just any apple pie; it would be the first made with our very own Bramleys!

Mum is a fantastic chef but I think her thing has always been pastry making; some people are just naturals. When I was growing up, she often made apple pie with apples from the garden. It was my grandad Donald's favourite and when we went to visit them or they came to us, apple pie was always on the menu. Mum used to heat it up and the crunchy, thin pastry and sweet fluffy apples with a touch of double cream is my childhood memory of heaven.

Of course, I have her recipe and now it's the château apple pie recipe.

....

GRANDMA'S APPLE PIE

Ingredients

For the pastry:
110g chilled butter, cubed
225g plain flour
80g sugar
Zest of ½ lemon (optional)
1 large egg, beaten

For the filling:
700g cooking apples, plus sugar to taste
Juice of ½ lemon (optional)

Method

First, make the pastry. Crumb together the butter with the flour and add the sugar. If you want to use lemon zest, add it now. Then mix in the beaten egg. Bring it all together in a ball, wrap in clingfilm and place in the fridge for thirty minutes.

Peel and roughly cut the apples into pieces. Don't cook them – just heat them gently in a large pan, adding sugar to taste, depending on the sweetness of the apples, and lemon juice, if you're using it.

When it's just hot, turn off heat and leave to cool.

Put the cooled apples into a buttered dish, approximately 28cm wide. (Grandma uses a 28cm glass flan dish.) Sprinkle over a bit more sugar. Now roll out the pastry and place across the top only. Make a few holes in it with a fork to allow the steam out and sprinkle with a little sugar.

Bake for thirty-five to forty-five minutes at 170°C. When baking, put something underneath in case it leaks.

You can also use Granny Smith apples and less sugar instead of cooking apples in this recipe.

....

Making the pie was hilarious. Mum really wanted to show Dorothy her tricks of the trade but Dorothy was having far too much fun with the pastry and the flour. Mum had learnt from my grandma and I could see she was enjoying explaining to Dorothy to rub the ice-cold cubed butter into the flour with her fingertips to stop it heating up too much. Dorothy, bless her, listened attentively but then 'stirred' it her own way, creating a cloud of flour that coated everything. She looked so pretty and I told her so. Dorothy replied, 'Well, all ballerinas are pretty, Mummy.' Mum and I gave each other a knowing look at this precious moment!

With two pairs of hands in the bowl, and Mum and I mainly trying to keep the contents in there, we achieved the rubbed-in butter crumbs. From there, it was relatively easy as the wetter bits helped everything stick together. We ended up in such a mess that it took days to get the flour and water mixture (glue!) out of our hair but it was worth it!

We all sat down in the *salle à manger*, drank tea from china teacups and ate Grandma's fluffy apple pie. There was a real feeling of ceremony as the apple pie was sliced and served on a selection of our vintage side plates. Arthur and Dorothy responded to the choice of cream or vanilla ice cream with 'both', but they were not alone – so did Dick and Papi! To this day, Mum still says it was the best apple pie she has ever made.

Once I had been convinced that a dome floating on my work platform was a good idea (though I'm not sure how this happened?), I set about finding the best and most suitable geodesic dome we could afford. It was not about the cost or the best looking, although both of these points would be taken into consideration; it was about investing in something that was going to last and would work on a floating platform. I knew my job would also be to attach it safely to the platform and, as it was mobile and floating, I needed to think about this before purchase. I finally found a dome from a company called FDomes. We were dealing with people in the UK but the dome was manufactured in Poland and was shipped from there. With the internet, the world is a small place.

When it arrived, it was hilarious: hundreds and hundreds of pieces of metal, but each with a different letter on it. It was like the worst techno LEGO nightmare I could imagine but, rather than chuntering, I decided it made sense to insist that Angela built it with me. It was her idea after all! The instructions alone could take a week to digest but, eager to get on, we started. Angel sorted out the framework by letter: A to F. It was a pity the children were so young because if they had been a few years older they would have loved it!

Once the base was down, the rest of the structure happened rather quickly. We had a system and flew through putting it up; we even managed to complete the structure before we collected Arthur and Dorothy from school. We knew that the children were going to think it was incredible! Dorothy had just started to become obsessed with ballet and the horizontal bars were just the right height for her to balance. I had to say to myself, 'Do not let the children convince you to turn this into something else!'

Our floating dome was not huge but it was five metres in diameter. I got a very funny look from Angela as she was arranging all the components. I hadn't realised I'd been laughing so I showed her the diagram of how to erect the dome. After building the frame, we had to slide the cover over, which involved someone pulling a rope attached to the leading edge of the cover . . . from ten metres beyond the dome! The penny took a second or two to drop. We were erecting the dome on our platform at the edge of the moat so ten metres beyond was fifteen metres into the moat – now that was going to be a challenge.

As Angela wouldn't get into her swimming costume, we put the very heavy cover in place by manhandling it standing on step ladders inside the dome. I took time to fully attach the frame to our pontoon, so there was absolutely no movement as we tugged and yanked on the cover. Once we had got it all on top, gravity was helpful and soon we were attaching the cover to the frame.

The final installation task was to put in the woodburner. Once done, it was no longer a pruning pontoon, it was a dwelling on the moat. Thereafter, it was all up to Angela to make it special. A light made from a scrap bit of metal and hung in the dome, along with a home-crafted terrarium full of shells, and it was all but ready for us to spend a night on the water as a family!

The dome looked fantastic. It was modern and angular in style and I was completely in love with the contrast with the historic château. Originally, when we were ordering the dome, we were after a dark green covering but it was not available so we opted for light grey. Thank goodness because it looked exactly right. A lucky accident.

The inside was charming; the large triangle window stole the show. I had purchased two new emerald-green comfy chairs, which I placed by the statement window. When you sat there, it felt like you were floating on water as you couldn't see the edge of the pontoon. I try to add magic wherever possible but it really did feel like something surreal. You did not rock, you gently swayed, though not enough to make you feel seasick. I'd also bought a large modern bed with a geometric wood lattice for the headboard. It complemented the shape of the dome perfectly.

My favourite moment is always the cushion moment because it means most of the work is done and your dream has been achieved! I added in lanterns of all shapes and sizes, rugs, cushions and blankets. There was lots of texture to ensure this space felt cosy. I stood back and thought: 'Yes, I could camp here!' Excited, I then took some photos to add to the website. Château under the stars was in business!

You just can't launch a business like a floating dome without a test run and we had to show it to the family and then decide where we were going to moor it. Access was down a somewhat wobbly plank but, once inside, it was so safe and stable that the children ran around bouncing on the bed and trying out everything. It was getting late and our little ones needed their beauty sleep so it wasn't long before we were all on the bed getting comfy and calming down ready for a well-earned sleep. It was just so peaceful. We were on the still moat and the château lights were reflected on the water. It was perfect.

The *Waltons* moment we had in the floating dome that evening is engraved on my heart. The fire was lit, the dome was cosy and we were all together on a floating dome, snuggling. Arthur and Dorothy kissed each other goodnight and the sweet and gentle manner in which they did so made me melt. It's the happiest memory I have of the dome because, after this, the real dome work started.

We were finding our balance, working hard, enjoying family time and still managing to do a few things that we moved to France for! I have a list of things that I regularly search for on eBay or other areas of the internet, and one such thing is a duck press for serving ducklings Rouennaise.

Rouen is a very famous historic city two and a half hours north of us on the River Seine. It is on our route home from the UK, so we have passed through many times but never stopped to investigate. I came across dates of the city's very well-known food festival *Fête du Ventre*, which is 'the festival of the stomach' – it sounds more exotic in French, doesn't it?! For the first time since we'd been in France, we were free the weekend it was to be held so we booked an overnight stay in a hotel famous for its pressed duckling, a dish I'd heard of years before but had never tried. We checked into the Best Western Hotel de Dieppe, booked our table for the evening, and set off to explore the festival.

The streets thronged with people and there were food and drink stalls selling every possible local product. Being Normandy, *cidres* and apple brandy were in abundance and cream and butter were used with gay abandon. This is not an area dominated by wine and olive oil. Our shopping bag was starting to fill when we saw a large marquee that was about to start a cookery demonstration. Behind the demonstration kitchen there were numerous chefs all sporting very high, starched toques, the white pleated chefs' hats. We eased ourselves into a position to see and discovered it was a demonstration by master *canardiers*, the professionals who serve the Rouennaise duckling. The dish is also known as 'duck with blood', *canard au sang*, which is not frightfully appetising. The bird is served with a blood sauce that involves putting the majority of the partially cooked meat into a very robust press that allows you to squeeze out the blood to make your sauce. The ducklings used to be suffocated to ensure more blood was available and the pressing is done at the table in an ornamental press that looks medieval.

We watched, we took notes and we even tasted a morsel as they were passed around the eager audience. It was fascinating and whetted our appetites for that evening. We had eaten little and bought lots to take home and were seriously ready for our meal at the hotel.

We both got dressed up and our evening started with cocktails and canapés at a large table that was big enough for our demonstration '*par un Maitre Canardiers* using the *Recette Originale crée Par Michel Guéret en 1932 à bord du Félix Faure – Président Fondateur des Canardiers*', which basically means our meal was cooked by a 'master duckler' in the old way! It was wonderfully theatrical and by the end of the evening I had a cunning plan for how we could do it at home. We'd been searching for a proper Rouen duck press for years and they either cost too much or were on the far side of the world so I needed a plan B whilst we continued searching.

We have driven past Rouen many times on the way back and forth to the UK. It's a stunning city, very well known for its cathedral. I personally had never stopped here, there had been no reason to up until now, but finding out that they hold one of France's largest food festivals was as good an excuse as any!

Because we were going to a food festival that boasts thousands of stalls, I thought I would 'save myself'. That was a silly idea because when we arrived, I could have eaten a horse (although that is not a good expression here in France). The streets were packed, the stalls looked impressive and different smells came at you from every direction. My senses were being tormented! As you would expect at a food festival in this region, there was stall upon stall of fruits, especially apples, and cheese, bread and other gorgeously displayed produce in wicker baskets, cascading over tables. Meats, pies, crêpes, patisseries, sweets. And so many temptations, cooked and ready to eat in a bowl – take now and stop your hunger! I was overwhelmed and could not make up my mind. I'm not indecisive generally but today I was because this hunger deserved something tasty!

We took all our new knowledge of pressed duckling back home and the next week we cooked the wonderfully rich dish for Jenny and Steve as a thank you for babysitting to allow us to go to Rouen.

Apparently, there are rules when preparing Rouennaise duckling, however, we follow the maxim 'rules are for the obedience of fools and the guidance of wise men' and adapted our dish.

- The duckling has to be suffocated to maximise the amount of blood available – no, thank you
- The carcass is cooked very rare, 'bleeding' – yes
- The breasts are then removed – yes

- Carcass pressed to remove all juices – yes, but we had no press . . .
- Offal to be used to thicken the sauce – yes

Based on recipes that are nearly 100 years old, we made our very own Rouennaise duckling à la Château-de-la-Motte Husson.

. . . .

ROUENNAISE DUCKLING À LA CHÂTEAU-DE-LA-MOTTE HUSSON

Ingredients

1 duckling, about 1.5–2kg (plus the liver and the heart)
1 tsp Dijon mustard
2 tbsp breadcrumbs

For the sauce:
4 tbsp chopped shallots
1 tsp fresh thyme
A bottle of dry red wine
500ml veal stock
1 bay leaf
A glass of cognac
Juice of ½ lemon
A glass of port
50g butter
Salt and black pepper

Method

To make a Bordelaise sauce, reduce the shallots, thyme and red wine to a glaze (glacé). Loosen with veal stock, season and add the bay leaf. This Bordelaise must be strongly flavoured so test the seasoning and leave to rest for at least an hour.

Blend the raw liver and heart and press it through a chinois into a small pan. Add the Bordelaise through the chinois. You now have a 'stock Rouennais'. When you're ready for service, sear the duckling in a very hot oven for seventeen to twenty minutes.

When you get to the table, remember it's all about the theatre!

Flambé a largish glass of cognac. Add the stock Rouennais and heat to just below boiling point. Add the lemon juice, the glass of port and the butter, then whisk to obtain a smooth sauce. Cut off the duckling's wings and drumsticks, then take them into the kitchen to spread with the mustard and coat with the breadcrumbs ('devilled'). These can then go back into the oven at 180°C to cook through and crisp for six to eight minutes. Meanwhile, carve and display the breasts on a warm, buttered dish.

It's now time to press the carcass. In the end, I repurposed a robust fruit press and managed to extract a decent amount of blood for our very rich sauce. Add to the sauce, warming it through but without bringing it to the boil.

Pour the sauce over the breasts, serving on very hot plates, along with the devilled wings and drumsticks and sides of your choice. We chose plain, boiled but well-salted new potatoes and finely shredded savoy cabbage.

The meal was a resounding success. One duckling should have been for two people but we found it was sufficient for all four of us as the sauce was so rich. It's not a meal for the faint-hearted and in a typically French way you are not spared the fact that you are eating a once-living animal. It's as though you are being told to 'get over it' and enjoy this wonderful dish, and it is wonderful!

Angela and I still keep searching for a Rouennaise duck press so that one day we'll be able to do it as and when we please!

December arrived and it's our month to catch up with loved ones. For us, Christmas is never just about the big day – it's the festive period of celebration shared with loved ones that runs up to Christmas and into the New Year. We had been very busy in 2017 and, if we were honest, we had not caught up with as many people as we would have liked to, but family and true friends understand and it gave us a great excuse to have a lot of fun and festivity in December.

Our friends Hazel and Andrew were the first to visit. Hazel had flown in from London, wearing her superhero cape, when we first moved out here. We were not even in the château at that point and we went on a number of local adventures together. We waited for their arrival before we decorated the Christmas tree. It was such a treat for us and we could not wait to share this with them. Dick played Christmas carols, we drank port and loved 'Christmassing up the château' together! A home at Christmas is magical and that evening, whilst Andrew and Dick cooked, Hazel and I chatted together about life and what had happened since our wedding.

Then we had our Christmas party with Dorothy and Arthur's friends – well, mainly Arthur's because it had become apparent that Dorothy was fussy when it came to making friends. We were not sure if hosting a Christmas gathering for the children's friends and their families would become a tradition but it felt right. (Little

did we know, but come the following year, Arthur would request a Halloween party . . . and so the spooky château won over the festive château, as our annual children's party.) My mum, being the master pastry chef, made up lots of dough and covered 10cm cubes of it in clingfilm ready for cookie making. I had a drawing station in the playroom and a Christmas decoration station ready to take over from the cookie-making station when the cookies went into the oven.

We decided that our focus would not be a full-on meal, so we invited everyone after lunch. We made mulled wine for the adults and a warm drink for the children. There were mince pies and Christmas fruit cakes, and chocolate Santas and English sweets, just to be different! The house was alive; there was laughter, concentration and real enjoyment. Families stayed and we loved watching the teenaged brothers and sisters of the children's friends enjoy the activities as much as the younger children. At the end, everyone went away with a festive and full bag and we flopped onto the sofa and drank the rest of the mulled wine! It had been a blast and Arthur and Dorothy had loved it.

*

Once we had tidied up after the children's party, my big boy James and his wife Holly arrived from Cornwall with my grandchildren Indy, Pippin and Arrietty for a visit before Christmas. They brought their friends with them, who brought their children, so, as well as the three sets of parents, we had a one-, two-, two-, three-, four-, five- and a six-year-old staying, all feeling very excited about the build-up to Christmas. It was lots of fun. The days were a constant child-orientated mêlée and in the evening, when small people were bathed and asleep, we cooked and drank and managed to sort of be grown-ups. When they all headed back to England just in time for

Father Christmas to find them in their houses, we settled down for our Christmas at the château.

Finally, my dear brother Paul brought over my nan on Christmas Eve and the family festivities could really get under way. Paul could not get away from work any earlier but they were here in time to see the children's excitement at leaving Père Noël his mince pies and glass of port and, of course, carrots for Rudolph and the gang. We had spent that evening all making mince pies in the family kitchen, four generations together, and it felt so good to have everyone at the château. I think we even got Nan tipsy on sherry! There followed a relaxed and enjoyable period with absolutely no commitments and no deadlines.

Again, the lift paid for itself. Nan stayed in the honeymoon suite and at the end of every evening we simply put her in the lift! Allegedly, Nan was getting a little hard of hearing but she never seemed to miss a thing the children said. Dorothy insisted on holding her hand everywhere she went and loved sitting on her lap in the lift. For a petite lady in her nineties, she didn't think twice about lifting Arthur up onto her knee for a cuddle either . . . no mean feat!

December 2017 was a time of making memories. I still giggle fondly remembering Dick in his shorts and T-shirt because we had the heating cranked up so high for my nan – the château was truly like a sauna! We loved watching the relationships between the kids grow as well: Arthur and Indy are now great friends and Dorothy and Pippin too. Arrietty was not yet old enough to get involved the way the other four did, but she will do in time. As if that wasn't enough, Dorothy and Arthur both have a very special bond with their brother James as well and adore Uncle Paul. The château was once again a lively, lovely family home. It was everything we had dreamt of.

We saw the old year out and the new year in with a meal that lasted all evening. I'd grown up with the idea that Christmas was focused on the children and New Year was for the adults. So once the children were up in bed, we were going to have a mezze, which was really just an excuse to keep the food and accompanying drink coming all evening. Plus, Jeanette, Angela's nan, said she loved a mezze so, as she was the senior lady present, it was only fair that I honoured her wishes.

Preparations were not at all hurried and we made the decision that, when possible, we'd keep the same plates and cutlery. It was New Year's Eve, so we felt the food should be interesting and diverse, so we didn't limit ourselves to traditional mezze dishes of the Middle East or North Africa. We just prepared what we fancied.

- Crudités with dips – hummus, tzatziki, baba ghanoush, harissa mayo, tapenade, fresh chilli and lime salsa
- Fried tortillas with Little Gem lettuce, red onion, feta, tomato and guacamole
- Garlic prawns
- Spatchcock poussin marinated in garlic and rosemary
- Lamb meatballs spiced with ras el hanout and chargrilled peppers and aubergine
- Carpaccio of beef fillet on a platter with crispy salad shavings and horseradish crème fraîche
- Baklava, French patisseries and mixed chocolate petit fours
- Irish coffee – a tradition from Northern Ireland but non-Gaelic variations were on offer too . . .

We were still grazing when we paused to toast the new year. As Paul had the darkest hair, he 'first footed' for us and came across the threshold with a tray that had all that we could hope for from the new year: coal for warmth, a silver coin for prosperity, a piece of fruit cake for food and a glass of the finest Irish malt whiskey for good cheer. We waited until 1am to phone family in the UK to wish them a Happy New Year so we could all raise a glass together! We said goodbye to a wonderful 2017 and looked forward to the unknown but full-of-potential 2018.

CHAPTER 11

Growing

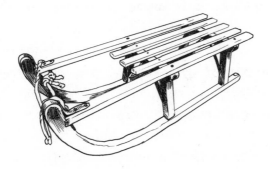

We started off 2018 content in the knowledge that our decision to go 'all in' was looking promising. Although the roof fund had nothing in it, we had eleven weddings in the diary, half a dozen food lovers' weekends booked and lots more ideas brewing! The diary was also full of appointments for viewings and tastings, and there were even more people on the waiting list wanting to visit.

As the dawn broke on the new year, we lay in bed talking about the year we'd just had and our one wish for the year ahead. Without knowing it, we *all* chose holidays! Again, Dick and I decided to aim for more balance, more 'us time'. But today was not the day for a long lie-in as we were taking all the family to Laval. The skies were a gorgeous blue that morning and, although it was crisp outside, the sun was already taking the edge off the cold and we knew that Nan and Uncle Paul would love a trip out to our local town.

Le Jardin de la Perrine sits at the top of the hill in Laval and goes a long way down the side as well! It's an epic park of four and a half hectares that boasts a 'harmonious botanical collection', which is divided into a French garden, an English garden and a rose garden. There are signs everywhere to give you details of the trees and there is also a small children's play area complete with roundabouts, swings, slides and a manmade rock with a cave inside to hide in ... There is also the most magical merry-go-round, which we have never seen open, manned or operational. It always has a thick plastic cover around it. It does, however, look lovely!

The park overlooks the River Mayenne and at the top there is a huge Hollywood-style sign that lights up at night saying 'LAVAL', which you can see from afar. In addition to the fantastic playground, there is a lovely area where they have animals and a large aviary of colourful birds, plus a book-sharing library. The park is very hilly, so Nan was in a wheelchair and we were taking it in turns to push her, although I was a bit twitchy that someone was going to accidentally let go when walking down the hill! Even though our château is glorious, it's nice to get out and see our local area. It felt like such a treat being somewhere idyllic on the first day of the year, together as a family.

The festivities had been indulgent. Apart from the usual eating and drinking too much, we had allowed ourselves copious amounts of time to enjoy family and friends. But now January was here, Arthur and Dorothy were back to school and we were getting back into our working rhythm. Wedding couples were eager to get organised, new enquiries were coming in, as were a *crazy* amount of food lovers' enquiries. In fact, I was finding the 'disappointment management' of this quite overwhelming. I hate saying no. I mean, I find it so hard that Dick jokes with me about practising saying 'no'. So I arranged a meeting with my husband to discuss

how we were going to manage our year and what we were going to add to our offerings.

It was becoming apparent that the weddings and food lovers' weekends were not allowing enough people to visit us and as more people became aware of what we had to offer and wanted to come, that was going to get worse. Our list of enquiries was stretching into the thousands and there was no way we could satisfy the demand. Offering weddings is obviously very niche and, although we were happy to do similar celebrations for birthdays, anniversaries, etc., it was still very focused on individuals and couples. Our food lovers' weekends, although very special, also only allowed a very limited number of people here at a time. We were receiving so many enquiries and Angela was finding it painful having to keep saying no without being able to offer a glimmer of hope of when we could fit people in. She detests saying no at the best of times, so we needed to find a way that we could say yes more often but keep the personal touch of our experiences and ensure none of the magic was lost. Not easy! We put on our thinking caps, got a drink in hand and brainstormed every option we could think of. After lots of discussions we agreed on three new offerings:

- Château under the stars – a chance to glamp in the château grounds
- Garden days – the opportunity to come and join us working in the gardens
- Days of decadence – a day of luxury and celebration. Basically, come to the château and be spoilt

Château under the stars was already happening (or so I was told). During the discussion, I found out Angela had already redirected a few early enquiries she'd had to turn down for food lovers' weekends that way. Although I expected nothing less, it did put quite a bit of pressure on us to get the dome and all the other facilities ready for guests to come and stay within the next five months. We agreed that château under the stars was the one activity that could happen even if we were not at the château. The plan was that our dome visitors would be entirely self-sufficient, which meant we needed to sort bathroom, eating and cooking facilities. We would of course chat if we were around but that was not a given.

The garden day was my idea, inspired by the volume of generous invitations and offers of help we had received already from garden lovers wanting to lend a hand. 'Why not get everyone together on certain days of the year?' I thought. We could all have a ball whilst really achieving something at the same time. I'd visited a garden on Guernsey that allowed volunteers to come and help so I knew people didn't mind working on someone else's garden. And we would be happy of the help. However, like everything else at the château, it could not just be *any* garden day – Angela wanted it to be special. Initially, we were going to have a no-cost ticket but that raised two issues: firstly, if people hadn't paid anything there was no commitment from them, so non-attendance could be an issue; and secondly, Angela could not get her head around having 'a quick and simple soup and a sandwich for lunch, then back to work' mindset . . .

As a result, the day evolved from a fairly simple idea into another château event. On arrival, we were to start with croissants and breakfast pastries, coffee, tea and fresh juice. Then there would be a morning work session, followed by a couple of courses for lunch (that worried me – what if people couldn't work after it?). Then the afternoon session working in the garden. After that, we would conclude with tea and cakes from our local bakers, a tour of the château and everyone receiving a handmade gift before departing. We wanted people to come and work with us, and enjoy being part of our journey, so we saw this as a way of making progress in the garden whilst allowing people to visit us and the château.

From a business perspective, we knew that we needed to charge enough to at least cover our staff and the catering costs. If not, our garden days could end up costing us thousands to host. We understood that people would have to travel and stay over, so to make the day accessible, we decided to charge £50 per head, which included 20 per cent VAT – to be reviewed when we understood the costs more fully. After all, we were going to need at least ten staff for the day to ensure everything ran smoothly and we could pull together a good lunch!

Our 'days of decadence' were based on the idea of a 'celebration day', not unlike attending a wedding but it would be open to individuals, couples or groups of people who did not know each other. It would be like an all-day supper club! Tickets would be sold per person and we decided on a capacity of fifty people. Even though we had space to host eighty at a time, we had learnt that fifty was a great, intimate number and that was what we wanted to achieve. Although we would not host these days until much later in the year, we needed to get tickets on sale for cash flow and to test the demand so we could work out the details. There would be lots of food and drink, tours of the exterior and interior and lots of chatting and having fun. The details and nuances were yet to be worked out, which is always the best bit, but first we needed to see if anyone was interested! Tickets for the day of decadence were £220 per person inclusive of VAT.

It was great to see our business grow and develop in new directions but we were most proud of the way our children were growing. Both were very happy and content at home and at school. Arthur was quickly becoming a sociable and loving little boy with the sweetest of souls. He was very tactile but also very strong and

his party trick at school was lifting up the school bench. As we spoke English at home and read it at bedtime, we relied on our local school to lead the way in French.

Kids' brains are like sponges but learning two languages before five is a truly remarkable task and quite a challenge. His teacher, Madame Jorre, could see that Arthur was not always as open and chatty as the other children and, as she had got to know him and how smiley he could be, she realised he was being hampered by his lack of French and was struggling to communicate with the other children. We talked to her about it and she could see it was breaking my heart to think that our special little man was not happy, so she took it upon herself to spend thirty minutes during their lunchtimes on his grammar and vocabulary. What a difference it made! In a couple of weeks, Arthur got it and flew forward and he has not looked back since. We are so thankful to his wonderful teacher. When I was Arthur's age, I struggled with English and my teacher, Mrs Osborne, gave me extra tuition. Her kindness has never left me and inspires me every day to give a little extra because it really does make a difference.

Dorothy was also flying . . . Well, gliding. She appeared to be the quiet one, always taking everything in, not missing a thing. She observed people and, unlike Arthur, who is straight in with a hug, Dorothy makes you earn her friendship. I like her style. Once you earn her trust, Dorothy is fun, loving and very loyal. The teachers adored her; she was precise and neat.

We were really taken aback one evening, however, when the teacher casually said that we should get Dorothy's ears tested because she wasn't speaking very much and the teacher wondered if this was because she had hearing difficulties. I had to work hard not to go into panic mode. Dick was typically blunt and told the teacher, '*Vous vous trompez!*' – she was mistaken. At home, we could not keep her quiet and we knew that it was still early days

at school. She was also learning a whole new language! My gut instinct told me that there were no issues at all and, as Dorothy was only three years old, we should all be patient. I tell my girlfriends very often to listen to their instincts, so I listened to mine – every child is different and learns and grows at different rates. Dorothy proved me right and when she speaks with our French friends now, they always comment on the fact that she sounds just like a little French girl. True to form, she is always chattering away.

Whenever possible, which was most Sundays, we would still sit down for our ritual of a Sunday 'French breakfast'. This involved Arthur, Dorothy and I going to the bakery in the village where there would be a lot of '*bonjour*' and '*ça va?*' to those we were on a nodding acquaintance with. While we were out, Angela would have collected a tray of goodies – crockery, cutlery, glasses, serviettes, fresh juice, fresh coffee, cold butter and some apricot jam, with a teaspoon to serve (it's not far off a capital offence to put a buttery knife in a jam pot in our house). And then we would all sit down together on a rug round a coffee table in the salon to ceremoniously eat our breakfast. The tradition was that we would break off bits of baguette that were 'armadillo-like' – crunchy on the outside, soft in the middle – apply slices of butter (Bons Mayennais *demi-sel* butter, made within a mile of the château with milk from the *département*) and then jam oozing over the edges. I would be the master of ceremonies as it was always messy and the children would always end up sticky. But as Arthur and Dorothy grew up, things changed slightly. Now they were allowed to choose something themselves when we were at the bakery, so that was added to the Sunday breakfast mix.

There was always a bit of pressure on them in the bakery as their decisions had to be made in the time it took for the queue to reach the counter and for me to order our staples. That would consist of some fresh bread for Jenny and Steve, a couple of baguettes – plain for me and traditional – for Angela, sliced sourdough loaves and a couple of croissants. While we moved ever closer to the counter, we'd talk about options. It was always a tough decision but invariably Arthur would choose a pain au raisin and Dorothy a *Suisse*, an unfeasibly large, soft, slightly sweet roll with chocolate '*pepins*' sprinkled through it. If it had proven a particularly tough decision, Daddy would sometimes also get the sugared choux balls or the apricot or lemon pastries, for him and Mummy to 'share'. I'm not sure if it would be true to say that we didn't always order cakes for Sunday afternoon as well.

By the middle of January, we had a handful of bookings for château under the stars, which, in hindsight, did put quite a lot of pressure on us. But at the time, my thought process was that we needed to start taking bookings early, otherwise the season would be finished and not marketed yet. What use is a floating dome with no bookings? The first booking we took was from Byron and Scarlett for Tuesday, 8 May. This was straight after a three-day bank holiday wedding for the lovely Matt and Hannah that was finishing on the 7 May. We had loads of time!

I understand 'going for it' and I understand the logic of timely marketing. I just don't know why we don't have the two-hour lunch breaks that so many people in France enjoy! From the outset, it's worth noting that our chief architect of château under the stars had never been camping, so glamping at the château did not have a baseline of sleeping in a tent. Rather, it was based on the image of a nice hotel room that was a bit outdoorsy. There followed numerous, somewhat heated, discussions about what people would expect. I knew I was wasting my time but I felt I had to fight the corner for all those of us who have ever camped! As with all our projects, once we agree we are doing something, we go straight into the planning stage and then onto the execution stage.

The plan was to turn an unused piece of scrubland on the side of the moat into a glamping site. We'd anchor our floating dome nearby and build a bridge to it. Then we'd clear another area, lay foundations and build another, larger, more spacious dome on dry land, landscaping and building a patio area. To that we'd add a pizza-oven-cum-barbecue and, lest we forget, a very comfortable shower and kitchen facilities – complete with coloured grout, of course. And to make it a tad more 'glam', we decided a wood-fired hot tub with bubbles would be nice. Oh, and did I mention that the only way to get there was to go around the walled garden? So a bridge at the end of the coach house would be useful . . .

*

Angela had loved the meadow in front of the orangery ever since we had first seen the château. There were some flowers spread amongst the grasses and it was a fitting backdrop for many of the wedding photos but, by the time the season was drawing to a close, the grasses had all sagged a bit and lost their colour and there was now little evidence of just how beautiful it had all been in the late spring and early summer. I had to find a way to make it look good for longer . . .

We were very happy allowing nature to help manage a lot of our land. When we'd been looking at châteaus that had sixty, seventy, sometimes hundreds of acres included there had been a part of me that yearned to be custodian of a reasonable parcel of land. However, I'd been partially self-sufficient on three acres and was not naive about what it took to use land effectively. Our twelve acres could be a full-time job but we didn't feel it needed to be overworked – though any area directly associated with our business did get extra attention! As you turn into the grounds, your eyes are immediately drawn to the château at the end of the drive, but we wanted it all to be special when you look around, too. Our orchard on the right was taking shape and every three or four weeks we cut the grass back. On the left you have the orangery with a meadow of long grasses and a lone tall cedar tree dominating the space. It was lovely but not beautiful, so we decided to lift it up a gear and give some wildflowers a chance in this space.

If left alone, the tight root systems of the many grasses in the meadow would not allow wildflowers to take root. It's a brutal world down there in the top layers of the soil and only the strong survive. I did lots of research and sourced a mix of perennial and annual wildflower seeds that would show results in year one but would also be robust enough to last into the future. To get them started, I had to level the playing field, or rather the meadow, so I bought a cheap *charrue* and set about ploughing and harrowing the area.

I've done some ploughing with modern tractors and even with shire horses but our little tractor was truly difficult as, no matter how I set the plough, it went in deep and turned over massive sods that turned the meadow into rough terrain even a four-by-four would have difficulty traversing. To try to smooth it a bit, I cross-ploughed and then, using an old rusty harrow I found in the barns, I raked it to within an inch of its life. It wasn't smooth but the ground was broken up, so then I called on my team of willing helpers to sow our sack of seeds. We spent the best part of an hour sharing the seeds and sowing them over the massive, muddy area, all the time chatting about how Mummy was going to love the flowers Arthur and Dorothy were planting for her. It was a great job for children and if we had any mishaps and I detected a pile of seeds anywhere, I simply scooped them up with a handful of the soil and threw it in a big arc to somewhere we hadn't yet been.

We couldn't wait to see the results of our work and I couldn't help regularly checking to see if grass was growing back or little flower seedlings . . . We had to wait a couple of months but this was the year our meadow was officially no longer a field . . .

The seed mixture we had sown early was intended to flower from May through to September, though the varieties of flowers included reminded me just how little I knew about wildflowers. Some I could recognise and some I could name, like meadow buttercup, red and white campion, corn camomile, cornflower, field forget-me-not, ox-eye daisy, foxglove, poppy, corn marigold, wild carrot . . . But there were also dozens that sounded like names that had come out of a medieval book of ingredients to be used by a slightly scary, wise old woman who lived in the little cottage in the woods. For example, lady's bedstraw, burnet, night-flowering catchfly, corn cockle, knapweed, musk mallow, yarrow, yellow rattle. With so many flowers all maturing at different times, it would be a real haven for our local bees and other pollinators, as well as looking stunning.

I'm not sure if they all grew but, by the middle of the year, we were treated to a meadow that appeared to have flower blossoms hovering above the denser grasses when you looked at it at grass-top level. Every time we felt we had seen the best, some more flowers would appear. Angela was really pleased with them. There were occasions when a lone unidentified flower would briefly appear to be adored, then next thing you knew it had gone. I'd done lots of research and when I explained that, to get the best results, we needed to plough again in late summer (i.e. before the end of the wedding season), I got a very simple, 'That's not happening.' Which was unambiguous at least! Needless to say, we waited until the end of September before the plough made another appearance.

Dick's ugly ploughed meadow truly blossomed into something spectacular in 2018 and it was the gift that kept giving. Arthur and Dorothy would regularly pick stems and give them to me in little posies. Yes, gushy Mum melted and we often had half a dozen glasses of wildflowers spread around the house at any given time. Dick and I were not sure if we would get the same flowers every year, so he suggested keeping a journal of what we found. And so we started the 'Château Flowers Pressing Book'. Pressing flowers is something that many people have memories of from their younger days – often an activity they did together with older generations of the family. Being a vintage book enthusiast, I especially love picking up an old book and finding flowers in there. The paper from the books absorbs the moisture from the flowers over time, keeping their delicate shape. The technique is so simple, yet so effective. When Dorothy and I took our first 'masterpieces' from the book and mounted them onto card, it was a very special moment; she had helped Dick sow the seeds, had picked the wildflowers with Arthur and then pressed them with me to add to the record of our history at the château. We could not wait to show them to Arthur and Dick.

*

It's in my nature to plan ahead and I knew we needed to get all offerings for the year ahead on our website as soon as possible. We were heading into the world of e-commerce and stock (i.e. tickets) management, so there was a little bit of learning required here. After lots of research, we went with an e-commerce system called Magento, which worked very nicely.

We added tickets for three garden days (in March, April and October); three days of decadence (in June and July) and a couple of dozen dates for château under the stars (sadly, we did not have that much capacity for this after the weekends for weddings, other events and family commitments were blocked out. We didn't want anyone staying in the domes when another event was going on unless they were part of it.

It was going to be a year of expanding our offerings and testing the waters. Within two weeks of uploading our château events, everything apart from the March garden day (which was going to be pretty cold) had sold out. That was a very nice feeling. Okay, we still needed to put the work in to plan, organise, renovate and build lots of elements but we had some funds to play with.

We were shaping our business and deciding what mix of activities we wanted to do. 'Wanted to do' is a really important concept because we had no intention of turning our home into a wedding factory or just turning out endless events. Of course, we had to make hay while the sun was shining but we also wanted balance.

I suppose this is probably a good time to clear up some misconceptions about our earnings. We have had to be very realistic with ourselves about what we could earn and what we could achieve in the future. I have been a television presenter since 2003 and when making television at the château, we get paid to 'present'. It's a 'talent fee' for making *Escape to the Château*. We get exactly the same amount now as we did for the first series, when it was an unknown venture. It's great as a revenue stream and better than a poke in the eye but most certainly does not cover the cost of the renovations we film during the making of a series. Our hospitality business and the other work we undertake at the château has been allowing us to grow year on year and supports everything we do. *Escape to the Château* is observational in nature and we have been adamant that we will not be 'directed' or 'guided' to do things that we would not do of our own volition. This stance has ensured that we have kept our integrity because no one can tell us what to do and how to spend our own hard-earned money.

We are not naive; the television exposure is great and it has been wonderful to stimulate the market of people who would like to come to the château. It helps people to understand the provenance of Angela's designs and shares the gentle good humour and values of our lives here at the château. We have to keep reminding ourselves when we have a 'strategy meeting' – a grand way of saying a chat about the future – that our move to France was all about ensuring a special family-orientated way of life. We only ever wished to do about twelve weddings a year, maximum. Our plan was to live our lives with a family-centric, two-hour lunch break mentality . . .

Well, we are definitely family centric and we know we'll get there when it comes to long lunch breaks and less work! One of our key tenets to grow our business was to have some diversity, in order to allow us to do all the different things we like, to keep us sane and to ensure that we have financial security so that if for some reason a revenue stream was to dry up, we would have other things to fall back on.

CHAPTER 12

Tresoire

With the year ahead looking busier than ever, Dick and I chatted about having a space in the château where I could have my sewing machine set up – a kind of craft room and an area to showcase personal treasures that were special to me. I had boxes upon boxes of vintage and crafting stuff and, even though we had a château with lots of space, it felt like a lot of it was still crammed away. I wanted to be able to bounce from event to family and from family to event, but with everything in the attic in boxes it was not ideal. I used to bring my sewing machine down to the honeymoon suite in between weddings to allow me to work on projects. But it wasn't an efficient way of working and it added extra time onto everything. And meant it was easy to lose things if they were constantly being moved around – losing things in a forty-five-room château really does your head in!

One day when the children were at school, Dick and I took a walk around the house, looking at places to have my craft room. Some places were still up for grabs but a lot had actually already been marked up for projects we had planned down the line. Before we knew it, we were in the attic. But standing in the central room looking out felt good. It was peaceful and the view out the window was to die for. Yes, it was a long way up, but in a way, that was not a bad thing. It would keep me fit and if someone wanted to disturb me, it would have to be important enough for them to walk up ninety-three stairs to do it. I've always loved the attic of the château and it did not take long for us to agree we had found my space. And as we walked happily back down the stairs together, Dick turned and said, 'No baths up here!'

It was ridiculous but the château was filling up! Angela needs her space to be creative. Not an office. Somewhere to be surrounded by inspiration and to have fun. She needed to smile as she came through the door and hum to herself as she worked. We have lovely views out of every window but the view from the top of the building looking down the driveway takes your breath away. Leaning out the window reminds you how high the building is. Sadly, there were no electricity sockets or lighting and the lime plaster had come away from the walls when there had been a problem with the roof in the distant past. However, it was a good size and, more importantly, Angela liked it!

Like all tasks at the château, we started with clearing, cleaning and the infrastructure. Angela would need easily accessible sockets and good lighting. We agreed very early on that the walls could retain some character and did not need to be perfectly flat. That made things a lot easier. So instead, we just put up plasterboards to stop the dust and there was very rudimentary plastering of the joints. I could feel builder mate Steve twitch but good enough was good enough! We put in a lot of double sockets and I insisted on a sunken socket in the floor in the middle of the room. Much later, when Angela's work desk made it up the ninety-three steps, the socket was proven to be a sound idea!

Sun comes through the window from about midday but a workroom needs good light and no shadows. LED panels were a fairly new concept but I thought they had the potential to provide the lighting required. As each one acted a bit like a sky light, the light did not come from a single point and so the shadows were minimised. We put in four panels and there were officially no shadows in the main work area in the middle of the room. The room was functional and with a lick of white paint everywhere, all that was left to do was to gather all Angela's treasures together.

There is a law of renovating that says, 'All the heaviest, most awkward items have to live in the most difficult to access and out of the way places . . . '

When I was growing up, Mum used to take me to the local material shop. I always remember the colours, the rows of fabric, the boxes of buttons, the displays of cottons. It was a complete visual feast and a treat, and afterwards Mum would always buy me an iced finger bun at the bakers! I'd never been to anything like this with Dorothy. Since her birth, I've bought nearly everything on the internet. She has been to many second-hand places but not an old-school haberdashery and I quite fancied taking advantage of the fact that we live so close to Paris, the home of fashion and couture. It felt almost rude not to go. I booked two tickets for a girls' day out to Paris for a trip to Ultramod, the oldest haberdashery in Paris, so that I could show Dorothy how they stored reels and rolls of fabric.

As we gave Dick and Arthur a big kiss, they were already getting ready to have an adventure of their own; there was a real sense of excitement. Dorothy and I both dressed up in kimonos and I drove us to Laval station. This was a big deal for me. I've watched Dick lots of times when he has parked in the underground car park at the station but I've never known how he gets the car in a slot because the spaces and corners are so tight. If I'm honest, it was the only thing on my mind as we set off that morning and, once I had managed to get parked and not scratch the car, I felt like a weight had been lifted off my shoulders.

We found our seats on the train, got ourselves settled and snuggled up. We were going on an adventure and the train journey felt full of the unknown! Taking Dorothy to Paris was glorious and incredibly bonding. We have never explored a city together before. She does not know London and, at first, she was a little overwhelmed by so many people walking very fast. For me, it was simply fantastic to be in a melting pot of culture again. It was a visual delight and full of all the sounds, smells and sights that I missed.

We walked around the streets, looking at incredible shop displays, popped into a few shops, stopped for a drink and a snack – and got the kind of service you might expect in Paris – and saw some incredible lifestyle shops. I was busy taking notes and pictures the whole time and was completely inspired to find old bread racks that would look perfect on display in my newly named *tresoire*! I was raring to get back and start getting my space organised.

The icing on the cake was of course the visit to Ultramod, the oldest haberdashery in Paris. If you are a crafter, you have to go. They have two shops opposite each other. The original shop was for milliners and the shelving displays are still all original and the most beautiful you will ever see. The haberdashery opposite was added in the 1920s and is vast. Every wall is covered from floor to ceiling with island upon island of buttons, cords, braiding, decorations, cottons, cloth. It blew my mind. We bought a little something in both shops to remind us of our visit. Dorothy and I decided we were going to make a rainbow hat together once the *tresoire* was finished and ready.

Surprise, surprise, on the way back to the train station we also ended up with yet another *Frozen* outfit and a fake joke poo for Arthur. I mean, you can't go to Paris and do no shopping. Just essentials, of course.

With the decoration in the *tresoire* completed, we investigated the attic and outbuildings for some storage solutions for Angela's treasures. And, of course, Angela checked out the *brocantes* and charity shops. Soon a pile of likely contenders was congregating in the boot room. We had:

- The old van de vin drawers from when it was a mobile shop. However, they had undergone a transition: the very decorative mesh had been painted and, instead of being on the bottom of the drawers, they were mounted vertically, so the decoration was the back. We then added smaller shelves and dowels to allow lots of bobbins and jars to be stored on them.
- An old ladder. It was so fragile you definitely could not step on it but once it was cleaned and varnished, it became a great storage solution, with material draped over every rung.
- A beautiful old wooden step ladder, which we varnished to make a lovely set of shelves.
- Metal racking with bakers' drawers, which were cleaned and painted.
- An impressively heavy, solid, metal set of zinc-coated mesh shelves.
- And a large table – it must have been for dining originally but it was perfect for Angela to sew or work at (fortunately the legs were also removable for upwards transportation!).

The move upstairs was a team effort as many hands were needed to ensure no wallpaper or paintwork was scuffed as we made our way around the twisting, narrower stairs of the fourth and fifth floors. I have to be honest, there was a bit of foul language, especially with the zinc shelves that had to be carried above the height of the banisters . . .

The straw that could have broken the camel's back was a sideboard complete with a 100kg marble top that turned up on a delivery van from Emmaus. I gave the driver and his mate €50 each to help us carry it up some stairs to my wife's *atelier*. Initially they said payment wasn't necessary but they accepted when I pointed to the window at the top of the château, and after the two journeys – the first to take the wooden carcass, the second to deliver the work surface – they had definitely earned it!

Like most tasks, once done, the pain is all but forgotten. Though I have made it clear that anything to be brought down from Angela's *tresoire* is to be a one-man lift. Otherwise it can be thrown out the window . . . Angela and I both know I'm not joking!

The space was finished and ready to start filling and it looked huge! This was not a fancy room; it was a functional white room but it had exceptional lighting and a great view and I knew already it would be a brilliant place to work in.

I spent evening after evening filling up the shelves and drawers. It could not be rushed and I had literally dozens and dozens of boxes to go through. We all do it, we keep things and only in time do we know if they are special to us. My boxes were bulging with so many memories: items from my childhood, clothes from my parents, pictures, props, wedding stuff, children's clothes, business items, a sewing kit that I have had since I was five, my first ever pair of tailoring scissors (which cost me the same as half a week's rent in London). Treasure after treasure, memory after memory. I had so much storage space up there that filling it was a complete pleasure.

It's often only when you look back over time that you remember what you have achieved. Looking through all these items and special memories, I knew one thing for sure: I've done okay at filling my life and, boy, have I made some interesting things in my time!

But without doubt, the best things I have ever made are the kids and I could not wait to show them my special space. Dorothy got to see it first because we had a hat to make following our trip to Paris and, not long after, Arthur came up as well. Seeing my *tresoire* from their eyes was gorgeous. Neither of them could believe that I had kept every drawing they had ever done and they were both fascinated by all the displays. It is my treasure trove and it is special when we go in there because they know that they cannot go in alone. I also quickly learnt that big jars of buttons and beads should go out of reach of *les enfants*.

*

Following our New Year's wishes, we were on a mission to make some family holiday memories. Dick had promised Arthur and Dorothy that we would build a snowman this year, but with no snow in the Loire Valley so far, he decided that if the snow was not to come to us, we would go to it! I liked his style, did some research and found a lovely family-friendly ski resort called Super Besse, so I started searching for somewhere to stay. But last-minute accommodation during school half term can be a bit of a challenge . . .

Angela had found us a very special 'eco lodge' a couple of miles from the main resort. It was a small group of cabins set in beautiful countryside. It took most of the day to drive to Auvergne but, as the family dozed in the car, any tiredness I may have had was dispelled by the sight of the amazing ancient volcanic mountains in the latter part of the journey.

The wooden cabin was snug, warm and comfortable and from the back of our cabin the valley sloped down to a stream and a little lake. We were at sufficient altitude for there to be lots of ice but there was only a little snow about. But we were on a mission and wouldn't accept anything other than snowy snow being snowy! There was no messing around. At the first opportunity, we got in our car and started driving up to Besse-et-Saint-Anastaise. We all started cheering when it started snowing – and then snowing some more! When the road became harder to see we found a deserted layby that had six inches of snow in it. So we pulled in and prepared ourselves to go out in the cold. The children looked like little Michelin men with all their layers under the waterproof, windproof coveralls we had bought them so they could play in the mud. Angela had a padded ski suit and, complete with Barbour and flat cap, I looked like a lost English country gentleman – but I was warm! We were quite sheltered in the valley so amid lots of laughing and giggling we made our snowmen/women and had a prolonged snowball fight. The sun was shining by the time we had finished and we got back in the car and turned the heaters on full blast. Everyone had that ruddy glow that fresh air and a bit of exercise brings. We could see the resort across the valley and much further up the mountain so we went in search of hot chocolate and hopefully something to eat.

Dick takes giving his 'word' very seriously and was adamant that we would make Olaf and Olivia (we had made up the fact that Olaf from *Frozen* must have a sister like Arthur has). I was overjoyed and at peace that whatever happened now on that holiday, we had accomplished what we set out to do.

The snow ploughs must have been out in force as, despite the heavy snow, just fifteen minutes later we were parked up about 200 metres from the centre and were getting re-wrapped to head into a restaurant for some food. We managed to get the majority of our preparation done in the comfort of the car with the heaters still working overtime. When all we could see were the children's eyes, we were ready ... I opened the door and it was bloody freezing. Not just cold. It was painful. We had a couple of hundred metres to go, but the first bit was subject to the cold winds. I got the family lined up, backs to the wind, and we headed towards the sanctuary of a warm restaurant. We tried different combinations of carrying children but what worked best was when I was acting as a wind-break sheltering the family as they shuffled behind me. I felt like a mix of Scott of the Antarctic, breaking a trail, and Good King Wenceslas sheltering his page ... Needless to say, we entered the first restaurant we came to. Fortunately, it was perfect, all wood and alpine lodge feel, and we stripped off lots of layers and settled down to get our hot chocolate and a relaxing long lunch. It wasn't even lunchtime. Back in our part of France, sitting down for lunch after 1.30pm just wasn't possible but the resort catered throughout the day, so we made the most of it.

Auvergne cuisine is steeped in farming tradition and pork is the meat most often found on tables: dried ham, sausage, breaded or grilled pig's feet, salt pork with green lentils from Puy. The region is famous for ... drum roll, please ... cabbage! We love cabbage and I've even cooked Angela my very tasty stuffed cabbage, so when we discovered that this was a speciality of the region we were surprisingly excited. And as if it couldn't get any more perfect we discovered that another two specialities of the region were potato dishes – heaven!

We had a spacious booth table and the four of us sat side by side watching people and everything being served.

We were on holiday so started with *la grande assiette dégustation*, which was a platter of small dishes, including a rich dish of Puy lentils cooked with gently smoked lardons. I hadn't realised that puy lentils were from the region, I'd thought they were from much further south, but I read on the menu that they were 'grown in fertile soil, formed by volcanic lava, in Puy-en-Velay and are protected in the European Union by a Protected Designation of Origin (PDO) and in France as an *appellation d'origine contrôlée* (AOC) – you learn something every day! The mix of flavours meant something for everyone. We do try to all taste everything but we are also parents, so it's always children first, and when Dorothy loved the tataki of salmon, which was more of a salmon tartare, we stood aside and watched her devour it. The charcuterie was magnificent and so were the dips. The only slight complaint was that we were supposed to enjoy this with one bit of bread each, with no butter. That was never going to work so I chatted to the lovely waitress and explained we'd need more bread and my genetic make-up meant it was essential that we get butter too. Well done to her: our breadbasket was never empty thereafter.

Our main courses were a real mix. The cabbage was served in a broth and was stuffed with pork mince and herbs. We had a lovely chargrilled steak of Salers beef from Cantal, which came with *truffade* – potatoes with fresh tomme cheese from Cantal baked in the oven. We also ordered a 'safety dish' of burger and chips for the kids and a side of *aligot* (which is another tomme cheese and potato dish, but this time it's a creamy, gooey purée that just tastes naughty). And then I made the schoolboy error of ordering the final dish, *ris de veau*. I thought it was something that involved veal and rice (*riz*) but actually it was veal sweetbreads. And 'sweetbreads' sound so much nicer than saying it's the pancreas and thymus gland of a young calf; there is nothing appetising about saying you are eating a gland, is there? Preparation involves degorging – i.e. soaking in a strong brine – then simmering for a short period, pressing and then finally dusting in flour and frying. It had the texture of very soft liver and was not something I'd go out of my way to order again but the creamy mushroom sauce was lovely. We had so many flavours on the table so we all dipped in and shared (though I didn't see Angela fighting me for the veal).

We didn't need pudding so we ordered a café and a café gourmand and shared the mix of cakes, biscuits and mousses. As we braced ourselves to brave the outdoors again, we were pleasantly surprised that the wind had died down and, though cold, it was now lovely out.

Nature is incredible and there is something majestic and life affirming about spending time in the mountains. During our break away, we enjoyed numerous trips to the slopes, though we didn't actually attempt to ski. In the resort there were a number of 'soft play' stations. They were cordoned-off areas to protect everyone from runaway skiers and there was a vast array of different foam shapes to climb over, slide on and build things with. The snow may have been compacted but it was safe for the kids to climb, slide and fall. It was a lot of fun, even for the adults!

The resort was fantastic for families. Apart from the soft play that Angela loved – I mean, Arthur and Dorothy loved – there were several gentle uphill travelators that you could stand on to be transported to the top of a gentle slope. It was your decision how you wanted to come back down. We carried up all manner of doughnuts, sledges and discs for sliding on your bum . . . It was winter fun as it's very best. We would race down and back up, Dorothy and me against Arthur and Angela. When the kids then asked to go by themselves I could see the panic on Angela's face. But these nursery slopes were meant for children, so what could go wrong? So we gave them a little freedom. I stayed at the top because it was tricky getting off the moving pathway and that meant I was also available to supervise them getting onto their sledge, which invariably wanted to slip down the hill without them. Angela waited at the bottom, poised to catch them. Dorothy, because she was smaller, set off first, followed quickly by Arthur who was keen to win. I know we are competitive – to be fair, life is competitive – but Arthur and Dorothy have always had their own, very friendly competitions. On this occasion, because 'she started first', Dorothy arrived with Angela first and Arthur, who was watching Dorothy and not concentrating, managed an impressive tumble that involved rolling a bit . . . I could not help nearly crying with laughter as I looked at my beautiful, wrapped-in-many-layers wife, with Dorothy in arms, running up the slope, sliding and falling, to rescue her little man. Impervious to his rescuer's approach, Arthur remounted and raced past the two girls with a huge smile, claiming he was the winner!

I'm not sure how many times we went up the slopes but it was a lot! It didn't take long before Dick and I were sitting at the end watching Arthur and Dorothy do it all by themselves. Their wrapped-up waddling bodies, rosy cheeks and great big smiles were just so lovely it made us want to have a snow holiday every year.

CHAPTER 13

Garden Days

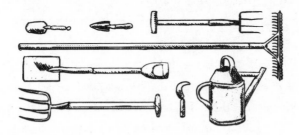

Returning to the château I expected (and hoped) the weather would change and that we'd find a covering of snow that would have made our trip unnecessary – which wouldn't have mattered as our trip to the Auvergne was everything we had hoped for and we'd had a ball. It didn't happen though; we returned to dark, cold days and so focused on the inside of the château, which had become completely familiar, warm and comfortable.

The routine of keeping the château 'at temperature' in the winter is soothing and it makes me smile. It's not a chore; it's part of the routine that reinforces the fact that we are meant to be here. We often talk about the château being our 'forever home' and that is more than words; it's a commitment that we felt from the first day we saw the château, before we'd even walked in through our massive, tired front doors. I sometimes do the EuroMillions Lottery and it is very telling that, if we won a huge sum, we would stay at Château-de-la-Motte Husson. We can't think of anywhere we would rather be. So, why enter? That's simple: we might be living our dream but we still fancy those two-hour lunches!

I was very excited when 10 March arrived. We had thirty guests coming to our first garden day and we mobilised all of our wedding helpers to ensure we were well staffed. They knew us, could find anything they needed and became our team leaders. Each had a little file that contained a map of our plot and a more detailed plan of the walled garden. It also included a list of tasks that were a possible start point for the day and I had included some diagrams of what I meant by a seed drill and how to plant out the way I wanted. We had lots of things we wanted to sort out and get ready for Nathan and Michael's wedding – our first wedding of the year – but I also had a list of things I wanted done to increase the garden's productivity. Our guests were to work in both the walled garden and on the island but the majority of the activity was to be in the walled garden, as that felt like it should be the focus for a 'garden day'.

I had been up early making sure the list of what had to be done and the timings and remaining tasks for the lunch were clear. We needed to prepare the cheeses for baking, finish off the spicy tomato soup and croutons, get the potatoes in the pot ready to be turned on and get the confit duck underway.

As the guests congregated, Angela checked off names and gave everyone a handmade work apron. Despite my fifty years gardening, I had no idea what a work apron looked like so did not pass comment on the very attractive vintage linen and cotton aprons with deep pockets for gardening bits and pieces.

After tea, coffee, juice and a croissant, we all gathered outside. Everyone was welcomed and I asked the very important question: how many people were drag-alongs? How many had come to make their other halves happy? It seemed we had three or four husbands this applied to but, by and large, everyone was a volunteer and very happy to be there! After thanking everyone for coming, and before I split people into groups, we headed off to the walled garden. Next on my agenda was confirming how many other Irish people were there . . . It's probably not politically correct anymore but I grew up when jokes were often told that made the Irish out as being a bit simple or naive. There was no issue with that, as most were made up by the Irish and kept simple so the English could understand them. However, I did make the point that we Northern Irish couldn't be that stupid as they'd all paid to come and work in my garden . . . just saying!

There followed a great day. I told everyone it was not an endurance test and no one was to do anything they were not competent or comfortable doing, but everyone entered into the spirit and got stuck in. Some of the workers were dripping in sweat from clearing, cutting and digging and everyone was surprised when I had to announce it was already time to wash hands and head to the orangery for lunch. I think most were expecting just soup and a sandwich but on the table we had lots of lovely fresh baguettes and local butter, some dips, cornichons and smoked mackerel pâté. Our workers attacked and were served cider or soft drinks. Some thought that was lunch and were surprised when lots of baked cheeses with toasted spicy seeds on the top turned up. Not long after that came vintage teacups of spicy tomato soup with herby croutons.

SPICY TOMATO SOUP

I was making soup for fifty but the principles are easy and this recipe is good for six to eight. Of course, it can also be easily scaled up, and if you have too much all you have to do is freeze it.

Ingredients

1½kg ripe tomatoes
3 cloves of garlic
Olive oil
Gastrique, to add depth of flavour (a simple gastrique is a sweet and sour sauce made of equal quantities of sugar – which can be caramelised, but I don't – and red wine vinegar, which is slightly reduced to make a syrup)
500ml stock (I prefer chicken but use vegetable to keep the dish vegan)
1 tsp chopped chilli (more or less depending on the strength of the chilli and your preference)
Salt

Method

Put the tomatoes on a baking tray, complete with stalks if they are on the vine. Poke the garlic cloves, in their skin, under the tomatoes. Drizzle with olive oil and roast in a 180°C oven for thirty minutes.

If you don't have any gastrique, make it now – put equal parts vinegar and sugar into a pan and stir until the sugar has dissolved. Allow it to boil for several moments, then it can be put into a clean flip-top bottle. It keeps well and adds depth to any tomato dish.

When cooked, put the chilli, tomatoes and garlic and tray scrapings into a large pan, having de-stalked the tomatoes and squeezed the garlic out of its skin. Add the stock and bring to the boil, simmering for ten minutes.

With a stick blender, or in batches in a blender, blend really well. Then pass through a sieve back into the pan. Taste and season and taste again – then add some gastrique. Depending on the flavour in your tomatoes, I'd start with four to six tablespoons. Stir, taste, add more if you think it needs it . . . then marvel at the difference a gastrique makes to tomato soup!

I make croutons that I toss in salt and herbes de Provence. This adds a lovely crunch.

. . . .

Then, when the platters of the main course came out, some actually groaned, but they did still eat the confit duck served with a port and plum reduction, buttery potatoes and roast veggies. We held back on the pudding as tea and patisseries from the village were to be served in a couple of hours.

It's hard to remember just how little had been done in the walled garden before that first garden day. I thought I'd started well but there was still so much to do. It's a big garden and the vast majority had not yet been turned over at all. Whole areas that were to become beds by the walls were cleared and dug over and the rotovator was kept busy. Some more pathways were cleared by taking up to six inches of earth, which nature had laid down over the years, off the top of them. The salad beds near the entrance were given some structure, marked out, cleared and dug over. We managed to plant some peonies in the flower beds and some more roses. Drills were made and seeds planted. Herbs were planted. There was a bonfire built to get rid of anything that would burn.

The afternoon session started gently but as the clock approached teatime you could see people rushing to finish off the bed they had weeded or dug and it was obvious that everyone had formed into teams that took real pride in what they had done for us. I'm quite sure when they watch the programme now they are checking the bit they did and making sure it's being well looked after. Tea and cake were followed by a gallop around the château in two groups of guided tours: one given by Angela and the other by me. I'm very sure they heard different perspectives of our challenges.

We love the garden days at the château and this first one set the tone perfectly – even our 'drag-alongs' said they wanted to come back! It's a lively day in the garden, complete with fresh air, meeting new people and having some fun, so what's not to love? And by the end we have achieved a man's month-worth of progress in the garden and that makes a real difference.

Dick's garden day was a roaring success and the word clearly got out that it was a lot of fun, as many of our guests re-booked again and again, and we simply could not arrange enough days to meet the demand. It also became apparent at Dick's garden day that we needed more tools for our participants – more than you would ever think anyone could need. So we added 'anything useful in the garden' to our long list of 'things we would like to find at a charity store'.

Whenever we're looking for anything, we start at Emmaus, then move on to *brocantes* or *vide greniers*. When we were looking for storage solutions one weekend, we drove down to Louverné, a commune in the Mayenne *département*, fifteen minutes' drive from the château. There was a *vide grenier* being held in the town, so we went in search of some bargains. The sale was set up in the grounds of Echologia, an eco-park we had not visited before, so we looked forward to seeing what was there.

This was a win-win as we got to go to a *vide grenier* and then got to explore a new part of Mayenne. Arthur and Dorothy like to grab a bargain just as much as we do, so we allowed them to rummage to see what they could find. We told them that if anyone found a copper pan, they would be given a €1 reward!

We were pleasantly surprised by the beauty of the area between Louverné and Laval; we'd assumed that it would be quite industrial but the eco-park is based in an area containing historic lime kilns. Lime was historically really important for building and there had been an immense amount of effort put into the construction of the beautiful stone kilns. Apparently, this had been one of France's largest lime-mining sites during the nineteenth century and had been operational from 1820 all the way through to 1963.

The backdrop of the kilns was majestic but sadly there were only about twenty stalls at the *vide grenier*. That did not stop our fun! I found an old cast-iron cauldron that was still usable, which I earmarked for making wood-fired popcorn. And Angela found some old magazines. She has millions of them already but somehow she still gets excited every time she finds some new old ones.

Like with most *vide greniers*, we found lots of things we wanted but probably didn't need: old French Scrabble sets, vintage magazines, a metal shopping list organiser. But the best bit was the lovely snack stall that served grilled local sausages in fresh baguettes. We were all so hungry; I'm not sure who finished first but I have a vague memory that we went back for round two.

*

Part of my eagerness to get organised was down to the fact that our wedding season was due to start early this year, with a March wedding for Nathan and Michael. Exactly one year earlier, we had

hosted Nathan and Michael for a food lovers' weekend, where they became engaged. It came as a surprise and a true compliment that, at the end of their stay, they asked Dick and me if we would also host their wedding. It's an honour to be asked and we take the responsibility very seriously. Now, a March wedding is not during our normal wedding season, which runs from May to September to give us the best chance of good weather, but they told us they wanted an intimate wedding, hosted indoors, so of course we said YES! The year had flown by since we'd first met Nathan and Michael and lots of preparation had gone into the big day, which was finally here.

When Nathan and Michael arrived, it felt like they were coming home – they had become friends of the family. They are both huge fans of blossom, so I had really gone to town with it; everywhere that could host blossoms did. Some of the containers were boasting tree-like blossom bushes! The cherry trees had blossomed early this year and I cannot tell you how much a silly thing like that stressed me out. I truly thought it might all be gone by the time the wedding was here. I even went and bought every bit of pink crêpe paper I could find, just in case we all needed to make faux blossom, which would have been great fun if we had had time on our hands.

Although it was going to be an intimate celebration, it was to be hosted over three days. Day one started late afternoon, with guests receiving a special, tried-and-tested-the-night-before blossom cocktail.

To make a cherry blossom cocktail you add a dash of cherry liqueur to a dash of brandy (or here in our part of France we use Calvados) and then top up the glass with some lovely bubbles, before adding a delicate piece of cherry blossom to float on top.

After cocktails, the guests retired either to the salon or the *salle à manger*. In the salon, there was a dress-up parlour with boas, pearls, hats, fascinators and champagne and patisseries. Earlier that day, I had found an old picture frame in the attic, which I quickly sprayed with gold to create a 'picture spot'. In the *salle à manger*, Dick had prepared a gentlemen's table full of terrines, whiskey and cigars (to be smoked outside!).

Our area of France is well known for its rillette and terrines. Rillette is basically cooked, shredded meat or fish preserved in fat. Unbeknown to me, I'd been making rillette for years but, being British, I called it 'potted' ham or fish. It was great to be able to prepare the dishes in advance – after all, terrines benefit from being able to mature a little. Because of the fat content in terrines and rillette, they are great with chutney or fresh, lightly pickled vegetables, which also add a bit of colour to dishes that can be a little 'brown'. We had salads and baguette to accompany these and slowly barbecued smoked legs of lamb – our kettle barbecue is in use all year round.

I moved between the two rooms hosting the guests but Dick had the gentlemen's table locked down, especially when he opened up his personal whiskey cabinet.

The following day, there was lots of nervous excitement in the air. The *salle à manger* had been converted into the wedding-breakfast area with two large tables from the orangery. It looked very grand and I adored dressing this room up, it felt really different.

The day started with bubbles whilst we welcomed guests. We had chairs arranged for the ceremony in the grand entrance and the atmosphere was peaceful and calm, with everyone talking quietly to one another. Nathan and Michael had both been given their buttonholes and all that was needed was for them to appear. When they arrived the peaceful chatting turned to roars of happiness.

The ceremonies that take place at the château are always different. They are made by the couple. I love my job as a celebrant because it's not about me – I'm just helping people say what they feel about each other – but I do have the responsibility of making it all happen without a hitch.

The wedding party always feels some anxiety or nervousness during the waiting time. I spend this time with the groom and by the time the ceremony starts, I try to make sure they are relaxed and have enjoyed the arrival of the bride. I don't let them stare straight ahead; they have to savour the arrival of their beaming partner. It's a memory not to be missed. Each occasion must be taken as it unfolds. Brides renowned for their punctuality have been forty-five minutes later than expected and usually confident brides, and a fair number of grooms, have been unable to say their vows through their tears. By the time the ceremony is sealed with a kiss and everyone is cheering, we've laughed and tears have been shed, but importantly, everything that was to be said and promises that were to be publicly declared have been, and the party begins in earnest.

I can't explain the pride I have when Dick is being celebrant. I feel it at every wedding and the pride does not subside or reduce because he has a few under his belt. Each couple has their own journey and story, and Dick plays the role with such authority, together with gentleness and sensitivity. He is perfect.

Nathan and Michael's wedding marked the start of this year's season for us. When they looked at each other it was intense and charged with deep adoration. Their ceremony was very moving.

The celebrations carried on and the meal was a treat. It was similar to that of our traditional wedding, in that the food came out in waves, but with the added complexity that it was being served out of our tight service kitchen. I kept my eye on everyone throughout and carried on topping people's glasses up. When it came to the speeches, the intimate setting allowed Michael to chat softly. He was great at public speaking. Nathan followed and I got the sense that this was an impromptu moment. 'It's everyone's dream to be swept away by a prince and get married in a castle, Michael,' he said. 'And you are my prince.' And with that, everyone reached for their hankies.

CHAPTER 14

Celebrations

Spring was well and truly in force; the grounds were changing again at a daily rate and wildflowers were appearing all the time. I don't know why, but I just expected returns of the same. But the foxgloves were coming up in different places, as were big areas of ox-eye daisies. Nature, especially spring, always makes me feel alive, but this year, with so much love charging the château, I also felt reflective. Nathan and Michael's wedding confirmed that Dick and I were a good team and we *loved* our jobs. It may have been that I was turning forty in a couple of weeks and I was seeing all my girlfriends for a mega celebration, and that when I arrived back it would be our dear friends Jon and Miguel's wedding at the château, but I was a bit overwhelmed with emotion that the house was literally (cheesy line alert!) full of love.

Angela and I were delighted to hear that Mum and the girls were coming for Easter. The timing was perfect. They arrived straight after Michael and Nathan's wedding and left just before we headed to London for Angela's birthday.

At home, we always had a turkey for Easter Sunday but that could have been because there was one left over from Christmas ... In France, *Pâques*, Easter, is an important festival. I don't remember the Easter Bunny being around when I was young and with a sister called Bunny, I'm sure I would have remembered? The reason for its importance is obviously as a religious celebration but it is also a traditional gathering for families – religious or not. As Easter Monday is a national holiday, everyone enjoys a long weekend and we have it on good authority that the French traditionally cook a large Easter meal with a leg of lamb and 'set a lively table' to honour the coming of spring. So that was our plan, too.

Knowing that Dick's family used to dye eggs when they were younger, I thought it would be fun to do the same this year. I wanted to create a keepsake for everyone. Egg dying is very easy. First, you put everyone's names on stickers on the eggs. Then you boil the eggs in water with lots of food dye in it. Once the dye has been absorbed, take the stickers off and, *voilà*, the names are there. I had picked up little terrariums in a craft shop, so I finished off the design with a floating butterfly, a little quail egg and a little chocolate Easter egg. It was very simple but the perfect place setting for Easter and very fun and attractive.

Pudding was easily taken care of, as every bakery had a variation of *la brioche de Pâques*, which is a more densely flavoured (typically orange blossom and anise) circular loaf or a simple brioche plait that is served with butter and jam.

Ahead of the family arriving for the weekend, I went off to buy the meat and trimmings from our local butcher at Grand Frais, our favourite food shop. When I arrived, the butcher brought out the rear portion of a lamb: the saddle and both legs, a double *gigot d'agneau*. I stopped him cutting it up and bought the lot. We did after all have a huge oven, a big family to feed and a wonderful copper roasting pan that it would fit in.

With springtime flowers springing up all over the château, I added to the table setting 'spring in a teacup', with primroses, pansies and daffodils. I hung some of the decorated eggs that Dick's family had made when they were young together with my new dyed eggs and, with everything cascading, it looked wonderful and smelled amazing. Jenny and the girls loved watching Arthur and Dorothy do their Easter hunt and seeing the decorations they had given us last year in use. A château is a great place to hide Easter eggs. Dick and I always try to hide them in a way that makes them blend in. The right-coloured egg sitting on a book, for example, all but disappears. It does mean that we tend to keep finding eggs for weeks after the hunt but I think that's just an added bonus. As the children dashed around, up and down the stairs, in and out of the rooms, I could see Jenny watching and enjoying every second of it. Moments like that last forever in your mind's eye.

After the chocolate excesses of the morning, Dorothy and Arthur were not frightfully hungry but the rest of the family did justice to the roast spring lamb, roast dumplings, roast potatoes, roast parsnip, buttered swede, peas and carrots, cabbage and bacon, mashed potatoes, onion sauce and a lovely rich red wine gravy. As with most celebrations, it was a matter of sitting down hungry and getting up tired, though the lovely red wine could also have had something to do with that . . .

I was turning forty shortly after Easter and, although having a big celebration at our house would have been a lovely idea, I fancied getting away and spending time with my husband – just Dick and I, eating, drinking and walking the streets of London.

With Arthur and Dorothy in the safe care of Grandma and Papi, Angela and I left the château early the morning before her birthday and, as always, took one final look back as we headed out of the driveway. The dawn hadn't broken yet so the building was just a shadow over the slightly lighter sky, but it's as if we say a goodbye to our home when we go away.

We chatted and Angela worked on her computer with a mobile 'dongle' all the way on the drive up to Calais, through the Channel Tunnel and up the M20, en route to our hotel of choice: Hotel Café Royale. I do know how to make my wife happy so our first stop, apart from a pee, was at Angela's favourite curry house, Needo Grill in east London. It's opposite the Royal London Hospital and serves the best curry a nearly-forty-year-old could wish for. It must have been her birthday because we managed to find a parking place outside the restaurant after about twenty circuits, just as they opened for lunch. I don't miss the traffic or the parking issues that come with living in a big city! I ordered Angela and myself a jug of mango lassi, the mixed tandoori grill, a dal and a whole plate of lamb chops.

Eight years ago, when Angela was in labour with Arthur at the Royal London, our midwife told us to go for a walk to relax. We are pretty sure she meant around the hospital but we snuck out, crossed a couple of roads and had the naughtiest curry in Needo's. Under Angela's coat she still had her blue hospital gown on but it was January and no one noticed that she never took her coat off and was grimacing at regular intervals.

I smiled all the way through the curry. Dick calls me his 'cheap date' because for the meal of your life it costs around £15 a head!

We don't get enough 'us' time, so when we do, we try to make it special. We love the Café Royale, partly because of its timeless elegance, but also because the staff always make us feel really looked after and welcome. We have no needs or indulgences but a nice hotel room every now and again is our treat to ourselves. In the hotel, they also have an art deco lounge with the finest cocktails. It may be because we tend to go early in the evening but it's never very busy and, after a little walk around London town, we then headed on to the Green Bar for a tipple, or several . . .

The following day, Dick took back the 'cheap date' quote as we headed to Notting Hill for a 'posh' meal at The Ledbury. Brett Graham is one of the world's finest chefs in our eyes. He has two Michelin stars and his restaurant is phenomenal. We found ourselves repeating to each other, 'I think this is the best meal we have ever had,' several times that evening. We still talk about the menu to this day. It truly was the best meal we have ever had and, as well as appetisers, palate cleansers and sweet morsels, it included:

FIRST
Grilled River Teign oyster, potato butter and sea purslane
Golden beetroot baked in clay, smoked eel, sake cream and char roe

SECOND
Warm bantam's egg, celeriac, arbois, dried ham and truffle
Squid and barley risotto, cauliflower, sherry and pine nuts

THIRD
Cumbrian veal, salt-baked kohlrabi, wasabi leaves and smoked
bone marrow
Iberico pork, hen of the woods, smoked butter and rosemary

FOURTH
Chocolate, dark chocolate chantilly and clementine leaf
Aynhoe Park honey, quince, buffalo milk meringue and bee pollen

We love our grub. For us, in France, we concentrate on the best ingredients we can find, which usually means buying seasonal and local. We are adventurous in our cooking and in eating out, so we were really interested to see and experience what Brett and his team produced for us. Delicate handling of the ingredients and the masterful combination of flavours and textures set a standard that has not yet been surpassed. We couldn't have asked for any more. As service drew to a close, we had a chance to catch up with Brett as we had friends in common; I had worked and presented with Mike Robinson, a chef and restaurateur who was completely immersed in the world of high-quality game products and who had, in turn, worked with Brett for years. Our lunch and the subsequent chatting was a very memorable way to spend an afternoon together and we smiled and held hands as we headed out into the late afternoon. We love a lunch that lasts until teatime.

The following day was celebrated with my friends and consisted of high tea at the Café Royale followed by dancing at the Palm Tree in east London. My dozen best girlfriends joined the celebrations and for the first time in a long time, I was not the one hosting. I was busy hugging, storytelling and being bloody gushy . . .

My girl was forty, so high tea and champagne with all her girlfriends (and me) seemed a great way to celebrate. I had to pinch myself as I was the only bloke in a room of beautiful, powerful, successful ladies. If I had not been so secure in my masculinity, I could have felt inadequate; as it was, I just felt lucky and smiled a lot.

It was great to see old friends getting together. They were all transported back to their party years, though most were now a combination of at least two or three things from the following list: beautiful, successful, businesswomen, performers, entrepreneurs, mums, barristers, accountants. The warmth and feelings of affection were obvious, and it was so moving to be there as Angela did a little speech about each one of her friends individually. There were tears and laughter and shared confidences – how she met them, their 'best' moments since they were friends, how they'd helped each other in times of need. All the girls then took turns to chat about Angela. I knew everyone in the room already but I was still learning such a lot about this remarkable lady I had been lucky enough to fall in love with. One day, I'm sure they will tell Arthur and Dorothy how she played a part in everyone's journey. It's who she is. She supports and encourages people to go for their dreams and I discovered she was also a real party animal, as we finished our champagne and headed to the East End.

The Palm Tree in east London is one of my favourite haunts with its original 1940s decor. The owners, Val and Alfie, had made me a cake and more friends from all parts of my life were there, including my brother. I kept hearing, 'Oh, it's lovely to put a face to a name,' as pockets of friends met for the first time. Old East Enders played on the stage, singing old-school jazz. It was perfect and I felt completely loved.

The following day was Dorothy's birthday. Now, this was very unlike us but we were not there for the morning of her birthday.

Instead, we left London at 6am to drive to Disneyland, Paris, where we were due to meet Mum, Dad, Arthur and Dorothy. It was about the same drive for us as it was for Mum and Dad, so we all left at about the same time and, a little spookily, we arrived at our apartment within minutes of each other.

Excitement levels were through the roof. Dorothy already owned everything possible to do with *Frozen* and spent the entire next day singing 'Let It Go'. That evening, we had a fantastic meal in the village and all was rather lovely. But when we went to the park the following day, we discovered that not only was the main *Frozen* show cancelled, but that all Dorothy's favourite rides were closed for renovation. Then, we spent an hour and a half waiting to watch Elsa drive past on her float, only for her to completely ignore Dorothy's frantic waving. I had to say to myself, 'Let it go.' But then Moana glided past, a Polynesian beauty, and she hugged Dorothy and gave her a kiss. Dorothy looked around to us all, most probably to check we had just seen the magic, but we were all in pools of melted hearts. We couldn't thank Moana enough and within ten minutes, Dorothy had a Moana outfit on, complete with a Heart of Te Fiti necklace. Yes, Disney, I'm that fickle too.

After all the celebrations, it was great to be back at the château and focused on the events we had ahead. It took us a week to get over the London–Paris trip (that looks so much more glamorous writing it down!) but there was an awful lot of work to do to get ready for the wedding season. Repairs, painting, getting organised and making things better seemed like a huge job. This was the first time we were going back into the wedding season and it was a bit of a 'Christmas tree light' moment – where we really wished we had put things away better! It was all part of the learning curve. And before we even started, I'd invested in new carry carts for the cutlery and crockery.

Our second wedding of 2018 was for our dear friends Jon and Miguel. They both came to our wedding and were an amazing pair of helping hands and both completely fabulous. I knew them from the *collectif* I was in many years ago and Jon and Miguel's wedding was everything I would have dreamed of for them: fabulous, outrageous, like a carnival of fun. Everyone had made such an effort with their outfits and I guessed many had spent months designing their costumes. Because the theme was carnival and circus, there was everything from sexy showgirl to a rather scary clown. But the one thing they had in common was the amount of love and the shared intention to have a good time ... it was colourful and eclectic, daring and dangerous. A glass of bubbles later and the party was in full swing. Even though they are so cool, they are completely soppy, and so the wedding season began with a wonderful celebration full of laughter and love.

Jon and Miguel's wedding was a little different from any other we had done as we were also invited guests, so Angel and I were to experience the wedding breakfast and party from the other side. The catering responsibilities had been passed to a couple of chefs who'd discussed the menu directly with Jon and Miguel – all we did was provide the manpower and some direction on the facilities. We had a ball but it was like sleeping with one eye open – I could see Angela mentally directing the front of the house just as much as I was giving telepathic guidance to the kitchen. When we chatted and laughed together later it dawned on us just how much the château was in our blood and our psyche, and how important it was to us as a family.

Boy, this year had started with a bang! There had been many celebrations and so much rain, so getting château under the stars completed had been a big challenge. But we were now on our final push because in eight days' time we had our first guests arriving: Byron and Scarlett (and for three of those eight days we were hosting another wedding).

When, after late nights, early mornings and frantic working, château under the stars was *finally* finished, we reflected that it had not been easy. In fact, over the past couple of months, the whole area got messier – a lot messier – as we had had nothing but rain. We managed to get most of the hard landscaping down and we took delivery of the bigger, much heavier dome. At least we were on dry, if a bit muddy, land. However, the conspiracy continued and after the game of giant Meccano, pulling the skin over the dome was thwarted by the fact that the far side where we were meant to pull a rope, to pull it up and over, was a marsh. It started out as a marsh but now it was so sinky we could easily lose the children in there.

Luckily, we had more help at hand, so we overcame our problem by having more hands on. Going from a five-metre to seven-metre diameter in the domes was a huge step up; the weight of the covering had more than doubled, so manhandling it over a frame that was over twice the height of a man was a sweaty, straining thirty minutes, even though there were five of us. As we wrestled it into position, we finally saw how big the space was – it was impressive.

I could not get over the difference in size of our large dome. It was double the floor space and was very tall and airy, nearly twelve feet high. It felt completely luxurious and this time I had chosen a cream inside liner, which made the dome feel like something from the 1970s, as well as being quite futuristic.

Because of the months and months of rain, the weeks we had planned to be working on the domes had slipped past, so Dick ended up calling in some extra hands to help. One of our workers, Craig, assisted getting the concrete base down for the dome to go onto and, once it was up, we realised that we needed a floor, so I chose a real wood floor that we painted cream . . . The window looked partly towards the château, partly at the other dome and partly at lots of greenery. Even at this stage, it was looking bright, airy and unique.

But the outside landscaping, kitchen and bathroom work seemed endless. We were investing heavily in this area and it would take many years to make a return on it. It was once all mud but I simply did not want our guests to get muddy en route to the kitchen or for a midnight 'spend a penny' break, as the bathroom and kitchen were not connected to the dome, so after lots of discussions we put down a geometric paving area that runs from the domes to their facilities. The paving slabs are a light-grey square shape, edged with an art deco pattern with small black squares. When finished, it looked fantastic, and going that extra mile was definitely worth it as it still makes me smile today.

The bathroom and kitchen area were small but perfectly formed. Dick and I tried to think of everything. The bathroom was tiled using a rectangular crackle grey tile in a herringbone pattern. The grout was copper to match the copper bathroom fittings and, to finish it off, I had purchased a huge, round bentwood mirror and copper lights with opal shades . . . it looked stunning.

For the kitchen, we had a large porcelain sink, a small two-hob gas burner, two fridges (one for drink, one for food) and a splashback in the same château tiles we used in our family kitchen. It was charming and *very* functional . . . everything you could need when glamping.

The utilities were connected to those in the coach house, so there was hot and cold water plumbed into the bathroom and kitchen, and the waste was connected to Jenny and Steve's septic tank. As we were putting in the infrastructure, I extended the piping along the side of the potager wall as, at some time in the future, we may need 'facilities' over near the circle of trees that would make an amazing tree house.

On the Monday, the day after the last guests from the wedding departed, we all headed over to the château under the stars to finish the final touches. The wood-fired hot tub was put in place; I dressed the dome with the soft furnishings – hanging chairs, rugs and a handmade hanging macramé display. We added furniture, plates, drinks, napkins, salt, pepper. The list was long, but we really wanted to make sure we had thought of everything.

At the end of another long day our brains and bodies were exhausted but as the sun went down, I knew we had broken the back of what needed to be done. Tomorrow, with fresh minds, we would do the final check.

Somehow, despite the weather and the mud, we reached the making-it-all-pretty stage before the first guests arrived, so what had been a disaster area was now respectable, if not yet perfect. We'd dodged a bullet there!

Our glamping area was meant for al fresco dining, not roughing it, so I designed an outdoor cook station that was inspired by lots of my experiences cooking outdoors. It is built from stone and has many different capabilities. There is a domed pizza oven that also acts as the chimney so things can be left in there to smoke; a conventional barbecue with a grill over coals; a pit with controllable air flow to allow for 'clam bakes' – it is constructed so you can even roast a whole lamb or pig in it . . .

It would never have crossed my mind to go camping with big double beds, ceiling fans, armchairs or a sofa, which just goes to show how little I know! Though I knew enough not to be surprised by the stocked fridges – one for local specialities and the other for drinks.

After months and months of rain, the sun shone and we literally were finished minutes before Bryon and Scarlett showed up. They could not believe their eyes! They had seen no pictures of the 'added' facilities and had assumed they would be spending a penny in a compost toilet with only the floating dome as accommodation. Dick shot me a look that I will not forget but the effort had been worth it. They had a choice of sleeping accommodation – the floating dome or the larger, airier land dome – their private seating area with barbecue capability and wood-fired hot tub, a kitchen with stocked fridges and luxurious toilets and showers. We felt it was special and everything that I thought a glamorous camper would want. We must have got something right as, to our delight, Byron proposed to Scarlett during their stay and, most importantly, Scarlett said YES!

Later that day, Arthur and Dorothy arrived back from a weekend at the beach with my mum and dad. They came running into our arms screaming, 'Mummy!' 'Daddy!' like they had not seen us in weeks. We hugged them tight whilst they both chatted at a hundred miles an hour about their amazing weekend. We thanked my mum and dad and gave them some fresh bread from the bakers and a bottle of milk – we knew they would want a nice cup of tea.

Mum and Dad living in France with us and taking the children away had given us the opportunity to get château under the stars over the line, along with hosting Hannah and Matt's wedding. Our twenty-hour days just would not have been achievable without their support.

We were on a complete high with everything we had achieved. We never take for granted how lucky we are and, as Dick always says, 'The harder you work, the luckier you get.' We were smiling from ear to ear and completely exhausted. The evening drew in and the sun began to set. We had never seen the château and the domes look so twinkly – the lanterns were flickering in the moat and the moon and stars lit everything up. It was simply magical and the picture of perfection, and, apart from the odd owl saying goodnight, it felt peaceful too.

Afterword

We often think about the saying, 'Living is what you do while waiting for your dreams to come true.' We have packed a lot of living into our time at the château in France, building for our future and always thinking about what we want to achieve next. But we have also made lots of our dreams come true, right from the time when Angela and I found each other.

We always try to savour moments that are unique and need to be stored away in our memories. We have so much. And maybe it's wrong to keep dreaming and working towards your next goal, but, as a family, we were about to head into probably the busiest period of our lives in a château that was now more than comfortable and set in the most beautiful of surroundings.

The château was definitely a home, and one that was full of love and happiness. All we felt for the future was optimism, and we couldn't wait to get stuck in . . .

Acknowledgements

Thank you

We may have not met you, but we have spent many a Sunday evening in your home – thank you for inviting us. You may have sent a letter, a gift, or emails of kindness and support, we may have seen you in the street and exchanged a little chat, even a hug – thank you. We read every piece of correspondence and, when life allows, take pride in replying. We see it as part of our history and one day, when Arthur and Dorothy 'get it', we will show them everything! Thank you for your love of our family. It has meant that *Escape to the Château* has continued to be made and we are now filming the eighth series, with our ninth already commissioned. We raise a glass to you and your family and thank you for being here with us.

Our Mums – the two Jennys – are the reason that we are who we are. They are completely biased, loving and have lived every step with us. Thank you.

Dad (Papi Steve) – for being the biggest kid, and best granddad . . . never grow up.

Siblings, friends and family – you cheered us on from the start. Your continued love and support keep us going. You know us, you know our integrity, our work ethics . . . thank you.

Partnerships:

www.TheChateau.tv – once upon a time, a gentleman called Paul and his amazing wife Emma came to an event at the château. We formed a partnership and, years later, this thrives through hard work, care and dedication. We are quite a team now! Thank you to Ella (and Simon) for looking after us all. And thank you to everyone for continuing to make the ideas and dreams we had right back at the start of our journey come true on the www. Thank you for being honest, lots of fun, generous, kind and hard working.

Lizi and Alan and our Two Rivers/Château TV co-production team. Lizi, without you no one would have known that we 'Escaped to the Château' – we are so thankful to be in your arms!

Homebase – for believing in us and together, giving it a go. Thank you.

The people that look after us:

The Soho Agency: Sophie – our TV mum and the reason we are together . . . What a year! We don't need to say much more – 2021 will not be forgotten!

Cliff – it may not be legal to write what we would sometimes like to write . . . thank you for looking after us.

Julian – thank you for being by our side through this process. Your calmness and wonderful knowledge of our industry is always so soothing – you have been amazing.

Orion Publishing – Vicky, it's been such a pleasure working with you on *Living the Château Dream*. Your hard work, kindness and complete attention to detail is remarkable. It is so lovely that our team at Orion completely 'get us'. Thank you.

Bells & Whistles – Bella, thank you for being with us from the start and caring so much. It's been some year and we cannot imagine anyone else looking after us with so much love . . . And, somehow, on the side, you manage to continually fill our press folder with lovely articles that capture moments in history for Arthur and Dorothy.

Sam Steer – the friend and artist who has brought so many visions to life. Our work and friendship go from strength to strength. Sophie and Lyra – thank you for sharing!

Team Château – Chloe, Tina, Steve and Denise, Sacha and Rob, Quentin, Meredith, Jane, Amanda, Sandrine and Chermaine, Lydia and Craig, Steve P. We have grown the perfect team. Thank you.

About Us

DICK STRAWBRIDGE is an engineer and an environmentalist. He began his TV career many years ago as a team leader on *Scrapheap Challenge*.

ANGEL STRAWBRIDGE is an entrepreneur who made her name in London with her hospitality business, The Vintage Patisserie. She first appeared on TV in 2010 as she sought investment on *Dragon's Den*.

Later that year Dick and Angel met and fell in love. They now have two children together, Arthur and Dorothy. In 2015, after years of searching for a new home, they invited Channel 4 to follow them on their journey as they bought a derelict château in the Pays de la Loire, and so was born the hugely popular Channel 4 series *Escape to the Château*. After extensive renovations on a shoestring budget, the couple married at their family home in November 2015. They are still living life to the full, and continue to restore, renovate and maintain their château.

In 2020, Dick and Angel published their first book together, *A Year at the Château*, which became an instant bestseller on publication.

🐦 @dickstrawbridge
📷 @the_chateau_tv
📘 @chateaudelamottehusson